VOICES
Women of a White Peak Village

Compiled and edited by Gillian Radcliffe

Parwich & District Local History Society

PUBLISHED BY

Parwich & District Local History Society
www.parwichhistory.com

© Gillian Radcliffe & PDLHS 2004
with the help of 'Awards for All: Lottery Grants to Local Groups'

ISBN No: 0-9548326-0-4

Printed by JMP 2000 Ltd. Burton upon Trent. Tel: 01283 566869

FRONT COVER: Two Ladies in Kiln Lane, Parwich.
BACK COVER: Postcard. "Just a Line from Parwich..."

Contents

Acknowledgements:

Thanks to all the contributors, especially Kathleen Allsopp and Eileen Ellis of Parwich W.I. who provided the initial material and inspiration, and many of the photographs, and Mary Whitechurch, whose books, photographs and writings have added both interest and structure to "Voices".

A special thank you to the women who sat in my kitchen and allowed me to record their voices: Kathleen Allsopp, Betty Stone, Sandra Chadfield, Eileen Ellis, Clara Evans, Ella Hopkinson, Valerie Kirkham, Barbara Lowes, Mary Rawlins, Betty Stone, and Catherine Elizabeth (Dolly) Wayne.

Grateful thanks also to Charles Allen, George Allsop, Patricia Bagshawe, Mollie Dakin (for some superb photographs) Angela, Sara and Vere Dodds, Roger Graham (for a large number of photographs and also written material) Charlotte Halliday, Violet Oldfield, Zelda Kent Lemon, Dorothy Marsh, June Nadin, Peter Rawlins, Eveline Shaw, Donald & Rosemary Shields, Ann Vidler, Walter (Ken) Wayne, Stewart Williams and George Woolley.

Thanks to Parwich & District Local History Society, to Rob Francis and especially to Peter Trewhitt, who compiled the list of "Voices" at the end of the book and has worked tirelessly at fund raising. Thanks also to my husband, Michael who has compiled the Index, cooked the meals and given me constant support and encouragement.

Gillian Radcliffe

Preface

*T*he idea for this book grew out of an exhibition of photographs and artefacts assembled by the Parwich and District Local History Society. A date was set to coincide with the Queen's Golden Jubilee, 2002, and the exhibition continued for most of the summer. With the help of the Parwich W.I. I asked people to look out their old photographs, invited them to come and talk about them, and recorded what they had to say. Since then, others have come forward to be interviewed, or have sent photographs or emailed their stories. Whilst all the participants have a connection with Parwich, the book does not pretend to be a history of the village. There are many more tales waiting to be told and photographs to be shared, and I hope that these may aired through the history society website, or be published in our magazine.

What comes through in the book are the unique, joyful, and sometimes poignant voices of the individual women who have so generously shared their stories. In the text, I have tried to let the authentic voices of the women speak, only changing the order of the material to give greater coherence to the story. Where the words have come from face to face interviews, it should be remembered that this is the colourful way in which people speak, not necessarily the way they would write.

The experience of compiling this book has been a rewarding one, though had I known that it would take me two years to complete it, I might never have begun it! Fortunately, contact with so many vibrant personalities and their stories has more than made up for this.

The book has been printed with money from Awards For All (which gives lottery grants to local groups), and also money from the Parwich and District Local History Society. While Parwich has been the main but not exclusive focus of the book, I believe the material has universal appeal and deserves to be read beyond the bounds of Derbyshire.

Gillian Radcliffe

THE TYMPANUM
now sadly deteriorating, above the west door of Parwich Church, dates from between 700-1100 A.D. and depicts Christ as the lamb of God. (Postcard from 1917)

Introduction

"Voices: Women of a White Peak Village" records the voices of women living in a White Peak village in Derbyshire, the White Peak being an area of the Peak District which is situated on white limestone, as opposed to the gritstone of the moorlands, known as the Dark Peak. It offers an insight into the lives of women and their families living in the village of Parwich and its environs, a place rich in history. The village remains unspoiled, its old houses of weathered grey stone nestling in a landscape of ancient habitation. On the surrounding hills are prehistoric burial cairns, Minning Low, Liffs Low, Wigber Low, Hawkslow, while in Cat Low, above the village itself, were found the remains of an Iron Age burial. A few miles away is the great stone circle of Arbor Low, which was a meeting point and ceremonial centre for peoples of the surrounding region.

The Romans enlisted the help of the local population to mine lead at Lombard's Green above Parwich, where the house platforms of a Romano British settlement cluster alongside a lead rake. The Roman road called The Street ran past nearby Minninglow and Pikehall, linking London to the north and west, and there were other Romano British sites close by at Rainster Rocks and Roystone Grange.

The 'Pecsaete', ('people who live in the Peak'), resided here in Anglo Saxon times, and are remembered in Parwich by the superb tympanum over the door of the church, as well as by graves and burials at Roystone Grange and Wigber Low, the latter of high rank. Moot Low, a meeting point for the Saxon Hundred, may be seen from the top of Parwich Hill.

In medieval times the village was surrounded by the monastic sheep ranches of Roystone Grange, Bostern Grange, Biggin Grange, Hanson Grange, Newton Grange and Mouldridge Grange. Roystone Grange belonged to Garendon Abbey in Leicestershire, and two grants of land from Parwich were made to it in the reign of Henry III. The poor climate of the thirteenth and fourteenth centuries must have created great hardship, with a reduction in the quality and yield of crops, causing villages like nearby Ballidon to contract. A population further weakened by the upheavals of the Hundred Years War and the Wars of the Roses capitulated swiftly to the ravages of the Black Death.

A stone manor house was built in Parwich in the mid sixteenth century but would have been surrounded by wattle and daub cottages. The church was probably the only other stone building in the village at that time. The seventeenth century saw the development of a prosperous rural middle class and the building of yeomans' dwellings like Knob Hall, and smaller houses in stone. This was accelerated by the enclosure of common land in the late seventeenth and early eighteenth centuries. From that time, we see the building of imposing farmhouses in Parwich, like Townhead, Flaxdale, and Hallcliffe. By the nineteenth century life had settled into a pattern of dairy and sheep farming, cheese making and market gardening in a village which for centuries was self sufficient, including everything from a chair bottomer and cobbler, to a coffin maker, and including several grocers.

Part of the unique character of Parwich comes from it having had absentee landlords from around 1700 to the early 1900s. This meant that although it was an agricultural village it

THE PARWICH FAMILY OF WILLIAM JACKSON HOPKINSON
Back from left: Harold, Lois, George Harris Campsie. Front left: Annie Gertrude (wife of George),
William Jackson. Foreground: Ethel May, mother of Mary Whitechurch.

was not an Estate village like Tissington, which was and still is in the demesne of the Lord of the Manor (Sir Richard FitzHerbert Bt.) Instead, there grew up a strong middle class of yeomen farmers like the Alsops, the Swindells, the Brownsons and the Kirkhams (and later Twigges and Buntings) who were able to build and hold land in their own right.

The lives of women in rural villages have never been easy, yet all those I have interviewed for this book remember their childhood and youth with a yearning nostalgia. They stress above all the freedom of a country childhood, so different from the constraints put on children today for reasons of safety. Though conditions were often uncomfortable and you had to be fit and strong to survive, the passing seasons in this beautiful countryside, and the sense of family and community more than made up for it. There are stories about life on the farm, the delights and the hardships; stories about wartime and evacuees, about nursing, schooling, and recreation, dances, outings, concerts, and the novelty of trips to the cinema in Derby. There are tales of walking miles to catch a bus to hospital when in labour, and the trials of being in a fever hospital. There is much about motherhood and being mothered, and the hard work of looking after a family without modern conveniences.

In the later part of the nineteenth and the early part of the twentieth century, there was a rigid class structure in Parwich. On the one hand were the gentry and yeoman farmers, and on the other, the tradespeople, farm labourers and servants. On the side of the gentry was Sir William Evans, who owned the Parwich estate but did not live here. Instead, family members, the Rev. Carr and his family lived at the Hall and his two daughters inherited the

estate. The Evans family, to whom Mary Whitechurch is related, lived at Darley Abbey, and references to them in Mrs. Curtis's book have been included to show the greater mobility of the gentry, as well as the often stultifying manners and morals imposed on the women of the late nineteenth century. Passages about Queen Victoria's visit to Derby, a boat trip abroad, or a description of the Great Exhibition were too good to omit. In the early twentieth century, the most common form of employment for unmarried girls was to go into service, though a few trained to be teachers. After marriage, women often worked hard on the farm, milking, haymaking, as well as engaging in the usual domestic pursuits. They would have churned butter, made cheese, steeped sloes, damsons, parsnips, dandelion, elderflower and elderberry to brew home made wine, and boiled jam using locally grown fruit. They would have baked Derbyshire oatcakes (which in earlier centuries would have been sweetened with local honey), as well as bread, cakes and lots of batter and suet puddings. Clothes would have been handmade on a hand or treadle sewing machine; and pastimes, before the days of television, would have included embroidery, tatting, knitting, rug pegging, crocheting, and quilting.

With the arrival of the twentieth century and two world wars, women's horizons broadened: this was their opportunity to go into occupations like nursing, to leave the village and discover the world outside. Such new found freedom applied equally to the gentry, whose womenfolk had been limited to socialising within their own class, and engaging in elegant pursuits like embroidery, sketching, and music. Parwich women also began to travel and work abroad. Early in the century, one (Lucy Lewis) went to serve as a

LILY MOORCROFT AND HER SISTERS, LUCY AND POLLY
Centre: Lily serves tea, demonstrating her social and domestic skills. The most common form
of employment for unmarried girls was to be in service.

missionary in the Congo, while another went to Abyssinia in the '20s, to work as a teacher-companion. During the Second World War women entered the forces, becoming officers, drivers, or secretaries in the War Office and later still one became a bomb disposal expert.

Of the women who feature in this book, some have lived in Parwich all their lives and have close family living nearby. Some came to Parwich only for holidays, and never forgot the experience. Others were born here, moved away, and then returned at a later date to live out their retirement in a place that holds precious memories for them. Some married Parwich men and settled here, bringing with them the riches of their experience of other places, and it seemed right to include all their story. The book is a history not just of one village and its inhabitants, but of the lives of individuals whose experiences have led them into a variety of social spheres, so that while some have fled the countryside, feeling suffocated by village life, others have sought refuge in its peace and tranquillity.

The book, which spans a period from the end of the nineteenth century to the present, shows how great the changes have been to village life. Today Parwich is a melting pot, absorbing and welcoming newcomers who have managed to change it in subtle ways without encroaching too much on traditional values. While the village may still seem remote, and was so until the development of modern forms of transport, it is ringed by big cities: Derby, Sheffield, Manchester, the Potteries, and Nottingham, to which some villagers now commute each day.

The book draws on the stories of over a dozen women, many of whom are living, but some of whom are deceased, like Helena Birkentall, born in 1875, whose memories of Parwich were published in the Parish magazine of Parwich in the 1950s. In one or more cases the surviving relatives of the women happen to be men. Ken Wayne gives us details of domestic life at the Sycamore Inn, and Roger Graham gives an account of his aunt, Miss Mary Graham, who kept the Post Office in Parwich. He also produced extracts from the letters of his grandmother, Beatrice, to her future husband.

One contributor, Mary Whitechurch, has never lived in Parwich, but her family have had a major influence on village life, having built both the school and the church. In addition, Mary's father, Gerald Lewis, gave the land on which the Parwich Institute was erected.

Mary's descriptions of the seasons in Parwich, told to her by her Parwich born and bred mother, Ethel Hopkinson, have been used to link sections of the book. Mary also provided the book, "Memories of a Long Life", by Mrs. Frances Curtis (née Carr) who, with her sister Susan Lewis (Mary's paternal grandmother) inherited the Parwich estate from Sir William Evans in 1892. Mary also lent me the *Needlework Book* of her mother, Ethel Hopkinson, and the book of *Receipts and Remedies* handwritten by her grandmother, Mary Emma Hopkinson.

The material has been organised under themes such as domestic life, wartime, schooling and so on, without adhering strictly to date order. Details of the contributors may be found at the end of the book.

The book opens with a brief description of her family by Mary Whitechurch. From then on, it is mostly the women who continue to speak in their own unique voices. What follows is a series of intimate portraits in words spoken from the heart.

Gillian Radcliffe

It may be helpful to say something about my father's forbears, the Evans, the Carrs, and the Lewis families, who all feature in Parwich history, as well as those of my mother, Ethel Hopkinson, who was born at Lenscliffe in Parwich in 1892 and lived there until the early 1920s. My mother lived with her parents, Mary Emma Hopkinson and William Jackson Hopkinson. Her father, my grandfather, was a cordwainer, or boot maker as well as being a lay preacher and later, Parish Clerk. He is buried in Parwich churchyard with his wife, and Annie Gertrude, one of their daughters. My grandmother, Mary Emma, wrote out her recipes in longhand, and many are reproduced in this book, just as she wrote them. My mother taught at the village school, as did another sister, Lois, before her. She was also church organist. She loved cycling, and had dresses made specially for the purpose.

Mary Emma Hopkinson

Ethel Hopkinson

My father, Gerald Lewis, lived at Hallcliffe. His mother (my paternal grandmother) Susan Lewis, née Carr, had inherited the Parwich Estate with her sister Frances Curtis, in 1892 from Sir William Evans who built the church and the school in Parwich. Frances is the Mrs. Curtis whose writing appears in this book. Susan was born in Parwich in 1833 where her father, John Edmund Carr, was vicar, and he and his wife Ellen (née Evans) lived at Parwich Hall. Ellen was the daughter of William Evans and Elizabeth Strutt, herself the daughter of Jedediah Strutt, business partner of Sir William Arkwright and later a mill owner in his own right.

A VIEW OF THE VILLAGE AND PARWICH HILL
The Hall is towards the left in the middle distance.

Susan Carr married Samuel Lewis, and their eldest son was the Rev. Claud Lewis who was unpopular in the village because he would not allow use of the school for the celebrations of George V's coronation. My mother, who visited the Hall to read books, told me how much she dreaded going there, as he made her curtsy to him. She used to hide behind the curtains to avoid him!

My father did not marry my mother until 1928, when he was living in the Channel Islands. She, rather daringly, was working in Abyssinia at the time, and he proposed to her by post! She was thirty-six years old and he was fifty-six. They settled in Guernsey where I and my twin brother were born prematurely, weighing only three pounds each at birth. My father had built a house on the cliffs, which had one of the best views on the island. In Derbyshire he had managed the Parwich estate for a while and owned the Creamery (the cheese factory) and the market garden in Monsdale Lane. In Guernsey he took up horticulture. I remember the big greenhouses in which he cultivated big arum lilies, and the sweet peas, daffodils and tulips he grew in the fields.

Mary Whitechurch

A GRAND LADY OF THE EVANS FAMILY OF DARLEY ABBEY
William Evans, a banker, purchased Parwich Hall and the estate from the Levinge family in 1814.

SPRING

With the coming of the spring sunshine, the roads were sometimes dry enough for the children to be running with hoops and spinning their tops. Soon there would be tadpoles to look for in the streams and later, sticklebacks and newts. The hedge banks were carpeted with celandines, daisies and violets. My mother especially looked forward to finding the sweet white violets in Monsdale Lane. Kingcups came early in the stream sides. She called them May Blobs, the local Derbyshire name for them.

Spring-cleaning was very hard work. The heavy chenille curtains used in the winter to prevent draughts were taken out and hung over the washing line, to be beaten with wicker beaters. The same was done to the carpets. Soda was used for washing paintwork; walls might be whitewashed. Lighter weight curtains, blankets and coverlets were washed. Most of the houses did not have running water, so water would have had to be carried from the village pumps for this and all other domestic purposes.

Mothering Sunday came in mid Lent and was much anticipated. By tradition girls in service were allowed to visit their parents on this day. Being Lent, there was less entertaining at this time and the girls could be spared ahead of Easter, Whitsun, and the busy summer. The younger children would be looking forward to seeing their sisters and enjoying a special Simnel cake containing currants, which was baked at this time. The children made cowslip balls to play with and of course daisy chains, sometimes interspersed with buttercup flowers. This could lead to the age-old game of "Do-you-like butter?" which my grandchildren play to this day.

At Easter time eggs were boiled wrapped in onionskins to colour them red and purple. I don't remember my mother mentioning chocolate very much. About this time hen's eggs would be laid down in isinglass, or water-glass, being more plentiful then and thought to preserve better than eggs laid down later in the season. They must be at least twenty-four hours from the nest to allow their temperature to equilibrate, and not more than three days old for freshness.

The cuckoo would herald Mayday; my mother spoke of going to the cuckoo gate in Monsdale Lane to listen to the echo. She also remembered Mayday celebrations, of crowning the May queen and dancing round the Maypole, but I am not sure that this was in Parwich. Could it have been at Tissington? May blossom (hawthorn) was thought to be unlucky if brought in the house, but was used to decorate the doorways. Children liked to eat the fresh young hawthorn leaves, as they tasted "hot". They were sometimes used in salads, as were dandelion leaves and watercress, which would be growing in the streams about now.

The early flowering coltsfoot was gathered for making wine. This must have been quite time consuming, as two pecks of flowers were needed for nine gallons of wine and one peck of flowers filled a two gallon container. In the spring several other wild flowers were also gathered for wine making, including cowslips, dandelions and elderflowers. The latter made a light sparkling wine. These flowers could also be added to gooseberry jam, when it was described as Muscat flavoured and was delicious.

Mary Whitechurch

Receipt for Coltsfoot Wine
For nine Gallons of Wine, two pecks of flowers.
Boil the water and pour it on the flowers.
Let them stand two hours well covered up.
To every gallon add 1 Lemon and 2 oranges
Three lbs of sugar to the gallon Crushed;
half a pound of Ginger and boil it with them.
Boil the lemon and orange peels with the Liquor, slice the pulp; add it after boiled.
Add a little Isinglass and 1 lb of Cut raisins
when you make the barrel up.
When the flowers have been steeped 2 hours [remove] them and if [not] the quantity of Liquor you want, add water. When you boil it put a spoonful of Good thick Yeast in and when you see it offering to work barrel it.
from the Receipt Book
of Mary Emma Hopkinson

Coltsfoot

In spring Nanny would take us for a walk every day, often up Slater's Lane to what we called "the Rabbits" because there were so many, and there would be primroses and violets and dog mercury growing among the outcrops of rock. We were brought up to know and recognise wild flowers, and they never ceased to thrill. Later we would often walk up the Bletches, sometimes to Tissington and back or simply walk through the top of our garden at Hallcliffe and up Parwich Hill. Halfway up there were comfortable rocks on which to sit and contemplate and view the village we loved. At the top was a wood planted in the shape of a cross, with a wall round it so tumbledown that cows could wander in and out. I have recently done that walk with Peter Trewhitt, the present owner of Hallcliffe, my childhood home, and I saw that the wall has been beautifully rebuilt.

Zelda Kent-Lemon (née Dodds)

I remember picking violets on Parwich Hill. There used to be tiny violets growing amongst the stones in Canon Carr's Cross [the cross-shaped wood on the hill]. We used to catch newts from the pond by the rose garden and keep them in jars. These days one could not do that any more. We gave them Anglo-Saxon names like Ethelbert.

Patricia Bagshawe

Syrup of Violet

¼ lb violet flowers. Pour 2 quarts of boiling water; cover it up in a stew pot and let it stand all night then strain it off and add ½ lb Fine sugar and let it ferment in a stone bottle and add ½ oz of Orrace Root.

Mary Emma Hopkinson

16

Patricia Bagshawe (right) and her doll, and her sister, Isma, in the gardens of Parwich Hall.

St. Valentine's Day means nothing today in the village, but the shop windows - five of them - of years ago, were packed not only with the "roses red, violets blue" variety, but also ridiculous caricatures intended to convey a nasty insult to the recipient.

Helena Birkentall

On the north side of the village the subsoil is all limestone, the pasture is short, but sweet, and all boundaries are formed of dry stone walls. South the soil is mostly of shale, often of quite an oily nature. Here are found no stone walls, but hedges interspersed with a number of forest trees, such as elm and ash. On the north there is practically nothing here except the large number of plantations, mostly placed in the neighbourhood of the farmhouses to give protection for man and beast.

One plantation has a special interest for my family. This is that on the top of Parwich hill, planted in the form of a cross, by Mrs. Carr, the wife of my grandfather, Mr. Carr, when he was vicar of Parwich. It was known in my time as "Mr. Carr's Cross", and in my own family as "Grandma's Cross".

Gerald Lewis

In late spring, when the jackdaws were sitting on top of the chimney, Mr. Braddock used to come out of Flaxdale House with a huge whip and you could hear him cracking it; and the birds would just hover away and then come back the minute he'd gone inside. They used to build in the chimneys and block them up!

Mary Rawlins

Dandelion Wine

Allow 2qts of dandelion flower to 1 gall(on) of water; 3lbs of dem[erara] sugar, 1 oz of ginger, 1 lemon , 1 orange.

Boil water and pour over the flowers; let it stand 12 hours then strain them; add sugar and ginger then let boil 1 hr. When nearly cold add 1 tablespoonful of barm to each gall then add orange and lemon sliced; when it [h]as worked an hour or two, put in barrel and stir every day for a week. Put (in) raisins and lump sugar and cork up. For 4 galls: 3 or 4 lbs of raisins and lump sugar.

Mary Emma Hopkinson

When my sister Vere and I were at the PNEU School in Ashbourne, we attended the start of the Shrove Tide football game in the lower Market Place just outside Bagnall's the grocers. It is a game that has its roots in medieval times, we were told; which wasn't in the least bit interesting to us when put beside the fact that 'Our Don' (Don Lowndes, the Parwich village blacksmith and poacher) was really good at scoring goals, especially the year when he hid his motor bike just outside the town and having gained possession of the ball, jumped on the bike, drove off and scored a beautiful goal for Our

Side, the Uppers, being those who came from above the Ashbourne Brook. The others were the Downers, a very suitable name we thought.

Lent was quiet, a time when the snowdrops were out and the FitzHerberts at Tissington Hall would have their annual Daffodil Party. On Good Friday there was a service in the church at 3 pm (this was a long time ago, when Mr Purser was the vicar). And then it was Easter Day! When we came back from church we could go out into the garden and find the Easter eggs. Many years later I realised that my mother never came to church with us (we went every Sunday to Matins with our father) because she rose early and went to Communion; and while we were at church she prepared the Sunday lunch or, joy of joys, on Easter Day she hid the Easter eggs! What was really exciting, a week or so later, was when one of us would discover an egg unclaimed on Easter morning, and that would be the most delicious of all!

Angela Dodds

Ashbourne Gingerbread

¹/₂ lb butter
10 oz plain flour
6 oz sugar
2 teaspoons ground ginger

Cream butter, sugar and ginger and sift in flour. Knead until smooth then pinch off walnut sized lumps of dough, roll into balls then flatten to 1" thickness. Cook in moderate oven for approximately 20 minutes.

If desired, cut dough in the shape of a man or an animal, with currants for the eyes.
Anon

Peter Harrison with Cracker

Shrovetide was a joyous occasion. After boasting of the number of pancakes they had eaten many of the children joined their parents and went off to see the traditional Shrovetide football game at Ashbourne. I went once, saw the barricaded shops, and the shivering men going in and out of the river. Saw a man's coat torn up the back, and was one of a waiting crowd who wondered where the ball was while the cunning downards had put it on the train and goaled it at Clifton. But still this old game goes on, rough and tumble as ever.

The old custom, still prevailing in Lancashire towns, of "Sunday School" processions in Whit-week, was observed in Parwich on Whit-Sunday. Every girl wore a white dress with brightly coloured silk sash and hair-ribbons to match. In all there would be 100 children or more, in those days.

Helena Birkentall

Parwich was a good place in which to grow up. We could walk anywhere at any time. Sometimes our father would drive us to Minninglow or Brassington Tops but our favourite walks were the local ones. We were enthusiastic about wild flowers, thanks to the PNEU School, and would see how many species we could find in the holidays. I loved the wild thyme and the cowslips and the quaking grass on Parwich Hill. We bicycled freely too. I found a letter my mother wrote to her mother, saying "how splendid" it was that my sister Angela, at the age of 9, had cycled to meet a school friend in Ashbourne and then home again. Our house was rarely locked and keys were left in the car.

Sara and Vere Dodds

On Whit-Monday the Women's Club had their procession with banner and band, and after a scrumptious tea there was dancing on the Hall lawn to the music of the band....

Ascension Day or Holy Thursday was the day, and still is, when Tissington people headed by clergy and choir go round to each of the five wells to thank God for the supply of clean drinking water which never failed, even in the great year of country-wide drought in the seventeenth century. We walked over to Tissington from Parwich in my early days and joined in the blessing of the wells, and one

Parwich. Daffodils on the Green.

thought of Parwich cattle driven with others over to drink deep of these crystal waters which ran freely then, as now, in that fateful drought [of 1921].

Helena Birkentall

Elderflower Wine

1 quart elder flowers

3 ½ lbs sugar (lumps)

½ lb Valencia raisins

3 sliced lemons

Put flowers into water in preserving pan and boil for 15 minutes. Pour into earthenware jar.

½ oz yeast

Add sugar, lemons, raisins. Stir until sugar is dissolved. When cool, sprinkle yeast on top of lemons. Leave to stand for two weeks. Skim off scum. Strain carefully and bottle.

Ethel Hopkinson

I like living in Parwich because the wildlife is really nice. I have seen hummingbird hawk moths, buzzards and hedgehogs. I saw a barn owl swooping past the Village Green one time. I have my own pond for tadpoles, which are now frogs.

Sam Webster (age 7)

I like taking Lexie to feed the ducks, and playing in the new playground. I like living next to Alexander and going to school. I like going to the pub for Sunday lunch and I like climbing to the top of Parwich Hill with Daddy before breakfast (sometimes). I really like going to parties with bouncy castles in the garden.

Thayer Linnell (Age 5)

The flowers of the blackthorn appear before the leaves so that we see nothing but the countless blossoms, and as these appear early in the year, in great profusion, the tree is a very noticeable feature in the hedgerow; the fall of the petals rivals the falling snow that is not uncommonly contemporaneous. It will often be noticed that we get a spell of sharp weather and cutting winds as the blackthorn is flowering.

F. Edward Hulme
From *Familiar Wild Flowers*, 1888

Angela and Zelda Dodds (left and right) bridesmaids at the wedding of Patricia Bagshawe (née Crompton-Inglefield).

Domestic Life

A woman's work...

Hare.

A kitchen in Roman Britain would have contained a raised hearth on which charcoal was placed. Cooking was done over this in tripod vessels or on gridirons. A beehive shaped oven would have been used for baking and roasting. Food storage was always a problem and most natives of Roman Britain would have subsisted on a meagre and monotonous diet of flat bread, bean pottage or porridge while their Roman masters feasted on snails fattened in milk, dormice fattened on nuts in earthenware jars, fattened pigeons with clipped wings, oysters, pheasant and goose. Meals in season might have included apples, cherries, plums, and pears, wild fish and game, and for the rich, pork, lamb and beef. Honey was the main source of sweetening. Stale meat was cooked first in milk, then water to improve the taste and, like vegetables, could then be flavoured with herbs such as coriander, cumin, pepper, lovage, caraway, dill, and basil. A ham, skinned, scored and doused in honey, might be baked in a pastry case with dried figs and bay leaves, while pudding might consist of egg custard or fried dates rolled in salt and stuffed with pine kernels, nuts or ground

pepper. To finish, lettuces might be served, as they were believed to induce sleep, a property of certain wild lettuces.

Gillian Radcliffe

For this information I am indebted to, **Food and Cooking in Roman Britain,** by Marian Woodman.

Throughout history, oats have been an important part of the Derbyshire diet. From Roman times and earlier, through to the nineteenth century, porridge or gruel was a staple meal of the poor. Philip Kinder, writing in the 1600s, noted that the "common inhabitants [of Derbyshire] doe prefer oates for delight and strength, above any other graine...It is observed that they have for the most part fair long broad teeth, which is caused by the mastication of their oat bread." Stephen Glover, Derbyshire historian, agreed with him, saying that "Oat bread and Havercake is the food of a large portion of the Derbyshire peasantry."

Food made with oats has the advantage of being filling as well as nourishing, a factor which endeared it to those labouring in the mines, especially in the cold, damp winters characteristic of the Peak District. Before the era of the railways, diet was limited to what could be grown in such a climate, but as Sir Humphrey Davy declared in 1813, "The Derbyshire miners in winter prefer oatcakes to wheaten bread... such nourishment enables them to support their strength and perform their labours better."

The poor were ingenious at finding tasty ways to cook and serve their oatmeal: oatcakes, Parkin, Thor Cake, Hasty Pudding, Frumenty and Lumpytums, the latter possibly a name for the indigestion which might follow such a meal! All would be eaten with cheese and washed down with ale; or a cold posset made from milk, eggs, spices, and currants, with ale used as a curdling agent. A strange custom was to put a wedding ring into this mixture, so that whoever retrieved it with a ladle would be the first to marry during the coming year.

'Lumpytums' were made by throwing the oatmeal into boiling milk so that it formed into small lumps. These might be eaten with treacle and butter. Joyce Douglas describes these as "like tiny, irregular snowballs... releasing a puther of dry oatmeal when chewed."

Gillian Radcliffe

For this information I am indebted to **Old Derbyshire Recipes and Customs**, by Joyce Douglas (This little book is full of fascinating information taken from original sources).

To boyle larkes or sparrows
A recipe copied from the cookbook of Jane Moseley of Brailsford, c.1700

Trusfe them fit to boyle and put into a pipkin, with a laderfull of mutton broth, a peece of whole mace, a quarter of nutmegge, a fagot of sweet hearbes, and a little young parsley pickt cleane and short.... put your parsley loos into your broth: season it with veriuyce, [crab apple vinegar] pepper and sugar, thicken it with the yolkes of two new laid egges hard [eggs that have been laid a few days, not hard boiled] and a peece of manchet, [a small, white loaf] strained with some of the same broth, till they be tender.... garnish your dish as you will.

Joyce Douglas

The terrible Napoleonic war was over before I was born, but my mother had vivid recollections of the misery then endured by the country, when bad harvests were added to the other causes of distress. Sound bread was difficult to procure, and she had seen loaves on her own table from which, when the crust was cut through, the contents ran out like treacle. If such were the inconveniences of the rich, it is fearful to think what the sufferings of the poor must have been. In one respect taxation took a most unwholesome form. The tax on light, causing all windows to be as small as possible, must have acted most unfavourably on the health of the populace. Early sketches taken of the village show what mere peepholes the windows of the cottages were at that period.

Mrs. Curtis

Francis Carr (later Mrs. Curtis)

Frances Carr (later Mrs. Curtis)

I can remember the tinderbox in daily use for obtaining a light before lucifer matches were invented. The matches of my early memory were thin slips of wood, about half an inch wide, with pointed ends dipped in brimstone. The tinderbox was made of iron, and within it fluttered a black, ghostly, filmy substance, which always inspired me with a sense of awe. There was a tedious process with flint and steel, which at last resulted in a spark. The spark kindled the tinder, and thus fire was obtainable. I can also remember the rush light, which stood outside the fender to serve as a nightlight during illness. The rush light was a small candle, made of rushes dipped in tallow. It was fixed at the base of a receptacle like a stove-pipe, about one and a half feet high, made of black metal, and pierced with round holes. The rays of the sunlight penetrated these holes, spotting the darkened walls and ceiling of the room with bright wafer-like circles of light - a weird appearance, not soothing to the eyes of a childish invalid.

Mrs. Curtis

To detect Bones, Jalop, Ashes, & c. in Bread
Slice the large loaf very thin, the crumb only; set it over the fire with water, let it boil gently a long time; take it off, and pour the water into a vessel; let it stand till near cold; then pour it gently out, and in the seiment will be seen the ingredients which have been mixed. The alum will be dissolved in the water, and may be extracted from it. If jalap

has been used, it will form a thick film at the top, and the heavy ingredients will sink to the bottom.
Domestic Cookery by Mrs Rundell
A new System of Domestic Cookery; formed upon Principles of Economy and adapted to the Use of Private Families.
['jalop' is a purgative]

The elder children in the larger families tended the younger members of the family, gathered firewood, and helped their parents considerably; the mother's work was never done. They cleaned, cooked, mended, and made garments, and their great reward was happy, contented men-folk, and rosy-cheeked children.

Helena Birkentall

To discover whether Bread has been adultewrated with whiting or chalk
Mix it with lemon-juice, or strong vinegar, and if this puts it into a state of fermentation, you may be certain it has a mixture of alkaline particles; and these are sometimes in large quantities in bakers' bread.
Mrs Rundell

Kneel On It
Do not throw away an old hot-water bottle - stuff it with old stockings and it becomes a useful kneeling mat
*From: **Take a Tip**. Manchester Evening News*

Eileen Ellis (née Steeples) right, and her sister, Joyce.

Life in the cottage in Creamery Road, with four girls, was very hard for mother, with none of the mod cons we have today. She was a gentle, kind mother, who always had time for us, reading to us each night, books like *Little Women, Lorna Doon, Tom Brown's Schooldays* and so on. She would also make all our clothes. Monday was washday, when she would get up very early, light the fire in the copper, then light the living room fire. The clothes were boiled in the boiler, then ponched in the dolly tub. Whites would be put in a bucket with the blue bag, to make them whiter, then everything would have to be mangled through big wooden rollers by turning a very big handle. Men's collars had to be washed and starched every day, and the shirts went into the wash once a week. If it was a wet day, everything would have to be dried round the fire on a clothes-horse; steam everywhere, and this went on all day. I hated Mondays!

Tuesday was cleaning upstairs day. Bedroom floors were covered with linoleum. This had to be washed on hands and knees, scrubbed occasionally, then polished. There were a few rugs by the side of our beds and the chamber pot underneath as we only had an outside toilet. Thursday was black leading day, another early morning for mother. She would spend an hour black leading the grate, before the coal fire was lit. I still have the bellows she used to get it going. The living room floor had black and red tiles which had to be washed daily. The carpet was coco matting which didn't half hurt your knees if you fell onto it. By the fire we had a peg rug; we all had to help making these rugs. I still enjoy using my rug pegger, and have a mat on the go. I imagine Great Grandmama must have done the same. On Sundays, high days and holidays she would have worn her black shoulder cape and skirt, a wonderful garment, hand embroidered with lace and jet. There was a bonnet to go with it, but I don't know what happened to it.

Saturday night was weekly bath night. The bath was made of tin. It used to hang on the wall outside and had to be brought indoors. Once again the copper had to be lit, to get the water for our baths which also had to be carried in, because we bathed in front of the fire. Afterwards, the bath had to be emptied and all the water carried back outside again.

Eileen Ellis

Ginger Wine

[made in the copper, but not on washday presumably!]

Put 6 Gallons water into a perfectly clean copper with 16 lbs of loaf sugar, the thin yellow rind of eight lemons, ½ to whole Ginger slightly bruised, ½lb raisins.
Boil for one hour, skim carefully and pour off into a large vat till the next day.
The liquid must not be left in the copper overnight.
Strain it next day into a perfectly clean sweet cask and add to it the juice of the lemons, 1oz isinglass

and two tablespoonful of thick frothy yeast. Stir once every day until the fermentation ceases. This is generally in about three days, then bung it up and leave undisturbed for 6 weeks, then strain the wine off into another cask where it must remain for a month at the end of which time it is ready for bottling; some people add 1 quart of brandy but this is quite optional and without it the wine is excellent.

Mary Emma Hopkinson

My mother's exercise book of sewing projects contains patterns for some fascinating garments. Given the pencil sketch of an elephant at the back of the book, might it have been used by her in Abyssinia, where she was employed as a lady's companion and governess?

Mary Whitechurch

This drawing and the following examples of patterns are taken from Ethel Hopkinson's **Needlework Book.** Ethel, married to Gerald Lewis, was Mary Whitechurch's mother.

Chemise for a Girl

The chemise is now going out of general use on account of its excessive bulk, and is being replaced by combinations, but it is still used to a certain extent, and also the pattern serves as a type from which many other garments can be developed.

Materials: 2 yards calico, longcloth, or madapolam. 32" to 36" wide, at one shilling and sixpence halfpenny per yard.

Ethel Hopkinson

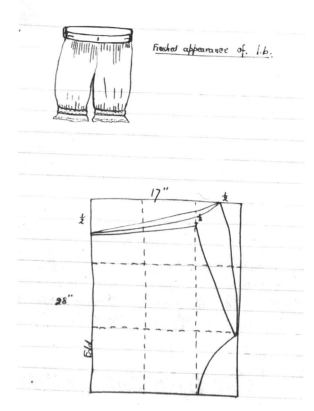

A pattern for bloomers

Mum made all my clothes. She'd have these catalogues, and she used to send away for loads and loads of material, then she'd make me dresses, and Granny dresses, and herself dresses. She knitted my school cardigans when I went to the Grammar school, and she used to darn socks, Granddad's socks, Dad's socks, things like that. When I went to school, Mum made me dresses with pants to match. Mum was brilliant really cause she was good at dress making, she was a good cook, she could knit, and she could sew. Dad's wearing pullies that Mum knitted for him years ago, the sort without sleeves with 'V' necks. He's still got some of those for working in now. She went on knitting until a few years before she died, until her hands got that she couldn't do it.

Valerie Kirkham

For keeping moths out of clothing

Mix half a cupful of alcohol the same quantity of spirits of turpentine and two ozs of camphor ; keep in a stone bottle and shake before using. The clothes or furs are to be wrapped in Linen and crumpled-up pieces of blotting paper dipped in the liquid are to be placed in the box with these.

Mary Emma Hopkinson

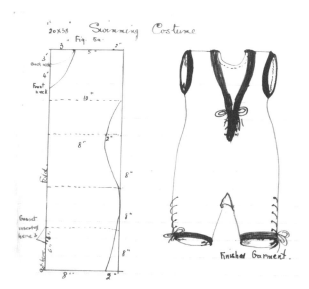

Ethel's pattern for a swimsuit.

My granny did quite a lot of sewing, and she taught me how to cook and sew, but the one thing I could never master was crochet. I could do all sorts of knitting, Fair Isle and so on, and I made all our clothes, even men's shirts.

Barbara Lowes

Weather-way-side and the Flaxdales lie together near the Alsop Road. They may be the fields where flax for linen was grown. Older folk in the village now living have seen linen which has been grown, spun, and woven in Parwich.

Helena Birkentall

New Calicoes...

If new calicoes are allowed to lie in strong salt water an hour before the first washing the colours are less likely to fade.

Cloth saturated in kerosene and dipped in whiting for cleaning tinware is much better than anything else used.

Mary Emma Hopkinson

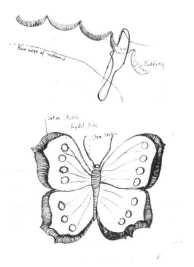

An embroidery motif.

Ethel Hopkinson's design for 'crawlers' was clearly what the best-dressed Edwardian toddler should be wearing.

A design for crawlers.

We had a range at Slate House with a big griddle pan hanging down from it on a hook, and Mum used to cook oatcakes on this round, flat pan. We had a lot of Yorkshire puddings, Yorkshire pudding for the main meal, and Yorkshire pudding with treacle and milk on for afters. A side of bacon was hung up in the living room.

Barbara Lowes

Pudding: Miss Langford

1 cup flour, 2ozs suet, 1 tablespoon of Treacle, a pinch of Soda, grate of nutmeg, lemon grated, pinch of Salt, ¼lb Raisins, Milk

Mabel Fletcher

(Mabel Fletcher was Barbara Lowes' maternal grandmother)

At first we did the ironing with flat irons. You put them on the fire to warm up. We had two or three of those, and then later Mum had an old type electric one, very antiquated really; you just put the lead in the top and that was it. I suppose Granddad's collars were starched, because people wore shirts with button on collars then. We had a kitchen, a living room, and what we called a front room that nobody ever went into except at Christmas! Granny and Granddad used to get up at six o'clock and have a cup of tea and a piece of bread and butter, and then at half past eight or nine o'clock they'd come in for a cooked breakfast. Lunchtime would be a snack. Dinner was at teatime, and you always had meat and veg, and puddings that were suety things with fruit in, or jam or treacle, or really big apple roly-polys. Mum had a pudding cloth and she used to roll everything up, tie it, and put it in the pot to boil; or she made big sponge puddings with jam on, or treacle. I mean if you ate those now, you'd think gosh, how unhealthy, eh? I can remember having that sort of diet. Farmers, used to have supper at maybe nine o'clock as well. On a Sunday it was always cold meat, cold potatoes and whatever else you'd got left from lunchtime.

When he went to market, Granddad wore knee britches with brown boots and, what do you call them, that you put round your legs made of leather? Gaiters. He used to buckle

Members of the Calladine family by the kitchen range

them on. The trousers buttoned down the leg from the knee. Grandma and Mum always wore dresses and what Mum called overalls, but not the ones you fasten down the side; you put them over your head and tied them at the back. Mum wore a smock for milking, but I don't remember Grandma wearing one. When they went out they always wore hats, especially to funerals.

Valerie Kirkham

Furniture Paste

2 oz Bees Wax   1oz white wax

½ oz Kestile [Castile?] soap

½ pt turpentine

Shave fine; put in a jar to dissolve

then put turpentine over it

Mary Emma Hopkinson

At the age of 86, Mary Anne Shaw came to live with her daughter, Esther Brownson, at Brentwood in Parwich, bringing memories of her life as a young wife and mother. Mary Anne was married in 1863 to Owen Shaw, a mill owner, and lived at Northfields in Lockwood outside Huddersfield. The household at Lockwood was well run, and maids were an integral part of life. Mary Anne depended on her *Mrs Beeton's Book of Household Management*. Afternoon tea was clearly a ritual. Tea was taken from a wooden caddy and poured from a silver teapot balanced on a stand over a spirit stove. The maid was summoned by a brass 'pinger' bell. Clearly, Mary Anne lived a leisurely life as a housewife and tutored her daughters in the gentle art of housekeeping without ever having to do menial work herself.

Ann Vidler

There was meat at weekends, but I wasn't particularly interested in food when I was young. I do remember that Aunty's cabbage tasted absolutely marvellous! It was fresh from the garden and a little bit undercooked, as it should be, and she put lots of butter in it, chopped in. I can remember the cabbage but what we were eating with it I don't know! We grew vegetables at home, but there was just something about this cabbage that was memorable.

I remember the range, and food cooking in the oven that was at the side of the open fire, and the big pot that was used for boiling the clothes in, hanging from a hook over the fire; and there would be two saucepans on the fire on trivets, and an oval type of saucepan, like a preserving pan, that would have two different things in it, probably a stew steaming away and a pudding just sitting in the water. This was very different from home where Mum used to make oatcakes on the gas cooker on an iron shelf that had come out of the old range. She made these on washing day. There would be oatcakes when we got home from school as a special kind of treat, all rolled up with golden syrup inside, hot and straight off the griddle.

Betty Stone

My grandfather always used to kill a pig at Christmas, hang it up and salt the hams in the big thrawl with saltpetre which cured it better round the knuckle bone. I used to stir the blood. My mother used to make savoury ducks and black pudding. To make it you need groats and seasoning. I remember getting this big enamel bucket and stirring the blood by the fire, and stopping it clotting until it cooled down. Mother used to make huge bowls of black pudding and brawn. I make brawn here sometimes. You get a pig's head (I do half of one) and the trotters, which jellies the brawn. Then I buy some shin beef and put it in a big casserole and cook it slowly in the oven; and keep working it round. You cook it until all the little bones come out then you press it into a basin and oh, it makes lovely brawn.

When we'd made the black puddings we used to render the fat. We put it in the oven on trays, and melted it down, then we poured the lard into big, brown stone jars. We kept rendering it until there was nothing left, and that was your scratchings. My father always said the ones you buy in the pubs in packets are not the same! Our stove was an old black leaded range with a fire, and a boiler, and an oven. On the top you'd have a hook and a plate to cook things on. In fact I cooked my wedding cake in the oven of the big black range and I've often wondered how I gauged it right. It was a three tier wedding cake. I got married in 1960.

Mary Rawlins

When we were travelling with the fair there were lots of chores to do, like cleaning the caravan and polishing the brass. We stayed in one place for a week: we'd travel on a Sunday, build up on Monday, Tuesday and Wednesday, finish off on Thursday, open Thursday night, Friday night, Saturday afternoon and Saturday night, then pull down on Sunday and travel to the next place. We lived on sandwiches, but if we got into a place where we could stay a fortnight, oh boy, then we could have Sunday lunch cooked on the Hostess Range in the caravan.

Washday: you did your washing outside; so what you did, you got three iron stakes in the ground and built the fire in the middle and put the zinc bath onto it, filled with water. You hotted it up, put some wash powder in and

threw in the whites, and as they boiled, you took some of the water out of the bath and put it in the dolly tub. Then you took the whites and ponched them in the dolly tub and put them on the rubbing board, then put them into a bucket at the side. Then the water went back into the bath to keep hot. Mother used to wring out the clothes as much as she could then put them through the mangle. I can see her now, because I'm mangling and taking her blouse through as well and she's shouting stop, stop!

Clara Evans

Clara Evans' mother, Mrs. Sykes, outside her caravan in Parwich during Wakes Week.

To render wood incombustible:
Alum, tungstate of soda, washing soda; any of these if dissolved in water will render wood which has been thoroughly permeated by them almost incombustible; but nothing will prevent heat from permeating wood.

Mary Emma Hopkinson

In my aunt's house there would have been a kitchen range, and on one side would be the oven and on the other side a little boiler which would heat a bucketful of water. There had to be a fire all the time to heat the water

MISS OADLEY, LATER MRS. SYKES (CLARA EVANS' MOTHER) OUTSIDE HER FIRST CARAVAN.

and to cook. The range was fired with coal and we used to go out and collect sticks: that was exciting, just picking up dead wood. We never pulled anything off trees or out of hedges. We would take a sack to put the wood in and carry it back. I came to Parwich in summer and I never stopped to think what life was like in the winter here, when the winters were much colder. My mother talked about the boys going to work over the fields and actually walking over the top of the stone walls because the snow was so deep.

And oil lamps; I remember the smell of the lamps being cleaned: methylated spirit did the glass and then the paraffin was put in and the wick trimmed; that was a ritual in every household, every morning. How dangerous, thinking of it now, with all the children in one small room and a paraffin lamp which if knocked over would cause a pretty horrendous fire!

Betty Stone

Furniture Polish Varnish
Put 2oz Dragons Blood broke in pieces into 1qrt rectified spirits of wine
let the bottle stand in warm place shaken frequently
When dissolved it will clean Wood, Mahogany
Mary Emma Hopkinson

Our family originated in Ireland. They came over in the 1600s. I have a manuscript on my wall on parchment showing all about the Brownlee family; and I've got this old book as well, and my mother's got a sampler. I've got the old warming pan that was put into my bed to heat it up, and there's an old tobacco tin that used to be my granddad's, and two little copper gills that came from Mr Gibson's house, the Fold, when that was a pub.

Barbara Lowes

I was born in the old fashioned caravan. I'm afraid it no longer exists, it rotted away. It was all wood. It had cupboards and fretwork and cut glass mirrors, and bunk beds with sliding shutters, and the top one had a big cut glass mirror which slid back. That was mum and dad's bed and the bottom one was just panels, which was my brother's and my bed. When we got older we had to have a bigger van so Mother had one built, it was all her planning. Inside it was all cut glass (she loved that cut glass) and brass paraffin lamps. There was big brackets what came out from the sideboard and the lamp sat in the bracket; and on the ceiling the shade was all brass as well, and it'd got all these frills all the way round; and it was warm in there because we had a Hostess range, a combined fire and oven, a big one this time. Outside was the water can. I used to have to take that to houses to ask if I could have water, and when I complained it was too heavy to carry, father made me a barrow of wood with a couple of pram wheels on it.

Clara Evans

I gave up nursing when we came here. Harry didn't want me to go out to work, though people in the village did, and they wondered why I didn't go to work at Parwich Hall. I had quite a big house to keep clean, and two children and washing and all. I didn't have a dolly tub, which was what a lot of people in the village had. Instead I had a copper in the kitchen, which we used to light and boil the clothes in. Whites were soaked and then boiled, rinsed and blued. Washday was quite a day - it took you all day to do it, because while you'd got the soapy water you scrubbed all the kitchen out and the pantry.

Ella Hopkinson

Perfume Powder for Linen

½ lb Lavender flowers

½ oz each Dried Thyme and Mint

¼ oz ground cloves and caraways

1oz dried common salt

Mix all together

Put in silk or cambric bags

Mary Emma Hopkinson

I have a beautiful black beaded 1920s 'flapper's' dress, which I found in the attic of an aunt's house after she had died. I remember being in people's houses when the daughters were being presented at Court and were wearing their Prince of Wales feathers; it was a very elegant age. I was with the Rothschilds, and Peggy Ashcroft was living with them part time, and she was in "Rebecca", and she gave us seats to go and see her in it. A lot of her clothes and costumes were in the house, and at night time I used to open the wardrobe door and look at them and think, aren't they beautiful! But you see, that's all past, hasn't it? You see these young girls with ever such a pretty dress and then they've got these bumper boots on!

Ella Hopkinson

The Brownsons came from Scotland with Mary Queen of Scots in 1568; after her execution a branch of the family settled in Parwich. They lived in various houses: Hallcliffe, the Hall and Alsop Hall. Miss Mary Brownson lived and died at Town-head. After her death at the age of 96, a sale of many Jacobean relics attracted buyers from far and near. The Duke of Portland secured many of them, including the Portland goblet and a beaded pin-cushion, which bore the words embroidered in beads, "Up with Prince Charlie and down with the Parliament". Peacocks strutted across the lawns of Town-head, nesting in a great box high up in a tree. Their raucous cries heralded throughout the village the approach of bad weather.

Helena Birkentall

Esther Brownson

In 1907 when Esther and George Brownson, and Esther's sister, Annie, moved to Parwich, the small village was dominated by a rigid class structure. On the one side were the gentry, mostly wealthy farmers and landowners, on the other the villagers, most of whom were labourers on the land. James Brownson, George's father, was 'gentry', a wealthy landowner who lived in a substantial house in the centre of the village. Another relative lived in Townhead, another large house. Into this scene moved the newcomers, to a modest cottage which was rented, and a shop which was to provide them with an income. The dichotomy of being 'in trade'

Brentwood. The shop is on the left

and yet born into gentry and married into 'gentry' must have taxed Esther and Annie greatly, for they were proud women who were used to a leisured way of life.

Compared with Lockwood, Esther's childhood home, Brentwood, the house in Parwich seemed an unprepossessing stone built cottage with shutters at the windows. It faces on to a cobbled frontage and opens directly on to the street at the corner of the main crossroads. The front door opens into a small vestibule with a door leading to the right into the sitting room, a door leading from the left into the living room and a flight of stairs with old hand-carved banisters leading upstairs.

The sitting room was kept for 'best'. It had a deep window seat looking onto the street from where the pious could be observed on Sunday walking to church in their Sunday best. A deep cupboard full of books was recessed into an alcove. Also on the wall were George's smoking cabinet and a pair of pictures of pheasants painted by Esther's sister, Annie. A grandfather clock stood against the wall. In the centre of the room were armchairs, a settee, a dining table and chairs. The piano was in this room also. In the living room opposite was the range in front of which was Mary Anne Shaw's rocking chair. A scrubbed table covered by a chenille cloth

was in the centre of the room with green covered chairs around it, and a huge settee was placed in front of the window. From here the shutters were opened or closed by way of a catch through a hole in the wall. Leading out of the living room was a door into the shop.

To the back one went down steps into the scullery, with a stone sink, a copper and a well sunk into the floor. A slate lined stone floored larder kept all the food cold and fresh even in the hottest weather. Esther, Granny Brownson, was an excellent plain cook. Nobody who tasted her cooking forgot it quickly. She baked all her own bread, made delicious Parkin, Swiss buns and Bakewell tarts and served up the most delectable steamed puddings. I have a recipe given to me by Granny. It is known simply as 'Mrs Gainsford's Scones', Mrs Gainsford being Granny's friend.

Upstairs were three bedrooms, a bathroom with washbasin set into a washstand and a bath. Two lumber-rooms were part of the bathroom. It was in the lumber-rooms that Granny kept items such as two waist-high globes set on stands and a china doll that played the mandolin when it was wound up. Another item of interest was a bassinette, one of the earliest types of prams on the market and presumably the one used for daughter Muriel as a baby.

Esther and George Brownson

George Brownson

The garden and outbuildings were reached by way of the scullery. A door led out of the scullery onto a path and directly facing was a flight of old steps into the garden, which was on a higher level than the cottage. If one wished to go to the privy it was reached by a door leading out of the scullery. Again a flight of steps had to be negotiated before reaching a cobbled area behind the shop. The old stables, one of which was no doubt George's workshop, were passed before reaching the privy, so it was quite a trek to the loo, especially on a cold winter's evening when the steps were slippery. The garden with its outbuildings was laid out in a typically Victorian way. There were shady arbours, hidden seats, secluded from view and sheltered walks which would lead on into the unknown.

Granny was a stately woman: upright, quite tall and well built without being over-weight.

She had a mop of curly, auburn hair, blue eyes and a very fair complexion. She had always taken an interest in fashion and a change in circumstances was not going to alter the habit of a lifetime. Taking their courage in both hands, both sisters had their hair shingled in the 1920's when this fashion first signalled the approach of the liberated woman. They were the envy of their more conservative friends, Granny often recalled. The ladies lost little time in integrating into the village. Maybe they were astute and foresaw difficulties if they did not bridge the social divide or perhaps it was a gregarious nature that prompted them to enter village life. Whatever the reasons, integrate they did.

Ann Vidler

How to remove Iron Mould from Linen

Mix a little oxalic acid and hot water together and rub the parts with the solution, after which wash the linen well.

Mary Emma Hopkinson

I went to live on Gibbon's Bank when I was married in 1963, and I lived up there for 11 years. We had no water and no toilet. Halfway down from Gibbon's Bank there was a tap and we used to get water from it, and we had an outside toilet at the back. We brought the children up there, and then we moved down to the council houses, Chestnut Cottages, and then to where we live now. They were great days up there at Gibbon's Bank. We used to pay three and six a week rent for it. I'd go back up there any day. We had hot summers and really cold winters. The children used to play on Gibbon's Bank when they were little. I had two children, Jonathan and Belinda. They loved playing in the woods: they used to play soldiers. I had Jonathan first, and when I had the next one I really wanted a little girl, and when Belinda came I was so thrilled. I could fancy her in frilly dresses with bows in her hair, but she turned out to be a tom lad! She'd never put her doll in the pram; she'd put the dog in it instead!

I used to do the washing outside. It was hard up there, when you had no proper water. We had these big zinc buckets to carry the water up in. We had a zinc bath hanging up on the wall outside, and we used to bath the children in front of the fire. It were great, having a bath in front of the fire. You'd never dream of doing it now; you wouldn't make the effort, but it would be lovely. And I can remember people fetching water from the Pump Shed, opposite Flaxdale House. There used to be a lady called Miss Roberts who lived where they had the post office, and she used to fetch water from across there, all dressed in black, a black dress. It was hard work; you had to be young, strong and fit.

Barbara Lowes

Barbara and Alan Lowes at Gibbon's Bank

John and Belinda Lowes

Our family moved to Parwich in 1947, when I was 10 and my sisters were 8, 4 and 1. Having moved from a house on the edge of Combs, near Chapel-en-le-Frith in North Derbyshire, we were excited to be in the middle of the village, on the Green, at Hallcliffe. Living in the house with us were two maids, who cooked and cleaned, and Nanny Williams, from Liverpool, who helped our mother with the little ones. Evelyn & Connie Kehoe, from County Carlow, were wonderful Irish dancers, and on Sunday nights when jigs were played on the wireless they would dance, light as feathers on their feet, although they were by no means slim.

Nanny stayed with us until soon after my youngest sister, Zelda, went to the PNEU School in Ashbourne at the age of six. I think Evelyn and Connie left about the same time. I was by then at boarding school in Hertfordshire.

Sara Dodds

After Peter and I got married and I moved to Parwich, Mrs. Braddock lived next door at Flaxdale House. One cold morning after I'd asked Denis, her son in law, to have a cup of coffee, the old lady bolted the door and he couldn't get back in. She'd got mixed up and thought it was her birthday, and that he would be taking her out for a little ride that day and a snack, but she'd got the wrong day, and she was so cross. So he says to me, "Can you be on standby to take the pane out of the window?" So I said, "I can't do that! Keep talking to her, coax her. Anyway," I said, "I'm going up to Mum's. You can ring me up if you're stuck." He'd been out ages, then all of a sudden she pulled the bolt back. So I said, "Stick a cork in the thing so she can't do it again!" We laughed many a time about it.

Mary Rawlins

It has been shown how slowly the evolution of man took place from cave to cottage, and from skin-clad savage to the woollen-clad, stone housed and well fed villager of a century ago. During the last seventy years, however, the wheels of progress have turned more swiftly than at any time in the history of Parwich.

Electricity with its gadgets of light, heating, cleaning and cooking, has ousted the farthing dip, paraffin lamp, dolly tub, dolly pegs, and the old-fashioned wasteful kitchen range of the old homesteads of the village. It seems as

The Dream Kitchen.
"House Proud" Products. Daily Mail Ideal Home Book, 1946-47

though the modern housewife has emerged from a period of dull, cold darkness to a life of light and radiant heat.

Helena Birkentall

It was good having small children in Parwich. My friends used to come on a Friday afternoon, so the children could all play together. By then of course Parwich was on mains water and electricity. I was scared stiff of electricity when I came down here to be honest. Well, I'd had nothing to do with it you see. I know it sounds silly; I'd got all the mod cons here, but at my home at Upper Moor Farm there was only the Calor gas and coal fires. People thought I was crazy, but it frightened me to death till I got used to it.

Mary Rawlins

Plumbing

People returning to Parwich looked out first for the tree-crowned summit of the hill. Once, both trees and slopes were blackened and yellow. This was in 1921, when the great drought of a fierce, hot summer burnt everything up. The water supply, which has been brought to the village of late years, would have been very useful to us then, when the rainwater supply was soon exhausted and we had to depend on the old wells to keep the village going. It is strange to remember that there was no bathroom or back-boiler in Parwich in those days.

Helena Birkentall

If you needed to go to the toilet in the middle of the night you'd have a chamber pot. The only thing I didn't enjoy was the privy: I was afraid of it, I don't know why because it was whitewashed and spotlessly clean. Everything was scrubbed and so on, but it was dark inside, with a strip of light over the door, and I remember taking a deep breath and getting out before I needed to breathe again because of the smell. There was a lid that went on the middle bit, and a box of lime with a little shovel in it. Well, I never needed that; I just could not look down there. Then I realised that young children who came to stay with us at Darley Abbey were just as frightened of the water from the cistern. It could be very noisy when the old fashioned chain was pulled and there was a sudden rush of water. They would open the door, reach as far away from it as possible, pull the chain quickly and shut the door before the water fell - reasonable I suppose!

Betty Stone

In the 1930s there were only two bathrooms with running water in Parwich *[the Hall and Hallcliffe]*. I remember as a child seeing men digging up the roads to put in the iron pipes for mains water. Before this, the Hall water was pumped up to the mere at the top of the garden, and people fetched water from the village pumps: there was one by Green Gates. Miss Alice Brownlee lived in the house below Gibbon's Bank and I remember her coming with her terrier Topsy to fetch water in a bucket from the troughs in Kiln Lane. She was old fashioned and rather eccentric, with her hair done rather like Beatrix Potter's. I remember one very hot summer we swam in the mere at the top of our garden. This was after we had mains water and the mere was used for watering the gardens. You couldn't drink it. Before mains water came we always drank bottled water, Malvern water.

Patricia Bagshawe

We had no mains water in the house at all. We carried all the water into the house. We had a big range in the living room with a copper with boilers on the outside, and we heated water on that. We had no bathroom. We had to bath in tin tubs in front of the fire - an outside toilet as well, which wasn't very nice. When you're little you don't like going outside in the dark! There was a two-holer privy at Fields Farm, at Ballidon, which is now Ballidon Quarry offices. My uncle lived there and they had a double adult one, and a child's one.

We had a gritstone sink in the kitchen, which you got to scrub and that's where you did your washing up and your washing. I don't think my mum ever had a washing machine at Dam Farm. We had a copper, dolly pegs, and a dolly tub, and we had a mangle: that was it. I remember the sewage system being put in

Parwich, in the 1950s I think. I remember them digging everybody's gardens up.

Valerie Kirkham

Today I live opposite Cat Low, which you say is an ancient burial cairn. That comes as a bit of a shock to me because I remember the horse and cart going round the village at midnight to collect the night soil and dump it up the side of the Low!

Kathleen Allsopp

I can remember them digging the drains for the sewerage in Parwich, and I can remember them digging trenches out, because my John was small and he was always falling in the trenches, and he would be say five? So it would be around the 1950s.

Ella Hopkinson

When I moved to Parwich, they were tarmacking the roads for the first time. Old Oscar and his steamroller were parked across on the Green. Until then, the lanes had been a sea of mud or dust depending on the season, and all covered in cowpats from all the cows that grazed on the Green. It must have been hard to fetch water for baths and for washday on Sunday nights, carrying it home in pails over the slippery road from the old pump shed which is now the bus shelter. Fortunately we had a pump at the side of the sink, and a boiler in one side of the range to heat it up.

Kathleen Allsopp

There was an old lady whose house we used to fetch water from, and stop for a chat. One day she comes and says, do you think you could do me a favour? Do you go to into the town often? So I says, well we usually go shopping on a Thursday. She says, do you think you could go to the Bank for me? So I says, that depends what you want from the Bank. I would like you to take me some money in and have it changed into the new currency, she says. Well, I couldn't believe what she did next. She got a sharp knife and cut a hole in the wallpaper, took out a brick and there was this box in the cavity with a thousand pounds in it! I says, well I don't know whether I dare take that much, but she says, please, please? So I trundle off to Yorkshire Penny Bank but they'll only take two hundred in one go; so then I go to every bank, and when I come back and tell her what I've done, she says, oh, I'm ever so grateful, here you are, here's something for your trouble, and she give me a hundred pound, and that money bought some of the stone for the bungalow we built in Parwich.

Clara Evans

When my mother, Millicent Wayne lived with her family at Rock House, they obtained their water from the trough by Staines Cottage. Every Sunday evening they had to fetch enough water to fill the big copper for washday the following morning.

Before mains water in the 1950s, the toilet facilities at the pub were urinals for the men, and three earth closets, one for the men, one for the ladies, and one for the pub family. The earth closets would be emptied on a regular basis and provide manure for the garden. On one occasion an elderly lady came into the pub most distressed, and a little difficult to understand. It turned out not to be the drink that was distorting her speech, but that her false teeth had fallen into the earth closet. Carefully, with sticks, the teeth were fished out from the human manure and after a good wash, provided a number of years' service.

Ken Wayne

Shopping

Eileen Ellis:
There were four shops in the village. Mrs. Brownson's was at Brentwood; Mrs Wibberley was at the present shop; the Norcliffes were at Jasmine House, and the Post Office was run by Mrs Graham and Miss Graham. Mrs Pollett sold everything, twist tobacco, etc. Wibberley's was a general store, and Brownson's too, and Miss Norcliffe had lots of sweets and was a general stores as well. We used to have to go and get an ounce of twist for Mr Blackwell every Sunday morning. He was an old gentleman who used to live in the cottages at West View. We used to love buying humbugs; and we got our fishing rods from Mrs Pollett.

Patricia Bagshawe:
Mrs. Graham and her daughter Miss Graham ran the Post Office. They had lots of cats that used to climb all over the counter, but mothers were not allowed to sit their small children on it. Harry Twigge, at Close Farm, had a trap to deliver the milk, and Wall's ice cream used to come from Ashbourne on a stop-me-and buy-one.

Valerie Kirkham:
A number of delivery vans came to the village. There was the baker's from Hognaston, and a Mr. Alsop from Ashbourne.

Ella Hopkinson:
The Co-op came out with bread on a Tuesday in a van. You ordered what groceries you wanted and it came in a box on the Friday.

Barbara Lowes:
There was the fish man: they called him Fishy Wilson. We used to say, "Fishy Wilson's calling!" He also had vegetables.

Valerie Kirkham:
He was from Mappleton and he came on a Tuesday. And we had the 'oil man', a mobile ironmonger, who sold everything, buckets, mops, brushes, soap. His name was Mr Corbridge and he came every other Monday from Bakewell.

Ella Hopkinson:
He sold oil because mostly people had paraffin stoves. He also sold cups and saucers and all sorts of things.

Valerie Kirkham:
There was always someone calling, butchers too: Peaches were coming then from Ashbourne, and Mr Hall from Hartington.

Ella Hopkinson
Three butchers came to the village. There was a shoe mender as well, who lived in the churchyard and had a little shop there. But you see in those days lots of men mended their own family's shoes.

Valerie Kirkham:
There was a lady who was a hairdresser who lived on Mount Pleasant and I used to have my hair cut there, and Mum used to have hers done as well. Mum used to cut Granddad's hair, and Dad's hair as well. It was the same with chiropody, Mum used to do Granddad's feet always, oh yes.

The shop at Brentwood was the family source of income. From the back of the shop butter was cut from a large block and bacon was sliced. On the counter in the front all the dry foods were weighed out on the scales and packed neatly into paper bags. Little was pre-packed in those days so shopping was a more leisurely business altogether, and Esther and Annie Brownson gleaned all the village news here. The sisters' partnership never faltered: when one was needed in the shop the other continued to run the domestic scene.
Ann Vidler

Do you remember Jim Webster? He had Buxton Dairy. Then he took a shop at Longstone, down the main street. He was married to Florrie Weston, and he used to come every fortnight round Parwich in a little Austin Seven, selling whatever he could in the drapery line, round all the people in Parwich.

Ken Wayne

There were no supermarkets, and Daisy Bank was miles from any village, so the groceries came by van, all the way from Bakewell to Cobblers Nook, where we picked them up by pony and trap, driving down the 'Measured Mile' and crossing over the railway line.

Kathleen Allsopp

Having been very poor, my mother was always conscious of how she spent money, and always arranged to have our school shoes mended when we came to Parwich because the cobbler put on country soles which were very thick and very heavy, and lasted a long time; but as one got older and a bit self conscious, it was quite embarrassing to have these really very clompy shoes. When we got home, people would say, "You've grown since your holidays!" I don't remember the cobbler's name but he was just above the shop, up by the school. I can remember because we used to climb over the garden wall to Shaw Croft, which is now where the professor lives; and just a little way down was the cobbler, and his workshop was at the front of his little house, and we'd go and talk to him and watch what he was doing. He mended horse gear, harness, and we used to go and watch the blacksmith as well, up Smithy Lane. I'd never been so close to a big horse: what wonderful creatures! The blacksmith would just lift up the foot and pare with a huge knife, it seemed to me cutting away the horse's foot, then put the iron shoe straight onto the foot with clouds of smoke rising up and the horse standing there quite patiently, perhaps with a young boy at it's

head talking to it, perhaps a nose bag on for something to eat. Yes, that was the sort of thing one could only see on this sort of visit.

Mrs. Beatrice Graham outside the Post Office

Miss Graham's mother kept the Post Office at Sunniside and in 1982, when I came to live in Parwich, it was still exactly the same: only the step had worn a little more. The bell still clanged, the counter, everything was just as I remembered it, and Miss Graham looked exactly like her mother, plumpish, with fluffy grey hair, very upright, very stately and yet a motherly looking person. Of course when I came as a child, her mother would have been as old as Miss Graham was when we came back here probably. I remember there was a little farm attached to the Post Office, a small holding, and there were a few cows, because we used to buy milk there and that astounded me, to go to the post office to get a pint of milk!

I remember being asked to go to another shop to buy a pound of treacle. Well, I loved doing errands, so off I went to the shop and asked for a couple of things plus the treacle. I think the lady was Mrs Brownson, and she said, "Yes, well give me your jar!"
Well that floored me. "I haven't got a jar", I said.

"Well, you can't have treacle without a jar! You had better go and get one."

So I went, and had to tell my Aunt that you can't have treacle without a jar, as if you exchanged a jar for the treacle: and my Aunt said,

"There it is on the table. I've put it out for you!"

Well I thought treacle came in a tin for goodness sake! So off I went and the treacle was in a little barrel with a tap, and when the 1lb. jar was full, that was a lb. of treacle. My Aunt hadn't given me anything to put on the top of it so I had to carry it carefully.

Betty Stone

Ben Mogue with the milk.

Every Friday morning Mrs. Tipper used to deliver the post. She took over from Mr. Slater doing Alsop en le Dale. She and George Tipper lived in the little cottage next to the Pinfold. Every Friday morning, when she got back from Alsop en le Dale, she used to come down to the Sycamore pub for two big packets of Birds Eye cod fillets for Miss Graham's cats. Everybody used to dread going to the Post Office because of those cats sitting on top of the counter.

Ken Wayne

Miss Graham, who ran the Post Office, was a lady, she really was, a most gracious lady.

Eileen Ellis

My parents lived in Shaw Lane (what is now Shaw Cottage). My mum sold fish and chips on Friday and Saturday, she had a proper stove installed and the fish used to come fresh from Grimsby by train to Alsop station and my brothers used to collect this with a trolley.

Irene Wilton

Mr Harry Twigge came every morning with his pony and cart to deliver the milk. It would be ladled from a churn into our jugs. The butcher also came to the back door and the weekly joint, usually a sirloin, would stay getting blacker and blacker in the meat safe outside the kitchen door until Sunday. The laundry van came once a week as well – this was long before the days of washing machines. There was a cobbler in the village who drove a motorcycle with sidecar.

Sara and Vere Dodds

At the Sycamore pub, we had the first ice cream permanently on sale in the area, in Parwich, the first frozen food, and Parwich rock. I bought a hundred weight of that. You know Blackpool rock? Well ours was made in exactly the same place. I used to have to buy a hundredweight from one of these wholesale groceries, because Parwich Wakes were coming up - threepenny and sixpenny sticks, and we had it on't lawn at front of pub, and it stopped there for a week. I've got a disc made like that *[indicates a wheel shape with his hands]* which says 'Parwich Rock' on it, and the price, '3d and 6d' in't middle. They were all firsts you know, in Parwich.

Ken Wayne

One regular passenger *[for the train at Alsop Station]* I remember particularly. She lived in Parwich and kept a Greengrocery and General Store and was known to everyone as "Ma Pollitt." Once a week she went by train to Manchester. She had a light horse and a two-wheeled cart. The railway staff tethered the horse on a flat bit of embankment where it grazed all day and then harnessed it ready for her return on the 6.35 milk train from Buxton, loading up the goods she had purchased in Manchester.

Alsop en le Dale Station

Boxes of cakes, chocolates and sundries arrived by train for the shops at Wetton, Alstonfield and Parwich, and in springtime boxes of day old chicks which had to be delivered on the same day. The newspapers, arriving on the 8.10 a.m. train, were collected by Esther Lees who cycled over from Parwich, leaving her cycle by the roadside near Alsop village, walking up the footpath across the fields to save going round by the main road.

Charles Allen
(Compiled by Stewart Williams)

(Charles Allen's father was Stationmaster at Alsop from 1913 to 1938 and Charles worked there as a temporary porter. Esther Lees became Esther Flower, Grandmother of Valerie Kirkham (née Flower) who grew up at Dam Farm.)

Mrs. Brownson's shop, across the road from Flaxdale House, used to have slot machines for chewing gum outside on't walls of shop, a penny coin for Wrigley's chewing gum, and a slot machine for Woodbines, five in a packet

for tuppence. 'Course, Frank Wayne and Arthur Wayne, Owen Bradbury and quite a lot of us lads, used to smoke. You could put tuppence in and get the first packet out, then you'd keep jiggling the machine, and they kept on coming out!

Ken Wayne

There were no supermarkets and people didn't really go shopping. Once a week the grocer would come out from Ashbourne and deliver orders. He would ring us up at Hallcliffe and ask what we wanted, and the list would be by the telephone for whoever answered to read out. If there was something extra, then we would have to ring him. The butcher delivered as well but all of our vegetables were grown by our mother in the garden; and we had fruit too, apples and plums and damsons, and gooseberries, blackcurrants, pears. The garden was our mother's greatest joy in life. The milk came from one of the farms in the village and was delivered every morning by the milk man in his cart; he would stop the cart by the Green, clamber down and take one of the old milk churns on his back; he would then walk across our yard, round the side of the house to the kitchen door where our mother would have put out the number of jugs she wanted filled. Then he would walk back to Monty and the cart. Once or twice Monty got bored and set off on the rest of the milk round by himself.

Parwich Shop, today, a Spar grocery.

Mrs. Rose Dodds with her daughters, Sara (with Monty) Zelda, Angela and Vere.

The village was very small but self-sufficient. We had the shop; it sold all the basics, including the really important ones like liquorice sherbets and bottles of dandelion and burdock. We had the cobbler, the blacksmith, Mr Spencer the Stonemason, and Mr Cundy the Carpenter. We had the bus which belonged to the family who had the petrol pump and which went once a week into Ashbourne on market day; and there was the Post Office too, run by Old Mrs Graham, and after she eventually died, by her daughter Miss Graham, who we also thought was very old. The counter was very high and it wasn't easy to see over the top; we had to stand on tiptoes when asking for stamps or whatever it was our mother had sent us to buy; and the whole Post Office, just a room in the Grahams' house, smelled dreadfully of cat:

there were cats everywhere, and the smell seemed to mean that they never went out, which seemed strange when we all lived in a village where there was no traffic and no cat thieves about.

On the way up the road to the Post Office we would pass the telephone box – quick nip inside to press Button B just in case someone had forgotten to claim their penny refund. There was the Pub too, the Sycamore, but of course that was a mystery to us; we could go in through a side door and down a passage, where we knocked on a little wooden hatch; the shutter would open and we could ask for crisps or whatever it was we wanted (Smith's crisps, plain ones with a little screw of dark blue waxed paper in each packet containing the salt). If you were brave enough to look through the hatch you could see into the bar where there might be two or three men sitting over their pints of beer – I don't think I have ever set foot in the bar in my life, but later when we were older our father sometimes used to take one of our boyfriends there for a drink. That was men's business; we would have to stay at home and help prepare the lunch.

Angela Dodds

At the end of the holidays, which I always spent in Parwich, I went back to my home at Darley Abbey. Dad was a sheet metal worker by trade but come 1922 and the big slump, there was no work, so he took on this little Post Office. The cottage was a Toll Bar in its time, on the A6, and the wage was very small. Mum wanted to try a shop but Dad was very hesitant, but eventually they agreed and they started very simply with a few jars of sweets and some tins of biscuits, and gradually built it up into quite a good business. It got a lot of passing trade; soft drinks were good, but then the road widening came and the cottage was in the way, and so it was demolished. After a very long fight they did get a very small amount of compensation for loss of livelihood.

In 1933 my parents built on the opposite side of the road and gradually built up the business. It was the only shop for a mile in either direction. They made their own ice cream, and lemonade which was drunk on the premises, and we put some chairs outside on a big forecourt. Sunday was very busy as there would be up to twenty cyclists from various clubs who would come from Matlock on their way to somewhere, and it was a convenient stopping place. They obviously talked to members of other clubs saying, if you go that way there's a nice little place. It

was very hard work and though it was good to see it growing, I never wanted it for myself. I wouldn't have liked to keep a shop. Then of course came 1939, rationing, shortages, and they just managed to keep going.

Betty Stone

The value of money has changed a lot. Even with a farthing I could still buy a farthing's worth of lovely toffee, and nowadays farthings have been forgotten about. Children would have a penny or tuppence. I've been in the shop and I've heard children say, (now this is four or five years ago), "What can I have for twenty pence?" and I thought, fancy, twenty pence, but they couldn't get very much for 20p today. Now they have pocket money in pounds. When I was still at school I used to go up to my granny's to do her shopping on a Saturday morning, and it was the same every week, a little piece of beef about three shillings, and that little piece of beef would be as big as what we'd pay three or four pounds for today; but it never varied, a little piece of beef about three shillings, and then carrots and things like that.

Ella Hopkinson

I can remember when I was a little girl and Mr. Steeples used to run the bus and pick up parcels from Bagnall's, quite a big grocers in Ashbourne. My grandma used to have a parcel sent up and it used to arrive on Mr. Steeples' bus on a Saturday. She often used to go into Ashbourne but she couldn't carry everything. It was a different way of life.

Sandra Chadfield

Sunday

In the old church...[t]he rood-loft was removed from the chancel to the back of the church, and it became the minstrels' gallery. Here bass fiddle, flute, viola and the old box harmonium led the choir until the new church was finished, when the present fine organ replaced the old orchestra. The harmonium for many a long year was the chief musical instrument in the school. The musical part of the services was keenly appreciated by choir, orchestra and congregation alike. It is related of one enthusiastic chorister that his wife's patience at the length of the choir practice had completely given out. She sent her small son, who called at the foot of the stone steps leading to the gallery, "Is our father up there?"

Helena Birkentall

On Friday last the new church of Parwich, built at the sole cost of T. W. Evans, Esq., of Allestree Hall, Derby, patron of the living, was opened by the Lord Bishop of Lichfield. The day was observed as a general holiday, and the weather being fine, a large crowd of people flocked into the picturesque village, which was appropriately decorated for the occasion. At the west gate of the churchyard was a triumphal arch of evergreens with the motto, "Glory to God." Other triumphal arches spanned the streets, all bearing mottoes expressing the good wishes of the inhabitants and tenantry towards their excellent landlord and his good lady... Between the afternoon and evening services a public tea was provided in the very picturesque schoolroom, also built by Mr Evans.

Derby Mercury, October 22nd 1873

A visit from Mr. Wilberforce...

I was born on April 23, 1830, in the Derbyshire parish of Parwich where my grandfather *[William Evans]* was the principal landowner, my father *[Rev. John Edmund Carr]* acting as clergyman. My parents left the parish when I was three years old, so of course I have no memories of my own connected with the place. But on my first visit there, after coming into possession of half the property in 1892, I found several old inhabitants still living, who had vivid remembrance of the eleven years my parents had spent in the district.

An old woman talked to me and my husband with unbounded gratitude of the benefits which accrued to the parish during their abode in it. She told us how my father and his curate used to invite all the men of the place to be present at "family prayers," which for their benefit were held in the large kitchen. There the men who could not read heard nightly a passage from Scripture with a short exposition, and learnt to join in prayer. Our informant told us how when prayers were concluded, my mother gave to each man half a loaf of bread and "a good big piece of cheese," on the supposition that they might have missed their supper at home through being present. No wonder the kitchen was crowded!

I was shown a substantial cottage which my mother had built for a schoolhouse for small children, the elder ones being at work. Here a "dame" of excellent quality was installed, and diligently she taught the children to read their Bibles, to write, to work out easy sums, and in the case of the girls, to sew admirably.

A great event during my parents' residence at Parwich was a visit from Mr Wilberforce, the great philanthropist politician, and religious

VIEWS OF PARWICH

Centre, St. Peter's Church; top left, Smithy Lane; top right, Close Farm with Wheatsheaf (once a public house) and Hallgate cottages; lower left, the Wesleyan Chapel in Dam Lane; lower right, Parwich School and the Hall.

reformer. At the time when his influence first made itself felt, religion appeared to be almost extinct in the upper circles of Society. His book, *A Practical View of the Christian Religion*, had a wonderful effect in awakening careless persons to a sense of their responsibilities. I have heard the remark made that this book, combined with Mr Wilberforce's personal influence, revolutionized London Society. At the time I speak of he was a Member of Parliament, together with my uncle, Mr Evans, of Allestree, a kindred spirit, and they worked together for the suppression of the Slave Trade. To the great joy of my parents, Mr Wilberforce accepted an invitation to visit them. The day after his arrival, my mother had asked her most distinguished neighbours

to meet him at dinner, probably at any time between five and six o'clock, and the previous hours were spent in a visit to Dovedale and Ilam Hall. In the library at Ilam, Mr Wilberforce discovered some ancient volumes or manuscripts, in which he became so engrossed that my mother (who was growing uneasy at the lateness of the hour) could not induce him to leave them. The London gentleman had evidently no idea of the earliness of country hours. He was so absorbed in the ancient books that he would not listen to any persuasions, and when at last they did make the start for home my mother realised with dismay that it was impossible for them to reach home before the guests should have arrived.

On entering her drawing room she found the company, in full dress, sitting round the room awaiting her arrival. "What could I do? " she asked, in telling me the story; "I could only say to them, 'I have brought him, he is here, I could not help it, you must forgive me.'" I never heard what happened to that dinner. In spite of this inauspicious commencement the evening was a grand success. Mr Wilberforce put forth his most brilliant conversational powers. The guests were delighted, impressed, carried out of themselves by his gifts and eloquence, and went away expressing to my mother their warmest appreciation. They left about ten o'clock, and my parents supposed it was bedtime, but the Londoners considered that the evening was only just begun, and more conversation ensued. Towards midnight Mrs Wilberforce, quite unaware of the exhaustion of her hosts, got out her drawing materials! Here my recollections of my mother's narrative of this interesting episode come to an abrupt close – memory will help me no further.

Mrs. Curtis

I used to see two old oak chests in the chancel and wondered what they contained. It was said that the candles for lighting the church were stored there because the mice played havoc with them when they were stored in the cupboard on the wall. I used to see one, bolder than the rest from my perch in the gallery. It used to run out of its hole and take a nibble from the candlestick placed in its holder ready for lighting. But it must have satisfied the hunger of the poor little thing that looked as small and famished as any church mouse must do!

Joseph Thompson, 1833-1909

Sunday was spent going to Sunday school, morning, afternoon, and service in the evening. We were all dressed up in our Sunday best, and weren't allowed to play games. But we used to look forward to MAZZA coming round with his ice cream, and if we were <u>very</u> lucky we'd get a tuppeny one. Mazza was an Italian man who sold ice cream from his motorbike and sidecar.

Eileen Ellis

Mothers' Union Parade; Parwich bringing up the rear and Mrs. Beatrice Graham with the banner.

I have in my possession a pencil sketch of Parwich Church, made by a little girl cousin, a few years older than myself. In the foreground the child has introduced a large tombstone with this inscription: "Here lies the Duke of Wellington, who hanged himself for having let the Roman Catholics into power." This was the child's own idea, and gives a glimpse of the passionate indignation aroused by the admission of Roman Catholics into Parliament.

Mrs. Curtis

MOTHERS' UNION, PARWICH, left to right: Mrs. Hansford, Mrs Slater, Mrs. Steeples, Mrs Calladine and Rev. Hansford.

The font stood inside the chancel. The stove in the middle of the Church. Women clattered up the aisles in their pattens and men used to cover their faces reverently with their hats during their private devotions before the service. There was no merit then in turning to the East, though a low curtsey towards that point was dropped by several women. In the square pews each knelt with his back to others, unaware of the bad orthodoxy of such a practice. Christenings were managed by means of a pewter dish containing a little water. Weddings were celebrated before the High Altar, that was, a plain oak table.

Communion Sunday was an event of importance coming, as it did only once every three months. All the respectable couples walked in, arm in arm, dressed in Sunday best, drab knee breeches and gaiters and black coats with such a display of pure white neck cloth that no other occasion warranted. The Churchwarden at this time was diminutive, who by some irony of fate had a very tall, handsome wife; she was caught in a tangent I suppose having been much disappointed in a former love affair. Mr. Fisher was here then, you remember him? Poor man, he was harassed with poverty all

Parwich Wesleyan Methodist Chapel and congregation, on its 50th Anniversary, 1899.

his life, overworked and had a plague of a wife who drove him crazy. I do not know if we have ever improved on him!

Joseph Thompson

The Wesleyan Methodist Chapel celebrated its centenary two years ago, and the Vicar of Parwich took part in the services celebrating the event. High up on the rock known as Lenscliffe, it has stood for over a century, and across the road is a rock of similar height which appears as though some convulsion of nature had split the original rock. Here week by week the services to the Glory of God have been carried on by god-fearing men and women.

Helena Birkentall

My children went to Sunday School on a Sunday afternoon, and while they were there, I made sandwiches in the summertime. Nearly every Sunday we walked up to the top of Parwich Hill and had a picnic. We'd go anywhere for a picnic.

Ella Hopkinson

Our Sundays were not festive. In order to allow the servants the utmost possible rest from work, our comforts were abridged and our meals unappetising. Some godly heads of families went so far as to forbid even a hot potato, and allowed no conversation except on religious subjects. Where the family included young people a day of silence was the result, and a strong reaction naturally followed.

Mrs. Curtis

Mary Rawlins (centre) Biggin Church Centenary Queen. Mrs. Inglefield (left).

I was chosen as Biggin Church Centenary Queen when I was eleven. I wasn't going to go in but they said oh, yes. I had to wear a long pink dress and a crown, oh quite a posh affair. We had to go on a dray. Mrs Inglefield crowned me, the old lady.

Mary Rawlins

Each year we waited excitedly for the Chapel Anniversary. This meant new dresses, new shoes, ours usually being black patent with ankle straps, and with white ankle socks. I can remember being very jealous of my friends Peggy and Jessie Simms, as they were allowed to have Sahara sandals. These had open toes, were strappy, and had a little heel. We all had to learn a poem for this special occasion and on our great day we had to stand up and recite it to all the congregation. The chapel was always packed full at these times. We had one special recitation about the tragic death of a collier's child, which brought many mothers to tears. It was called, "Little Jim" and it was Frankie Gibbs who always recited it. Of course in those days children often died, of diphtheria and so on.

We used to have to be churched after we'd had babies. It was about cleansing and about thankfulness for a safe delivery. My friend Kathleen wasn't allowed back in the house until she'd been churched! It would bring bad luck! I remember my sister Joyce and I went together because we had our babies, two little girls, the same night, with an hour between them.

Eileen Ellis

Mum or one of my Darley Abbey aunts made gingham dresses, and she would also make my best frock for Sunday. There was this ridiculous thing where one had to have a special outfit for Sunday, which was so stupid as you'd grow out of it so quickly you'd get no wear out of it.

Betty Stone

My grandmother was quite religious and she used to have a lot to do with the Chapel. She played the organ there, and I played it after she packed up. In fact there should still be an organ in there that belongs to me. It was my granny's and when she died it was left to me, and if they ever close the chapel I think I would like it back. It is a nice chapel; I wanted to get married there but I couldn't get a licence, so I had to get married in Ashbourne.

Barbara Lowes

In the days of which I speak, [circa 1840] the line of demarcation was drawn clearly and strongly between the Church and the World... When a young person left "the World" and became "serious", a most tremendous sacrifice was involved. Her dress, in the first place, must, by following the latest fashion but two, become a matter of habitual mortification. Amusements in every shape, all light literature, all secular companionship, must be renounced, and especially the hope of matrimony, as there were not curates enough to go round, and the few who were eligible were rendered unattractive by the worship paid them by the muslin-clad young ladies whose tea parties they adorned... The girl who became "serious" rose early, so as to have two or more hours of Bible study before breakfast. Her morning was probably spent in her district round, often collecting for some society - a most painful duty. Her time was

further occupied in Bible classes, cottage meetings, and especially visiting the sick in all weathers. Many were the deaths among devoted women from the habit of sitting beside sick beds with wet feet.

Mrs Curtis

Harry and I always took the children to church. As my Harry used to say, in villages years ago, it was always the lord of the manor who was important, the vicar, and the schoolmaster. Our vicar had a lot to say about where he'd been and what he'd done. Harry was cutting the hedge at Parwich Hall gardens and the vicar had got some friends staying with him and he was saying, "This is where Sir John Inglefield lives and I married all their daughters." Well he didn't!

I didn't belong to the Mothers' Union and I had no intention of belonging to the Mothers' Union. The lady who lived next door to me belonged to it, and she said would I go this one afternoon, it was something special, and I said yes, but I'm not joining, and as we were coming out the vicar's wife said to me "Mrs Hopkinson, now we do want you to join the Mothers' Union, you will think about it?" and she was saying it because Lady Inglefield was standing at the back of her; and I said "No, I'm not joining", and I thought, if she's saying this because she knows Lady Inglefield is behind me and she thinks I should join because my husband works for Lady Inglefield, that made me even firmer that I was not going to join. Well, I never fancied it, but I did join the WI because they do things. Most of the people in the village did belong to the Mothers' Union and they must have got quite a bit out of it, but it never appealed to me and I can be determined sometimes!

Ella Hopkinson

Dressed for Confirmation.
(Roger Graham's family album)

The solemn day of Confirmation will never fade from my memory. My toilette was viewed as a matter of immense importance. Everything I wore was snow-white, clear "book-muslin" dress, white kid gloves, and I especially remember the exquisite glossy white silk kerchief which completed my toilette round the neck. On my head was a dainty little cap. The caps of the girls were understood to be for the protection of the Bishop's hands (Rowland's Macassar oil was very freely used in those days) and I have often heard the remark, "How very unpleasant it must be for the Bishop confirming the boys....."

Nothing further of that day remains in my memory, but my first Communion, not long after, was marked by a sad mistake, for which my mother blames herself greatly. She had not instructed me to take my gloves off, and consequently I received the Elements in a pair of thick woollen Berlin gloves."

Mrs Curtis

Parish News: The Patronal Festival:

We look back upon another very happy and lovely Festival and all the services went very well. We are especially grateful to our Choirmaster Mr. Fearn, for the lovely little Anthem he had written and composed, and to the choir for singing it so well. The "family" service in the afternoon was quite successful (although one could have wished that more families had joined with us!) but it was a venture "well worth while"! And we appreciated the message that our beloved friend and Bishop - Bishop G. Sinker - gave us. With his permission we would correct one thing that he mentioned (and on which he had previously been misinformed), and it is that as a Parish we DID SEND MORE THAN £1 last year for the Church's Work overseas, and the bishop was pleased to know this.

Rev.F.G.Hansford. 1961

Lid of the Parish chest (17th century) Parwich church.

Gardener's Cottage, Parwich

mauve-blue cranesbill, wild roses, pink and white, nettle leaved bellflower, ox-eye daisies often known as marguerites, poppies and cornflowers. Later would come the harebells and heathers. Near the stream sides, yellow and purple loosestrife and meadow sweet bloomed.

Mary Whitechurch

SUMMER

Jam and jelly making began early in the summer with strawberry, raspberry, and currants, black and red. Runner and French beans would be salted down. June brought the haymaking. The hay was raked into long lines, turned by hand with two pronged forks and built into stooks to dry. These were then loaded onto the horse drawn hay cart. Sometimes the children were given a ride home if the hay cart was not loaded too high. About this time the glow-worms would begin to show their soft green lights in the evenings. These are not worms, but are small beetles, the unwinged females shining their lights to attract the winged males. The children were fascinated by them and built little rush cages in which to carry them as lanterns. The hedge banks and fields would be carpeted with flowers, foxgloves, red campion,

SWEET-BRIAR

Keep Your Milk Cool

Use the sock treatment for keeping milk icy cold during the hot weather. Wet a pair of socks, wool preferably. Put the legs over the milk bottle, and dangle the toes in a basin of cold water

Take a Tip

ANNIE CALLADINE ON THE MILK TRAP WITH BABY ARTHUR.

53

Summer brought the village sports day, an occasional cricket match, and the summer fête at the Hall. As we grew up we helped with various stalls, mine usually being the shove ha'penny one.

Angela Dodds

Raspberry Vinegar

To one quart of fruit add one quart of cold vinegar; cover close and let it stand twenty-four hours. Then pour off the liquor and put to it a quart of fresh fruit; cover close and let it again stand twenty-four hours. Repeat the same the third time then boil up the vinegar with 1 lb of lump sugar to each pint until it becomes a syrup. Bottle. The finer the quality of sugar the clearer the syrup.

Mary Emma Hopkinson

[Mary Whitechurch says that Raspberry vinegar was taken during pregnancy. It was thought to strengthen <u>and</u> relax muscles!]

In summer, my Aunty Mary made wine, as many did, mostly from hedgerow and garden things, rhubarb, damson, elderberry. It came out if there were visitors, and there was always a special wine for the children, which was non-alcoholic elderflower, and it was absolutely delicious, slightly sparkling and really very good. I've tried to make it several times but it didn't work for me. It's like a cordial. I've got some recipes, but I wish I'd asked Aunty for her recipe before she died. I don't think I used yeast because that of course would make it alcoholic.

Betty Stone

Elder Flower Champagne

2 heads elderflower; ¹/₂lb white sugar; 1 gallon water; 1 lemon

Pick the heads when in full bloom and put into a bowl, followed by the lemon juice. Cut up rind (no white pith) sugar and vinegar. Add the cold water and leave 24 hours.

Strain into strong bottles. Cork firmly and lay on sides.

Drink after 2 weeks.

Ethel Hopkinson

My childhood days were idyllic as we were so free, and so safe; not like today. In summer, Mother would pack some sandwiches for us and a bottle of home made ginger beer, and off we would go down the meadows with our fishing rods, which we bought at Mrs. Pollett's shop, which used to be like Aunty Wainwright's in "Last of the Summer Wine". We'd go with our fishing rods and jam jars and catch a few minnows and frog spawn, then make our way to Bradbourne Mill, where we would have our picnic and paddle in the ford, rushing to open the gate for the cars coming through. If we were lucky we would get a few pennies thrown to us.

Eileen Ellis

Life on the Farm

I was born on Gibbon's Bank in 1913, so I'm ninety years old. I lived in the end house until I was about four, and my grandma lived there as well. From there we went to Ballidon, and then to Aldwark, and then I came back to Parwich just as the war started. I can't remember anything about Gibbon's Bank. My earliest memory is from when I lived at Ballidon. It was heaven! I remember playing with my friend, Ethel Holmes, who was the same age as me. We went on the rocks and played houses, with dock leaves for plates, and daily bread (cow parsley) for curtains. I've always been happy, no matter where I was.

It was lovely on the farm. Depending what sort of farm you'd got, there was ploughing and thinning turnips, all that sort of thing - not a very nice job but you did it, cutting the cabbages off when it was all icy. Then there was haymaking, and that was a lovely day; but we were praying for it to rain so we could leave it! All the family went out to do the haymaking and we used to be throwing hay about, and I used to be loading it onto the wagon. I was thrown off loads of hay, and one particular occasion I was winded; I couldn't get my breath.

I remember when I was at Aldwark and the bull ran me. I always fetched the cows in for milking and there was a gateway where the cows gathered, and I just turned round and there was the bull right against me. I'd got a little stick in me hand, and I hit him right across the face, which was a silly thing to do, and it broke, the stick did, and I ran! I ran down the field with the bull after me and I can remember turning round and seeing him coming. We'd got a dog, Jimmie, and I just got to the wall and I shouted him, and as soon as he came, the bull turned. But you can tell how close it was: it ran right up the side of the wall. If I would have tripped I'd have been dead and gone. There must have been somebody watching over me then. The bull was always with the cows and it was a mad bull really 'cause George, the farmer, had stuck a pitchfork in its nose. It was fastened up in the shed but it broke loose through the door. Twice it ran me up the yard, and I just got through the little gate. I still have nightmares about it.

Catherine Elizabeth (Dolly) Wayne

Wind Galls to cure
Best alcohol tincture of arnica
British oil and oil of tar each 2oz
add slowly Sulphuric acid $^1/_2$oz
Mix all together
Mary Emma Hopkinson

Marketing the produce of the farm is very different today from the days when there was no motor transport and only limited railway facilities. Milk was made into butter and cheese and sold in the Town Hall at Ashbourne. Together with live and dressed poultry, green cheese, eggs and other produce, the butter and cheese were displayed in baskets on spotless cloths and were sold to buyers from town and country. This was on market day and the farmers' wives spent the sale-money on the week's necessities before driving home in the horse-drawn milk float or "trap".

Helena Birkentall

My grandfather, Alf Brownlee, was a farmer and he lived at Slate House on Smithy Lane. He had fields right up from where the Evans live, from Townhead. On the other side of the road there is a gate that goes up the fields.

There used to be a track that went right up to the top, and all those fields used to belong to Slate House, as well as the field opposite. They used to have hens in there, and when my granddad was very poorly and couldn't get about, he used to give me a shilling to go up and feed these hens. My granny was really tight and she wouldn't give me anything, but my granddad would say, "Here ducky, here's a shilling, go and feed hens for me." We also had cows and a couple of pigs in what they called the hovel. As you go into the yard of Slate House it's on the right hand side. I used to go across to my granddad in the cowshed and he'd fill me a tin of milk from the cow. It were so warm! I couldn't drink it now like I did then. It had little hairs in it, and it were 'orrible. I think that's why I hate milk so much.

I can remember going hay making at the farm, and riding on top of the hay cart. They used to just chuck the hay on with hayforks.

Hay making at Upper Moor Farm.

Those fields I told you about, above Townhead, we used to come down the hill from there on top of this cartload of hay. We'd be wobbling about and falling off but it were great! We used to take a picnic up with us and sit under the hedge bottom and eat it, and we had lovely summers and hard winters in those days, not like now. It's not seasonal now; too much rain.

Barbara Lowes

Fish Sauce

To a bottle of Port wine add half a bottle each of sherry, Walnut and Mushroom Ketchups, the juice of four small oranges, half a pound each shallot and horseradish, two ounces of mustard and a quarter of an ounce of cayenne.

Mary Emma Hopkinson

Caring for poultry was often regarded as an occupation for women and children on the farm. As a child, I remember helping my granny prepare the mash for the hens, sniffing the warm, yeasty smell of stale bread, warm water, and grain as she mixed it in the big bread crock. Together we chased recalcitrant hens into the coop over slippery ground, or searched for eggs laid in unusual places. In 'Poultry Notes' from the Ashbourne Telegraph of Friday, October 28th, 1927, the following advice was given:

"...Those nasty foggy nights we are now encountering are as objectionable to your poultry as they are to you. You appreciate the little extra tit-bit at supper, so will they if they get it. Biscuit meal, scalded and dried off with middlings, or preferably Sussex ground oats, will solve the problem. It is not merely a question of generosity or kindness on your part. The extra attention will keep the birds in perfect physical condition... Many cases of scouring... have been observed when birds have eaten sour or cider apples. Personally, windfalls are gathered, just a few being left for the fowls' amusement, and it is a wise precaution.... Care that is taken in the collection, storing and packing of eggs will be amply repaid by enhanced prices when buyers realise that the supplies you send can be relied upon".

Gillian Radcliffe

Mrs. Beatrice Graham and friend feeding the turkeys.

There were chickens in the croft at Dam Farm and at one time I think my uncle sold the eggs to Thornhill's from Great Longstone, who would collect them and take them to their egg packing company. They'd come once a week with all their packers; they'd have a big case and they'd pay you so much per dozen.

Valerie Kirkham

White Hands

In order to have white hands, a good soap, aided by a pinch or two of cracked oatmeal, may be used for a thorough cleansing twice a day and if needful to still further cleanse them, warm water- not hot- will do the necessary. Once a week they should be rubbed front and back and between the fingers with a slice of Lemon. If the hands are inclined to chap camphor ice may be applied at night and white gloves worn to increase the softening effect. The best Camphor ice is a home made preparation of pure white wax, melted and stirred to the consistency of cream, with the addition of several drops of spirits of Camphor. Holes should always be cut in the palms of the gloves to allow ventilation.

Mary Emma Hopkinson

From the letters and postcards I inherited after my aunt, Miss Mary Graham's death, it appears that her father, my grandfather, was a farmer, mostly self-employed in yearly tenancies. This resulted in my grandparents having at least eleven different homes from 1898 to 1913, which must have been very disruptive for the children, and exhausting for my grandmother. An article in the Ashbourne Telegraph written at the time of my Aunt Mary's retirement says that her father was "involved in work with farm implements." The family moved from Co. Durham to two villages in Yorkshire, and then on to the estate of the Duke and Duchess of Sutherland, at Golspie, North Scotland. Later, they went to Oxfordshire and Surrey and back to Co. Durham, followed by four villages in Derbyshire before reaching Parwich, where they remained for the rest of their lives. By a strange coincidence, both my wife's grandparents and mine on our father's side were farmers, and both lived on the same farm at different times, though my father never told me this. My wife spent many summer holidays at the farm at Etwall with her uncle (her parents having died by that time) and the words New Close Farm are stated on the gravestone of my wife's grandparents in Etwall Churchyard.

Roger Graham

A young helper at Upper Moor farm.

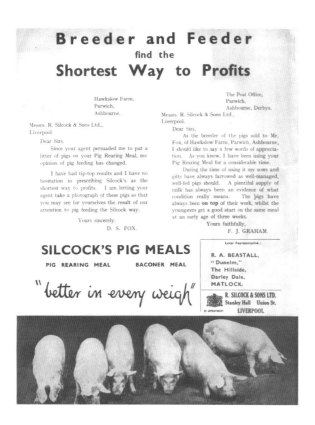
The above advertisement contains a letter written by Miss Mary Graham's father, Fred Graham, from the Post Office in Parwich, in which he claims credit as the breeder of the pigs, pictured above, which he sold to Mr Fox of Hawkslow Farm, Parwich. While rearing his pigs on Silcock's Pig Rearing Meal, Fred claims that his:

> sows and gilts have always farrowed as well-managed, well-fed pigs should. A plentiful supply of milk has always been an evidence of what condition really means. The pigs have always been on top of their work, whilst the youngsters get a good start on the same meal at an early age of three weeks.

The letter from Mr. D. Fox of Hawkslow, also on the advertisement, pays tribute to "the tip-top results" obtained from feeding his animals on the same meal. He has "no hesitation in prescribing Silcock's as the shortest way to profits", and adds, "I am letting your agent take a photograph of these pigs so that you may see for yourselves the result of our attention to pig feeding the Silcock way".

Gillian Radcliffe

(Stone from the Hawkslow pigsties is now part of Peter Trewhitt's greenhouse at Hallcliffe!)

When visiting my friend Mary Graham at the Post Office in Parwich, the farming side was always a great attraction for me, as I followed Mr Graham and Mary around. Until recently I had the yoke that he and sometimes Mary carried the pails of milk on. Unfortunately worm had so damaged it despite using killer preservation, it crumbled. Time without number Mary called at my parents on the way home to Parwich, staying late. The carbide lamp on her bicycle never seemed to want to function and it was quite a joke that it had to be coaxed and primed and oh, the smell!

Dorothy Marsh

On some of the old maps you can see all the dewponds that were round Parwich, and the pingles, small corner pieces of land in the fields which the plough couldn't reach. Farmers grew things like potatoes and beans on these pingles which they used as part payment in kind for seasonal labour. The fields might be as much as three miles out of Parwich. There were some at Gorse Hill.

Kathleen Allsopp

Potatoe Sandwich Cake

Blend ¹/₂lb of Potatoes with 1oz butter, 2oz fine sugar, a little lemon rind and a few drops of essence. Beat two eggs thoroughly, and mix; then add nearly a teaspoon of baking powder. Butter four plates,

LILY BROWNLEE FEEDING THE CHICKENS

pour an equal quantity on to each, and put into the oven to bake and when the bottom is browned lift onto the top shelf to finish. When cold, spread marmalade on two of the cakes and place the others on the top. Sprinkle caster sugar on.

Mary Emma Hopkinson

My aunt loved animals, and while she was working with her mother in the Post Office, she was also expected to help look after the cows and 200 pigs. I think my grandfather may have moved to Parwich to farm initially from Church House (later called Jasmine House), until the move to the Post Office and its adjoining land. He also farmed other land in the village: I have an old insurance policy dated 1926 which refers to land known as 'Town Head' and 'James Acto', and Parwich people remember him carrying the milk in pails suspended from a yoke, and spilling it on the steep slope coming down from Townhead.

Roger Graham

When they called me up I could either go into munitions or join the Land Army. Many times since I've sort of fretted I didn't go into the Land Army. Well, I was reading this book about it and the things they had to do and I thought, thank goodness I didn't join the Land Army! For instance, I couldn't milk a cow: my cousin worked on the farm and he said, "Have a go, Dolly, have a go!" So I got the stool and got under the cow but he was looking through the cowshed window, making such fun of me I never milked any

more! I just cooled the milk. You had to put it into a receiving pan, and then there was water in a sort of a thing that looked like an old fashioned wash board. There was water in the middle of it and you poured the milk and it came all down these filters and it cooled it. George could get a churn and pick it out of the water as easily as anything. But one young chap fetching the milk said, "I can do that." He tipped up this churn of milk and it went everywhere: and George was very tight, ever so tight. Well, he nearly went mad! Milk went everywhere, you see. Well, it was money, wasn't it?

Dolly Wayne

Seventy years ago when I was young, the village was practically self-supporting in all the essentials of life. It could provide its own food, clothing, and houses for itself.

Milk could not leave the village proper because of transport, but was made into butter and cheese, and the by-products of whey, skimmed milk, and buttermilk were fed to the pigs of the farmer and his men. This meant bacon, ham, pork and at pig killing time savoury dishes for the larder. The number of pigsties in Parwich is amazing. There are seven at Hawkslow alone. Those farmers who could take their milk in floats to Minninglow Sidings were lucky. And to this day the siding is called "The Farmers Parliament."

Helena Birkentall

Dairy farming in Parwich

A cutting from the Daily Express shows that cows were still munching happily on the green open spaces of Parwich in October 1975, and no doubt some of them belonged to us at Dam Farm. My name is Valerie Kirkham and I was born at Church Gates and moved to Dam Farm in 1947 when I was one year old. My father, an electrician by trade, was brought up there, and helped his father with the farm work in the evenings.

There were five of us in the house, my Granny and Granddad Flower, Mum and Dad and me, three generations. During the day Mum and Grandma helped with the milking and I remember Granny used to sit me on a stool and milk the cows by hand while I waited. We had tying up for fourteen, ten in the front and four in the back. Then when we had the milking machines installed, we milked the ones in the cowsheds (now part of Dam farmhouse) by machine, and the ones in the back shed were milked by hand. Grandpa did those and Grandma did the ones with the milking machine.

Before there was water in the cowsheds, the animals were taken to the dam. We'd let them out two at a time, take them for a drink, and clean out the stalls. They were then walked to pasture on the Alsop road and down Pitts Lane. When I was little I used always to go with Granddad to fetch the cows, and as I got older, Granddad let me fetch them myself. We had two collies and if you took them, they'd fetch the cows for you. We sometimes had calves in Miss Graham's croft (when she was at the Post Office) and I'd go and feed them sometimes.

Milk was sold, unpasteurised, from the farm door. In the kitchen we had a bucket with milk in it; it had a ladle, and someone would come with a jug and say, "Can I have a pint?" and you'd pour it out. You wouldn't be allowed to do that now. I think sometimes we were healthier then. These days we are too hygienic and have got no immunity.

In spite of suffering from asthma, I remember the fun of haymaking, which provided the animals with winter fodder. Before the days of machinery, we collected loose hay and made two big haystacks in the croft at Dam Farm, putting the rest in the barns or out in the buildings in the fields where the young stock were kept during the winter. Some of the youngsters would help from the village, and when they'd finished they'd come back to Dam Farm, and there'd always be something cooked or something like cold meat for supper at maybe nine or ten o'clock at night.

Granddad worked with a horse to collect the hay while my dad was at work because he couldn't drive the tractor; he hadn't got a license, which sounds silly really if you're a farmer, doesn't it? Granddad loved his horse.

When I was home with my granny and granddad, we'd move the hay by hand; you'd have a rake and you'd turn it over, or a fork, and throw it around to get it dry; and in the evening Dad would go with the machinery and put it into rows, and someone would come and bail it for us. We had this great big sledge which we used to collect hay on with the horse and I remember my aunt and my grandmother had what you call a bonny rake, a great big wooden rake that two people would pull. The rake part was oval, with shafts on it and you would pull it across the field to collect loose hay after haymaking so that you didn't waste anything. It was quite heavy. It was the same with manure spreading; you didn't have a muck spreader, you just put it in a cart, took a horse to the field and told him to stop every so often so you could drop a pile out. Then Granddad

Horsepower: Mary Rawlins and friend with Mary's Grandfather at Upper Moor Farm

would go another day and throw it about with a fork, and that's how you spread it. It was heavy work. But when my dad came home he used to let me drive the tractor with him, and I can remember him saying, "Now keep in line with that tree when you drive the tractor, watch that tree and we'll have a straight line!" Great fun, great fun!

Valerie Kirkham

Sheep washing time was in June, and hundreds of sheep were driven to the sheep wash. Excited school children spent their dinner hour watching the sheep dropped from the pen into the water, where men stood waist-deep vigorously rubbing them. Then they were started up the ramp to the Green to dry in the sun and chew contentedly after their ordeal. (In later years the sheep-dip took the place of the sheep-wash, which now is derelict and empty.)

Helena Birkentall

I was born at Upper Moor Farm, Parwich in 1936. We were mainly doing dairy farming. I can remember the milking by hand, sitting on a three legged stool. Then we had to cool the milk. We had a churn and a big pan on the top, and a thing like a radiator, where water used to go inside and it was like all tubes; and you poured the milk in the top and it sort of run down, a bit like a scrubbing board really. Then you'd have a sieve at the bottom to sieve it into the milk churn, and we used to go with beakers and have a drink.

Mary Rawlins

In the early days people killed their own pigs and although I was very young when we had pigs at Dam Farm, I do remember a gentleman called Mr Webb who lived at what

is now Knob Hall, which was the Creamery then, and he used to come and kill the pig. We had these wooden benches, and thrawls, in what was the milk place at the back, and he used to cut the pig up there and hang it because we had big cellars at Dam Farm where we could hang meat. It was really cold: you didn't need a fridge. All you needed was something to cover everything. We never had sheep: Granddad thought they were stupid things which they are because if they get their head through a hedge they're gone and you can't really keep them in. So we just had cows and a horse. It was a great life, especially for a child, with a freedom undreamed of today. It was a matter of being there, and helping, and enjoying being on the farm, and I never wanted to leave. Those times were so good.

Valerie Kirkham

Sheep's Head Broth
1 Sheep's head,
5 part cold water,
half teacup rice,
2 tablespoons oatmeal, 1 carrot,
1 turnip, 2 onions, celery 2 pieces,
4 leaves sage, salt & pepper.

Wash head well; take small bone out, place in pan, pour on water and bring to a boil and skim clear; cut vegetables; add to the broth with rice; let it cook gently 2¹/₂ hours. Mix oatmeal with cold water; stir in broth, season it. Let it cook ¹/₂ hour longer, all together 3 hours. Dish up the head, put the brains in slit of the tongue; serve with parsley sauce.

Mary Emma Hopkinson

The first tractor, a David Brown. Upper Moor Farm

On the farm intensive mechanization has followed the introduction of petrol-driven engines. Tractors have taken the place of horses. On the roads the internal combustion engine has replaced horse-power. The first motor car to run through Parwich caused an amusing rush into the streets. What was not amusing was the terrified rearing of horses when they met the first petrol-driven engines. From that time the horse-population of the village gradually dwindled to its present low level.

One of the most memorable sights of my early life was the procession of farm-horses from the smithy to their respective homes. They were in most cases brought down under an escort, but the return journey was very different. The escort returned to the farm, and after shoeing, the blacksmith slapped the leader on the back and away they all trotted to Hawkslow, Low Moor, Hill Top, and so on. No loss or accident ever came to my knowledge. From Newton Leys the road to Alsop was a field-road, therefore horses both coming and going were led by a farm hand for there were gates to open and shut.

Helena Birkentall

There were cows still coming through Parwich when I was growing up. My uncle, Arnold Lees, was at Dam Farm and he used to drive his cows up through the village. In fact I used to do it when I was young. I used to drive them up the Alsop road. And Reg Twigge used to bring his cows down through the village to the cricket pitch. David Woolley was saying how they had to clean up the cricket pitch before they could have a game because of all the cowpats! And the Rowbothams had cows and there were some up Creamery Lane at Church Farm that used to go out into the fields there.

Sandra Chadfield

We made butter every week, in a little churn that fitted on the table. We had cream, butter, milk, and Grandma used to make what they call 'beastings pie' with the first milk after the cow has calved, a bit like egg custard, with a pastry base. I didn't like it but Granddad loved it. The milk was like when you first have a baby, sweet, ugh!

Valerie Kirkham

Syllabub under the cow

Weight a dairy bowl with some sugar, the juice of a lemon and a glass of white wine and pull into it as much beestings as you consider. Stir and abandon overnight, when, with a dusting of nutmeg on top, it will be ready to serve.

Beestings being the milk given by the cow after calving, and particularly rich and creamy.

Joyce Douglas

Outside Dam Farm. Esther Flower (née Lees)) with her mother-in-law, Ada Willa Flower.

Dam Farm today.

Childhood

Ken Wayne astride a toy horse. Boys were dressed the same as girls until breeched, that is, put in trousers.

My sister Sara says we moved to Hallcliffe in Parwich in 1947. I can't remember the date as I, Angela Dodds, can only have been 3, or 4 at the time. I do recollect one or two events before Parwich but not many; practically all of my childhood memories are of the village.

My overwhelming feeling about my childhood is its intensity. I loved Parwich and the surrounding hills and fields deeply, and my memories are all very physical. I felt I knew every tree and flower, every stone,

each ripple in the stream and muddy patch in the pond. Those years were full of colour and light and sounds. Does every child feel this way about his or her home? Do today's children feel so strongly about the outside world when inside there is television, video and CD players, and when parents think, and children are told, that the world has become such a dangerous place?

I first saw television at the time of the Coronation. My mother had taken my two older sisters to London to watch the procession while my father stayed at home with us two smaller ones. The Inglefields at the Hall had a television set – I seem to remember that it was purchased especially for the Coronation, just like many others across the country. We sat quietly, my sister Zelda and I, in the drawing room and looked at the small, fuzzy, black and white picture while the grownups chattered all around us. Somewhere about the point when the young Queen was processing down the aisle, her train held by a child I knew simply as the only boy in the dancing class I attended for a short time in Bakewell, we became bored and went out into the garden to play under the big chestnut tree.

Much more interesting, round about the same time, was helping my mother plant the young chestnut trees on Nether Green, along the road by the marsh. I thought of all the marigolds that used to grow there, and the fun we used to have crossing it, jumping from grass tuft to grass tuft but not minding at all if we fell into the mud. Each chestnut tree was fenced round with posts to prevent the cows from eating it. My mother believed very strongly that making something grow was a very important gift to the world, and she planted many trees, flowers and shrubs, in many parts of the world, throughout her life:

whenever one of us settled down somewhere with a garden, she would be there with spade in one hand, trowel in the other, ready to make yet another garden.

Another place we loved playing in was the churchyard. There was a huge chestnut tree there, perfect for conkers in the autumn. We would take them to school and play with them, and we girls would also carve little things out of them – small baskets with handles, cradles, faces. We would take the path through the churchyard by the stream and through a field (now part of the extension to the churchyard) to reach the cobbler's hut. I have no idea what his name was or where he lived, but he worked in his wooden hut mending shoes for all the people in the village - for all I knew he lived there too - and he was surrounded by a lovely mixed smell of leather and sawdust and polish. Once, on our way there, Zelda and I found a little drowned row of newborn kittens spread out along the bank.

We played in the church too: the creaking of the door; whispering to each other because it wasn't a place in which to shout – but running up and down the aisles and playing a few notes on the organ. We tried to peep into the vestry while our dog watched us uncomprehendingly. His name was Monty, as was one of the Inglefields' dogs, as well as the horse that pulled the milk cart (those were the days when the country had heroes!) Later on, we got to know exactly what the vestry looked like because we joined the choir, dressed up in our little blue choir robes and thoroughly enjoying ourselves. We used to climb up the church tower too, very nervously because the old wooden ladder at the top didn't feel very safe. And it probably wasn't!

A very important part of the village was the animal life. We always had dogs and cats –

Monty, Pingu, Kelpie, Tom, Oliver – all much loved, all buried at the very top of the garden behind Hallcliffe. As well as the milkman's horse, Monty, there was Kitty, the carthorse. One day she panicked and ran away from the man looking after her. I remember her thundering down the street and onto the Green, where she calmed down and allowed herself to be caught again. And the Inglefields had a Shetland pony called Wildeyes who was kept for a while in the field beside Hallcliffe. One day I was showing off to my mother and, having enticed Wildeyes to stand near the wall, I clambered onto his back – whereupon up went his heels and off flew I, much to my mother's amusement!

For a while the same field housed a whole lot of pigs. A bright memory is of the night when I persuaded my mother to let me stay up with the pigman (George Edward Twigge) to watch one of the sows producing a litter of piglets. Another time I went into the field to look at the pigs and the big boar chased me – I ran and ran and reached the wall, but George Edward was nearby and he ran after us and caught the boar, who managed to bite him hard before backing away. I can still see the deep wound and oozing blood – and I know that I saw white bone too, but my adult sensibility tells me I couldn't have done. My mother bandaged him up, probably told me off severely, and George Edward went back to work.

We climbed Parwich Hill regularly, even when it meant crossing the Mound and braving the herd of young pedigree Herefords that were often there during the summer – still in my eyes the most beautiful of cattle. Once when I was on the top of Parwich Hill I saw a fox crossing in front of me, which was breathtakingly exciting; and the area beyond the hospital at the foot of Parwich Hill was, my father told me, home to badgers, though I never saw one. There were rabbits by the hundred though, until the first, most dreadful wave of myxomatosis hit them, and we would find terrible, pathetic, half dead creatures unable to run away, unable even to see us. We would watch them in deep sadness, not yet then aware that sometimes to kill is to be kind.

In summer there was sports day, cricket matches and the summer fête, and all the while the church was there in the background, with choir practice and services and weddings and funerals – one slow chime for each year of the deceased's life - and on 11 November, Remembrance Day. In half sleeping, half waking moments I still live in Parwich, I am still 10 years old, I have no responsibilities, no worries. I may now be elsewhere, but Parwich is still my home.

Angela Dodds

Lily Brownlee with her son, Fred.

Flaxdale House, a Youth Hostel from 1933-1935

I used to play with Cassie Braddock at Flaxdale House, opposite Dam Farm. They used to come and fetch milk from us, so we were quite friendly. By then there were no cows in the barn at Flaxdale, but some calves in the croft maybe. But they never farmed. Mr Braddock did the garden and I remember the beautiful buddleia trees. When we were kiddies we always walked up and thought oh, butterflies, butterflies! You get so many different types of butterflies, more than you would normally see if you hadn't got buddleias.

Valerie Kirkham

My name is Betty Stone. I was born in Parwich at Littlewood Farm really by accident, on September 18th, 1922. My mother, Ruth Lees, was born in Parwich, on Gibbon's Bank, and most of her family remained here, but she left home and went into service at the age of thirteen and never really came back to live. She had various jobs before she finally became cook in quite a big house in Derby. Most of her working life was in Derby. She and my dad married just after the First World War, in 1920. At that time there was a dreadful shortage of housing and they could only get rooms, which was most inconvenient for having a baby, so Mum

68

came back to Parwich and stayed with her sister, Annie Calladine, for my birth; and then I didn't see Parwich again until I was four or five. Mum and Dad had a post office and shop in Darley Abbey, just outside Derby, and when there was any crisis at home I used to be sent off to stay with one of the aunts. My first holiday was at Littlewood Farm. My Auntie Alice (Mrs. Wood) lived just behind the shop on Shaw Croft.

I remember most about the village from when we came for school holidays from around 1927 or '28. I came regularly to Parwich for 16 years, just up to leaving school. There was a bus from here to Derby on a Friday, so Auntie Alice would come and pick me up, and the first time I arrived here I was absolutely astonished at how different it was from home. Home was not by any means luxurious, but we had proper sanitation and gas for lighting and cooking, and a bus passed the door into Derby every 15 minutes; but when I arrived in Parwich the first thing I noticed was no pavements.

Everything about the holidays here was different. I found it really very exciting to take the bucket to the pump on Pump Hill for drinking water! I used to go with one of my cousins and we would join hands, arms outstretched, to carry the bucket in the other hand and change over half way. And of course all the children washed at a stone sink in the yard - no running water in the house - so all the washing up bowls were put on the kitchen table to do the washing up. However did they manage? However did my grandmother manage? Ten children in this little cottage; she was washing nappies for 20 years! I admire her enormously. Oddly enough, the first year we returned here to live in 1982, the mains pipes burst in Creamery Lane - no water - so we had to take the bucket down to the standpipe at the bottom of Westview

Terrace and then I thought what it must have been like. It must have been very hard work.

I cannot imagine where ten children slept in such a small cottage, but of course they would probably have left home at thirteen. The girls would go into service, the boys to live on the farms, so as the new ones were coming in, the older ones were moving out; but even so, there must have been times when it was extremely difficult. I suppose they must have shared three to a bed at least, and of course the clothes they had could only be handed down so far.

We used to feed the hens. They were in a field away from the cottage and we quite enjoyed that as well, but we didn't collect the eggs. Uncle or one of my cousins collected them on the way home in the evening. I did learn so much about the countryside, all the different flowers and grasses. We used to be always busy, always occupied doing something. There were lots of little tricks one could do with different grasses - rather primitive craft - those ones with soft, fluffy heads which we'd take three of and wind them round and round, and make a decoration; and another one which had a little hard, black head, and you could twist the stalk round the handle and pull it and it flipped off, so you could see whose seed head would go the furthest, silly little things like that, all quite new to me and quite entertaining. I remember being out for a walk one day and my cousin suddenly rushed ahead and started to climb a tree.

"What are you up to Ken?"

He threw down a whole lot of bird's eggs and I was quite horrified, as I had been taught that you don't disturb a bird's nest and just take one egg; that was permissible in those days. When I protested about this he said, "Well, it's a magpie's nest and they are vermin and you have to do that." People still have a thing against magpies, don't they? They do attack smaller birds, eat their eggs and peck their eyes out but that's the way they are, and they're quite beautiful to look at.

I made lots of friends in Parwich because everyone spent most of their time outdoors doing nothing in particular, and there were all these cousins. I played imaginative games with my girl cousins. We would play shops, go round collecting seeds that became tea, and play schools, and on wet days we would play cards mainly, but that doesn't seem to happen very much these days. I know we played cards at home as a family - simple things like Beggar my Neighbour, and a variation of Rummy; it kept us amused for hours and hours.

I remember one time at Easter we had a trip. Mr Steeple's little bus took us to Eyam, to the plague service. I couldn't have been very old. I'd heard of Eyam but I didn't grasp what was happening on this occasion; all these people gathered on the hillside, and somewhere down below the vicar, in a surplice, was speaking. There wasn't much in the way of a public address system so I couldn't really hear, but it was quite an excitement for people to be having this trip out.

My cousin worked in Tissington at the time and I remember him coming in one evening over the fields, carrying his cap very carefully. He put it down on the table and said, "Don't touch!" The cap was full of about 12 plover eggs and it was quite in order to eat them, fried very lightly. You just had a little taste, not enough for a meal for everyone. Of course, Harry had a bigger share because he had collected them. Incidentally I haven't seen plovers around here. I saw some in the fields up near White Meadow earlier in the year but there are an awful lot of birds disappearing now. It's lovely to watch them when they are displaying, a wonderful sight.

Jam was made with whatever was in season. Gooseberries have always done extremely well in this village. Everyone used to have at least one gooseberry bush in the garden or allotment, and each year Aunty would send a box to Mum because I don't think we had gooseberries at that time at Darley Abbey. We used to walk down to the Five Lamps at the end of the Kedleston Road and wait there for the Parwich bus and collect this box of gooseberries and take it home.

Betty Stone

Mary Graham (later postmistress of Parwich) with her brother Billy, photographed while they were living on the Duke of Sutherland's estate at Golspie, North Scotland.

70

As for my mum, I think life was hard at that time for girls. I think they were always busy, they weren't children; well, they didn't do childish things, they did grown up things because they'd always got chores to do, hadn't they?

Valerie Kirkham

Blackberry and Apple Jam seedless

Put 1lb of blackberries into a jar and after well bruising stand in a saucepan of boiling water to extract juice, then strain well. Pare, core and slice 2 lbs of good cooking apples and to these add blackberry juice. When cooked to a pulp, add to each lb of pulp, ¾lb of preserving sugar, and to every 4 lbs of jam put the juice of one lemon and half the rind grated. Boil for 20 minutes, and put into pots. This will set in a thick jelly and being seedless will be much appreciated.

Mabel Fletcher

Patricia Inglefield (now Mrs Bagshawe) and her sister Isma (now Mrs Lutyens) with dolls and Patricia's cat, Woozer, whose real name was Miss Smoke.

I should like to record the following instance of the mystery that grown people's devotions are to children. My old home stood at the foot of a rocky hill, and was surrounded by terraced gardens, beyond which was a "plantation" of Scotch firs and other trees which ran for a considerable distance up the hill. My elder sister Bessie, four or five years old, failed to understand the petition, "Lead us not into temptation," and wishing to make her prayers a reality, she substituted habitually, "Lead puss not into the plantation" – a place of danger where she thought the cat might get lost.

Most people would imagine the *Pilgrim's Progress* to be a harmless book, but it was near to costing the lives of my two brothers. The hill, behind Parwich Hall, diversified with rock and bushes of gorse, was an ideal playground for children, but developed at it's summit into a desolate tableland, walled everywhere and of great extent. We had all just been saddened by a painful event. Our gardener's little child had wandered away up the hill, and had been found dead under a wall.

Imagine the consternation when, a few days after this accident, the two boys from the Hall went missing. Our mother was in an agony. The church bell and all neighbouring church bells, and every house-bell were rung, and the whole district was speedily dispersed in search for the missing children. They were discovered in the lone country energetically climbing a wall. "We are on a pilgrimage," they announced, "the Celestial City is only a little way off now, we shall be there directly."

I fear their mortification must have been great on being carried home. They were quite small children, about five or six years

71

Parwich Hill, site of "the Celestial City"!

old. I feel little doubt there was a thanksgiving service for their return, but the tale as told to me ends here.

In 1833 my parents moved to Holbrook Hall, six miles north of Derby, being unable any longer to bear the severity of the Parwich climate.

Mrs. Curtis

Barley Sugar

Take 5lbs of crushed sugar either for clear red or yellow; put the sugar into the pan with 1½ pints of water; there is no set quantity of water only do not overdo it. Bring it to a boil then lift it off and see that all be thoroughly melted, and be sure that it is so if the sugar is rough in the grain; give ½ a teaspoonful of cream of tartar, but if it is smooth a little less will do; put it on the fire again and put the lid on the pan for about 4 minutes; let it boil till it cracks in your mouth and does not stick to your teeth; do not let it get to cold on the edges; turn it over and roll in long pieces as long as your slab then break in ½ sticks. Is good for colds and coughs

Mary Emma Hopkinson

I've got a brother six years younger than me and he's at Upper Moor Farm now. He always says that I helped to rear him, made sure his ears were clean! We used to have quite a lot of children playing, even though we lived on the farm - eh, harvest times, and bonfire nights, we used to have marvellous times you know! We used to go in the wood and get trees that had fallen down and make a bonfire and a Guy Fawkes, and play all sorts of things. We'd make our own entertainment at nights. I did a lot of embroidery as I got older. We had the radio and of course we'd Tilly lamps, and later we got Calor gas and a real cooker.

Mary Rawlins

Mary Rawlins at Upper Moor Farm.

Mrs Sykes (Clara Evans' mother) with Iris and granddaughter, Kay.

Moving from place to place with a travelling fair, if we stayed somewhere for a fortnight we could have Sunday lunch, roast beef with Yorkshire pudding, all the trimmings, and either rice pudding or apple pie and custard; otherwise it was bread and cheese, bread and jam, with toast and dripping for breakfast. You'd be sitting there in front of the little open fire with a slice of bread on a fork and you'd get it nicely done and turned over when Dad would come along and pinch it. Well, father was the mainstay and he had to be looked after. I used to like to watch him shave because he used a cut-throat. He'd get his belt off, and on the front of the stove there was a rail and I can see him now, he used to have a piece of newspaper on the mantelpiece and he'd sharpen his razor. He had this shaving mug, and he'd wet his face and rub it all over with a Gibbs shaving stick, lathering it up like; then it was curk, curk, curk, really fast

with the razor. He used to say, "If I cut my throat you do realise you're going to get covered in blood!" And then he used to say, "Rub us a bit of blacking on me boots, duck" and we used to have to do the sole. Whether this stemmed back to his mining days I don't know, because when you knelt down you could see this part of the shoe and if that was clean you was of good character. I don't know whether there's any truth in that but that's the impression I got from a very early age. And if you left a bit of mud in between the top of the boot and the sole, he made you do it again. And he used to walk miles for a pint.

I remember going down the fields messing about with the dog, and I come back with this enormous horse mushroom and I says to my mother, what's this, and she says it's a mushroom. So Father says, "Give me that", and gets the frying pan out and it covers the bottom of the pan completely- and he eats the lot! I says to Mum "He's a greedy pig!" "Don't you dare say that," says she. Mother was law: what she said went. She never hit us and she never got cross with us but when you did anything wrong she'd get hold of your cheek and say, come on, get this done!

Clara Evans

Clara Evans

To clean White straw hats

Wash in soap and water then in clean water dry in air and wash with gum arabic or with well beaten white of egg or sponge over with oxalic acid solution

Mary Emma Hopkinson

In my teens I lived right out on the moor up near Glossop, and I used to go to night school to learn Marcel Waving. I had to pay one pound ten shillings every week out of my wages to buy a tress of hair to practise on. If Dad couldn't fetch me from night school I had to walk from the bus up this long country lane which was very scary. I used to call in at Mrs. Hardy's who would be ready to meet me with a candle in a jam jar to light my way home. She'd tie a piece of string round the lip of the jar and light the candle, but by the time I'd got round the bend to the piggeries and the first farm, my little candle would have gone out. Then I'd run as fast as my little legs could carry me, especially past Miss Brown's, an eccentric lady the children were all afraid of. One night I heard a terrible rustling: it was only a horse putting its head over a hedge but it made me run even faster! I legged it the rest of the way home. When I reached the farm cottage with a barn next to it, there were owls swooping and hooting and I was terrified!

When I was eight or nine years old I used to be scared of another lady called Mrs Burdikin. To get to our house I had to turn off left down an unadopted road that was all rough and stony and hurt my feet. Mrs. Burdikin lived in one of four cottages along there. She wore an overall with a filthy, double-breasted herringbone coat over it, and a dirty headscarf tied very tight over her long, wrinkled face, which was the ugliest you could imagine. You always knew when she was coming because she wore clogs on her blackened feet.

For the last eleven years I have lived in the centre of Parwich village where as well as seeing owls I have been startled by a possible 'flying saucer'. Mary Goldstraw and I saw one here some years ago. We were

A trip to Blackpool in Mr Robert Steeples' bus. Alfred and Beatrice Brownlee, Mary Ellen Allsopp, and Doug Allsopp

sitting on the wall outside my house late one evening when it went over Bradbury's farm towards Ashbourne. I don't know what it was but it had all different coloured lights.

June Nadin

To Curl the Hair

One lb Olive oil, one d *oil of rosemary.
Mix well and apply two or three times weekly. Will curl the straightest hair, if not cut too short.

Mary Emma Hopkinson

**d=pennyworth, or more likely, a drachm, 1/8 of an ounce.

My name is Eileen Ellis, née Steeples. I came from the village of Hognaston in 1929, which lies approximately five miles away from Parwich. I have a sister called Joyce, eighteen months older than me. When I was three years old we moved to the Garage, Creamery Road, Parwich, as it was then called. Dad bought a bus and was the proprietor for many years. Eventually, he had two buses and a taxi. His name was Mr. Robert Henry Steeples. Outside, we had two hand operated petrol pumps. Across the road was the coal house from which we also sold paraffin and so on.

I remember Dad converting the bus to a coal carrier on Monday mornings, taking the top off it and the seats out. In those days most villagers used the bus, as there were very few car owners. There was a service to Ashbourne on Tuesday, Thursday and Saturday market days, and a bus to Derby every Friday which called at all the little villages on the way, namely Ballidon, Bradbourne, Biggin by Hulland, and many more. The farmers' wives came with their baskets of eggs, live chickens and baby chicks, and dairy produce to be sold at the Derby market. Dad always brought a brace of pheasants home for Mr. Crompton-Inglefield who lived at Parwich Hall in those days. Then it was a task for Joyce and I to deliver them by hand. They were always covered with maggots and we hated it but we were rewarded with a silver sixpence which was left on the kitchen table for us.

Each evening we watched out for the bus, and alerted Mum so that she could get Dad's tea to just the right temperature for him to swallow it down and rush back on again, continuing his journey on time. My father was quite strict, and only had to look at us to ensure our good behaviour. We girls shared a bedroom, and I remember us all sitting up in bed with chicken pox, giggling at ourselves in the wardrobe mirrors.

When I was five years of age my sister Kathleen was born, and in 1937 my sister Helen was born. Dad was fed up, another girl! Soon after this I went to live with Aunty Kathleen in Hognaston, as Grandma had died and Aunty was lonely living with just Granddad. I only stayed for two years and returned to Parwich in 1939, when war was declared.

The games we used to play in the village were whip and top, shuttlecock and battledore, skipping, hopscotch, 'What time is it, Mr Wolf?' and rounders, and many more. Then there were Wakes, which are still going on. We were always dressed up in fancy dress for it. My mother used to organise the school concerts with Mrs. Cole, the vicar's wife. I remember practising for these at Flaxdale House. Kathleen Allsopp and I used to play there with Nancy Hinton and her younger sister, Josie, and we had dancing lessons up in the attic. We must have had music of some sort, an old wind up gramophone maybe? Henry and the vicar used to stand on the stage singing, "Oh, no John, no John, no!"

Eileen Ellis

"Shoes or wellingtons, Mum?" Kathleen Allsopp (née Brownlee) at Daisy Bank. Behind her, from left, her sister Sheila with Beatrice, her mother, her Aunty Lily Watson (née Brownlee) and Flo, daughter of Kate Wibberley who kept Parwich shop.

I was born at Daisy Bank on the High Peak Trail, the High Peak Railway as it was then, which transported materials from Glossop's quarry. My father worked at the quarry and if you take a walk there, you can still see the old, rusty rails. The building we lived in is still there too, but it's lost its chimney and is no longer a house.

Our house was built in the 1800s beside the railway, but people may have lived up there since prehistoric times. In the 1700s lead

Before the storm. Kathleen Allsopp at Daisy Bank

miners worked a big rake close to the old barn, and though Daisy Bank may seem an odd place for a stable, between 1830 and 1841 horses were kept there and were used on the railway, to pull the engines up from Cromford. The farm was originally known as Ballidon Moor Farm, but was called Daisy Bank because of all the moon daisies growing along the railway line.

My mother married Alf Brownlee and went to live at Daisy bank, and we were there until I was seven years old. There's an amusing photograph of me outside the house: I'm wearing a wellington on one foot and a shoe on the other! Other photographs show me dancing, all windswept, on top of the dog's kennel. It was wild and isolated up there, so beautiful. It was a lovely childhood, so innocent and all. The photographs would have been taken on the old black Brownie box camera No.2 which I still have. I also have the Kelly oil lamp that went by the bed

and didn't tip over. There was no electricity of course.

I could kill a rabbit before I could write. We used to set 'hangs', and I went with my father at night, then we'd look for them in the morning and my father would show me how to kill them. We used to walk along the railway line, and once Molly only just managed to reach a place where she could get off it in time before being knocked down by the train!

When I was six years old I remember a contest which took place at Daisy Bank between Thurston Dale and Denis Fox, to resolve a dispute which arose at a Point to Point meeting at Flagg. On the High Peak Trail, right opposite the lime kilns, there is a gate at the end of a straight measured mile, and Thurston Dale and Denis Fox had a bet to see to see who'd got the best horse! They raced this measured mile and everyone placed bets.

Some of our water was fetched all the way from Minninglow Sand Hole, a deep mere that had formed after the quarrying out of the sand. On the way to it we passed another mere where we could pick bulrushes. The sand hole was like a secret place, hidden from view unless you knew of its existence. It was beautiful, surrounded by trees and vegetation, and its waters reflected the clouds on a sunny day; but it was also very dangerous, as the sand could shift and the sides collapse, taking with it anyone standing on the bank. We used to dangle a bucket over the edge and let it down into the deep water. My mother warned us to be careful as the mere was 'bottomless', meaning that if you fell in, the sand would suck you under.

Kathleen Allsopp

To cure Rabbit Skins

Tack the skin down fast on a board well stretching it out before tacking.

Scrape the fatty mater of [sic] with a knife and dress it every day with the following mixture: 4oz Bay salt, 2oz Alum, 4oz corrosive sublimate [in] 2 gals Boiling Water. Let it get cold before using.

Mary Emma Hopkinson

When I was at boarding school, my mother wrote postcards to me, sometimes twice a week, and in my collection are the Parwich ones. Incidentally, I have always known it as "Parridge"! They are very gloomy black and

Gibbon's Bank. "In this picture you can see Mrs Mace going up to see her Daddy who lives in that little cottage on top of the hill. Her black dog is with her. He has not noticed the cat. I think the cat belongs to the hospital."
A postcard from Charlotte Halliday's mother, with figures added by her.

Charlotte Halliday with her brother on Parwich Hill

white photographs, probably taken long before the War, but she enlivened them with little figures and comments such as: "You can see Mrs. Mace going up to see her Daddy who lives in that little cottage on top of the hill" and, "I don't know who the children are in this picture, but I expect most of them are little Allsops." And they bring back memories of the Miss Brownsons at the village shop, and Mrs. Graham in the Post Office; of Sergeant Salt, the policeman, and Isaac Swindell, who helped mother in the garden; of Owen Twigge, who delivered our milk (and had a huge dog called Darren who bit me) and of Mr. Steeples' bus, which took us on our occasional trips into far off Ashbourne; and in my nostrils again is the delicious smell of a rather damp, ancient, stone-built house, The Fold, much loved.

Charlotte Halliday

There is a photograph taken in 1950 of me, Zelda, aged four, the youngest of Mr and Mrs Dodds' four daughters, Sara, Vere, Angela and me. I am sitting on the edge of the Village Green at Parwich, and our house, called Hallcliffe, is in the background. Like many people in the village, my parents rented the house from the squire, Colonel Inglefield, who lived at the Hall. Hallcliffe was a sizeable house, having nine bedrooms. In the early days we were a household of nine, with two Irish maids (Evelyn and Connie) and a nanny.

Our lives then were largely spent in the nursery where there was a cream coloured enamel stove which burned coal. The day would begin with breakfast at the table by the window, and then a spoonful of malt with cod-liver oil for each of us was taken from a large brown jar. We then lined up in front of the fire to have our hair plaited by our mother who had a clever way of doing it so that the plaits remained tight and tidy all day. In term-time we would go in the car to Alsop station where the train would take the others (and later me) to Ashbourne, to school. It was often so cold, and in the evenings, having again been to Alsop to collect my sisters, I would look up at the nursery window as we drove in to Hallcliffe, knowing there was a warm fire and tea waiting for us.

Zelda Kent Lemon

Zelda Kent Lemon (née Dodds) at Hallcliffe

It became my turn to take the train to school. It was a steady downhill ride to Ashbourne through breathtaking scenery, which we must have taken for granted, but now remember with joy. If there was nobody at the station to collect us at the end of the day, Angela and I would put a halfpenny on the line, wait for a train to drive over it, and then find the squashed coin, larger and thinner, and be ever hopeful of passing it on as a penny. As we became older, bicycles would be taken and left for us at the station so that we could bicycle home. They were awful old bikes without brakes, and I remember often falling off – the hills were very steep in places.

Hallcliffe, having three storeys, was a tall house, so it is no wonder that passers-by were horrified to see a couple of small girls astride its roof. A frightened voice would telephone our mother to inform her where her children were, but I don't remember ever being told not to do it again. Angela and I slept in a room at the back of the house, and the nightly routine would be to climb out of the window onto convenient stones which protruded from the wall, then onto a low roof and up its pitch while hanging on to a gutter. From there we scrambled to a higher roof, and up a gully to the very top. It was exciting to be so high up and we loved doing it. Daytime activity could involve jumping from our mother's first-floor bedroom window onto the lawn 20 feet below. We had to be very careful to jump out far enough to reach the grass and avoid the wide York stone path beneath. Another feat was to climb onto the narrow ledge which jutted out over the nursery landing; we would climb over the bannister and edge carefully along it, taking care not to look down. There was a boy called Robbie McMicking who was about the same age as me, and whose parents farmed at Parwich Lees. He came quite often to play, and once Angela tied him to one of the legs of the nursery table, telling him to stay there because he was a dog! He stayed, until rescued by a grown-up. There were apple trees to climb at the top of the garden, and there was the church. It had a belfry reached by a winding stone staircase, and at the top was a long tall wooden ladder up to the gigantic bell.

Because of Hallcliffe's situation, much time was spent looking out from its many windows over the Village Green. Every day there was Mr. Harry Twigge to see, black patch over one eye, carrying huge iron churns full of milk on an old cart pulled by a shaggy, blinkered pony. He would carry a pail of milk to the back door of Hallcliffe and fill whatever random jugs had been left out for him. Sometimes the pony would decide to wander away, or on to the Green to eat the grass. In the evenings, Mr Twigge would be seen following his herd of cows across the Green to grazing grounds somewhere at the other end of the village.

Then there was eccentric Miss Roberts who lived two houses to the east of Hallcliffe. We were fascinated by the spectacle of her walking each day with a bucket to fill her daily needs from the pump by the Village Green. She wore black, and I swear sometimes a tall pointed hat. She would shout loudly all the while, and on more than one occasion we saw her turn the bucket, full of water, up and over her head. Sometimes she would ask Angela and me into her cottage, where the garden was full of nettles and the house full of cats. We would eat fish-paste sandwiches and it was quite an adventure. The house between Miss Roberts and Hallcliffe was a place we also visited, and that was fascinating because in the garden up a steep path was an outside privy, with two holes to sit upon.

MISS OADLEY, A SELF-ASSURED FAIRGROUND CHILD

The church was opposite Hallcliffe and my parents took us every Sunday, either there or to Alsop where our father would sometimes read the lesson, and where Angela and I were allowed to leave during the sermon and play under the trees in the churchyard. Through the churchyard of Parwich church was a field with the cobbler's hut at the end of it where we would take shoes to be mended. The cobbler was fascinating too because he had a wooden leg. The brook beside the church was another place to play, and in the autumn we would collect conkers from under the big chestnut tree, and that is where my parents are now buried.

Sometime during the 1950's, Nanny, Evelyn and Connie left, and we were able to have our own bedrooms. I slept above the kitchen. I well remember that cockroaches were a hazard, and it was imperative to turn on the staircase light and make a lot of noise if wanting to enter the kitchen at night; there was always a rush of big, shiny black creatures clattering back to their refuge in the wainscots and it was then safe to cross the floor in unslippered feet. There was once a pest officer who knocked at the door to enquire directions to the Hall, and my mother invited him in to show him her problem with the cockroaches; he put powders and potions in the appropriate places which cured the invasion, and she was so pleased because he would not let her pay him a fee.

The most fun of all was had, however, at the Hall. Colonel Inglefield was now Sir John Crompton-Inglefield. He and his wife were wonderfully kind to our family. When television was invented and they had a set, Angela and I were asked up to watch children's television every Sunday. When it was over we would stay to chat until it was time for me to go to Evensong because I was in the choir.

I hope it is fair to say that my parents were popular members of the Parwich village community. My father was a true gentleman and was always polite to, and interested in, anyone he met. My mother was very creative and threw herself into village affairs, running the Women's Institute and being an active member of the Mothers' Union and the Parish Council, and entering produce and flowers from her wonderful garden in the Village Show. The house was full every weekend it seemed, with our friends staying, after we had all migrated to work in London. Our mother always found time to pick and arrange huge vases of flowers for all the main rooms of the house, and smaller ones for the guests' bedrooms.

The twenty years we spent at Hallcliffe were truly memorable and happy, and I think my sisters and I are grateful for the privilege of having lived in Parwich during all our formative years.

Zelda Kent Lemon (née Dodds)

An outing with Nanny. Patricia Crompton-Inglefield (Mrs.Bagshawe) and her sisters, Isma (Mrs Lutyens) and baby Caroline (Mrs Kilner) of Parwich Hall, with 'Na', Elsie Gordon Cameron

MURIEL BROWNSON
Muriel lived at Brentwood where her family ran the shop.

A young Edwardian boy. Reg Twigge and his parents, Lucy (née Moorcroft) and Frank Twigge

Note Reg's elaborate dress, the side-buttoned knickerbockers, off-centre buttons and big, starched lace collar. His mother's dress is quite plain by comparison and there is still something girlish about the outfit in spite of the boy having been 'breeched' long ago. His mother still puts a protective arm around him while the father stands to one side.

Muriel Marjory Annie, the only child of Esther Helena and her husband George Brownson of Brentwood, Parwich, was a child of small build with china blue eyes, a fair complexion and wavy auburn hair. As an only child in a cloistered household, she was nervous, and exceptionally shy and did not remember her childhood with affection. There was little to occupy her in the village because she was discouraged from mixing with village children, so she must have suffered hours of boredom on many occasions. Fortunately, she found friends in Dolly Bunting and Alice Fentham, daughters of local farmers, and Alice Twigge, daughter of the local doctor. Perhaps because she was an only child, Muriel loved animals. She had pet lambs, dogs and poultry, and always cared for them herself. Sadly, she was not encouraged to enter a profession or take up a career. As a girl, she had nurtured hopes of becoming a nurse but her mother thought her too 'delicate' for this occupation so she stayed at home to help to run the household until she married seven years later. Unlike her other female relatives, Muriel was not musical, artistic in the formal sense of the word, or a needlewoman; neither did she enjoy reading. The time spent at home must therefore have hung heavily on her hands. She had a flair for flower arranging and was a good plain cook, especially with pastry.

Ann Vidler

As the twentieth century progressed, clothes were simplified, making life easier for both mother and child, as we see from this picture of Roger Graham taken in the early 1940s.

84

When I was six or seven I was friends with Cassie Braddock who lived at Flaxdale House, and I used to go round there for jam teas. Mrs. Braddock was really strict with her adopted daughter, Cassie, and Cassie rebelled against it. They used to lock her into her room, so she'd climb out of the attic and shin down the pear tree; she was up to all sorts of things. Long after Cassie was married, Mrs. Braddock was still trying to keep her under her thumb. We used to play house in the sheds in the croft outside. There used to be a well in the back, where you come down the steps to the kitchen door, and to the left there was a trough. Inside the kitchen, there was a fire like a Rayburn. I remember when you went up the first few stairs there was a big picture of an Indian in all his feathers and things. Mrs. Braddock had an old desk, really old fashioned. She was a big churchwoman and practised the organ in the front room at Flaxdale House. She played in church sometimes.

Barbara Lowes

My brother Jack and I played mostly round the fairground but sometimes we managed to get away and go to somebody's house and play. I came to Flaxdale House in Parwich once when Cassie Braddock was about 11 or 12 and that's when she showed me the upstairs. I was fascinated with it being four storeys high. She slept in the attic and she'd got this violin and I pleaded with her to play something. She could play a little and to me it was magic because I'd never had the opportunity. Mother always said I had long, thin piano fingers, that's what mother always used to say. In any case there was nowhere to put anything in the 'van. All my clothes were kept in a suitcase on the foot of the bed.

Clara Evans

When I was a child I loved making mud puddings. No matter what toys you had there was nothing quite like it. It's good that things have changed, but what do people do with their spare time? My children always had a bedtime story. I always was there. I didn't even join the WI until David was 15. Course, Harry used to do a lot of overtime at two shillings an hour! He did hours and hours of overtime, and then eventually they did pay him.

Davey Crockett hats, that was all the rage. I went to a jumble sale and there was a fox fur there and as soon as I saw it I thought, Davy Crockett! So I bought it and made the boys hats. David used to go up Parwich Hill with his friend; people were safe then so you didn't mind the children going off, and they spent hours up there. I remember John was late one night. I was getting tea and Harry came home and he says, "Where is John?" He'd been home from school and changed his clothes. So then we started looking all round the village to try and find John, and Harry found him eventually, up near the Care Centre opposite Bell's Yard. He'd tried to climb under the gate and got himself stuck on some barbed wire!

Len Gibbs, when he was younger, used to go up and pinch apples from Hallciffe, and one day Harry caught him, well saw him, and the lad ran away and Harry ran after him. Len said, "I looked round and he was still coming after me and I still had to keep going," and Harry said, "Yes my lad, there was I chasing you for pinching apples and here you are now, sitting in my house, and my wife's cooking apple pie for you!"

Ella Hopkinson

One time, when we were in Parwich with the fair for Wakes, I was playing with Val Kirkham who lived at Dam Farm. We were playing happily, and she was riding this three wheeler bike up and down the little alley by the brook, and when she come up to me I says, "Can I have a ride please?" "No, she says, you can't", and she was riding backwards, pedalling away, and next thing I knew she'd gone in the brook. I can see the bike on the bank with its back wheels spinning. I ran and grabbed it, then I pulled her out and she went in and told her grandma I'd pushed her in the brook! She says to me, "I think you'd better go home", so I went, a sad little soul!

I used to go scrumping gooseberries near the White's garage which was a garden then with all these gooseberry bushes round the wall; and there was also an apple tree; well I didn't fancy the apples 'cause they looked scabby. So we used to sneak under't back of swingboats and get gooseberries. Mr. Flower caught me and he came to Dad and he says, "Look, don't let her go taking them; if she wants them tell her to come and ask me and she can have as many as she wants - but that wasn't the same was it? There was no element of surprise or the fear of somebody catching you!

Clara Evans

How to Clarify Meat dripping

Put the dripping into a pan with some water, and let it boil for ¹/₄ of an hour. Then pour it into a dish to get cold, and when cold make a hole in the dripping and pour off the water, Then use it for children's cakes; they are not rich and the dripping does not taste after being boiled.

Mary Emma Hopkinson

Mary Graham (right) with Beatrice, her mother, and brother Billy.

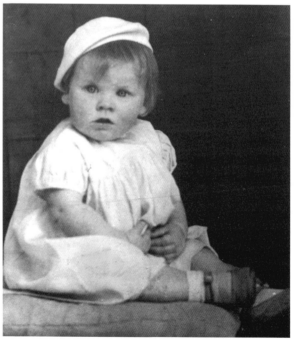

Valerie Kirkham

School

In 1861 the school and schoolhouse were built and splendidly equipped by Sir William Evans, a generous gift to the people of Parwich. The school was said, at the time, to be one of the finest village schools in the country, and looking at the good stone walls of local limestone the mullioned windows and the firm buttresses supporting the building and the clock (bell) tower, one realizes that the grateful people of the village may well be proud of their school. Many years after the death of Sir William, the school was sold and became a council school.

Helena Birkentall

Presentation: Miss L. Hopkinson, late assistant teacher in the Parwich School, was on the 12th inst the recipient of a silver Queen Anne tea set, presented to her by the teachers and scholars as a token of their esteem for her. Miss Hopkinson has served in the school for nine years and is now leaving to be married. The school was thrown open for the occasion, the parents and friends being cordially invited to see the children at work, and a great many availed themselves of the opportunity. Miss Hopkinson, on receiving the present, which was much admired, heartily thanked her friends and said that the tea set with its inscription would always recall to her memory the happy days of the past. After songs, recitations, and drills had been given by the children the proceedings closed with the singing of the National Anthem.

Press cutting, 1907, belonging to Miss Mary Graham. Source not identified.

Unlike the rest of her family, Esther (née Shaw) Brownson did not go to boarding school but went instead to a day school by pony and trap. Why this break from tradition was made is not known. Perhaps it has something to do with her father's financial position for he apparently 'went bust', or maybe his failing health was the deciding factor: he died at the age of fifty seven when Esther was only sixteen years old.

Ann Vidler

The education of my Aunt, Miss Mary Coultman Graham, Postmistress of Parwich, must have suffered with the many changes of schools due to her parents' frequent moves, (they had at least eleven different homes between 1898 and 1913). I have an old school report of hers from Littleover Church of England School when she was 13, in which her teacher writes, "Mary has worked carefully and intelligently, and has made very good progress. Conduct: Excellent."

Roger Graham

I did not go to school until I was six years old. When we moved from Daisy Bank and came to live in Parwich, all three of us attended school, myself, Mollie and Sheila. There were only three years and ten months between us, and two younger than me, so my mother couldn't possibly have walked from Daisy Bank with us. So I only had seven years schooling altogether. I left at fourteen, because there was no Secondary Modern and I didn't get to the Grammar School, but both my sisters went to the Secondary Modern because it had just opened by then.

I remember the one-up-one-down cottage, now demolished, which stood in the tiny space where the picnic table and flower bed

PARWICH SCHOOL circa 1935
Back row left: Walter Wilson, Donald Allsopp, Jessie Gibbs, Charlie Twigge, ?, Nancy Hinton, Tom Bunting.
Front row left: Irene Lees, Audrey Dale, Margaret Edge, Joyce Brownlee, Eileen Steeples, Jessie Sims, Mrs. Yates

are now outside Parwich shop. It had steps up it and you had to go outside to get to the upper room. It was a cobbler's shop. The school caretaker lived there and he had only one arm. We used to call him Inebegyny, I don't know why. He was also the postman and he used to chase us with a brush. We used to be frightened to death of him. There was a shed at the bottom of the school playground where he used to collect paper. We kept our distance from him, but when we were all going home at night he used to get into this paper shed and stand there and hit us with the knob on the end of his hand.

Kathleen Allsopp

It was my time to start school. We had a lovely teacher called Miss Walker. I evidently made a fuss and cried and upset my sister

Joyce quite a bit. Miss Walker used to cycle from Brassington every day, come rain, snow or shine. We had three classes, 1, 2, and 3. I can't remember an awful lot about class one apart from learning the three 'R's. We moved up to class 2 at the age of seven and our teacher was Mrs. Yates. She lived on the Village Green. She was very strict and would often hit you on the head with a thimble on her middle finger during sewing lessons, and if you put your head back, it went right down your nose! Joyce told her off one day for hitting me on the head with a ruler. She said, "Don't do that to our Eileen, she's got a headache," sticking up for me you see! Mrs Yates also played the piano, to which we danced *Sir Roger de Coverley* and *Pieces of Eight*.

At eleven years of age we moved to class three. Mr Hampson was the Headmaster. I quite liked him, although he gave me the cane once for talking in class! He was a great one for taking us on nature walks. We picked wild flowers, and then we had to press them in our nature books and remember the names of them all. He also taught us a lot of poetry, Wordsworth, Tennyson and so on. I remember he loved "Gunga Din"!

Eileen Ellis

My sisters, Sara and Vere, had had a governess to teach them when they were little, in our previous home at Combs, but after we came to Parwich, Sara and Vere went to the P.N.E.U. in Ashbourne, and Angela, aged four, took herself off to the village school where she learnt to read in a matter of weeks, and from that day hardly ever had her head out of a book.

Zelda Kent-Lemon

I went to the PNEU School in Ashbourne and travelled by train from Alsop en le Dale station. One of our parents would drive me and I would always hope it would be my father collecting me as the great game with him was at the turning off the A515 Ashbourne-Buxton road* to switch off the engine and see if the car could coast all the way into the garage at Hallcliffe. It usually worked with a lot of leaning forward and coaxing the car up the hills.

Sara Dodds
*The Parwich Dale route, presumably

At Parwich school, we two younger ones learned to read and write under the inspired teaching of Mrs Yates. She lived two doors away from us on The Green and I would climb over the wall at the top of our garden, cross over next door's garden and go and knock on Mrs Yates' kitchen door, just to sit with her and listen to her talking.

Angela Dodds

The village school was considered unsuitable for Muriel Brownson, so she travelled daily to a small private school for the 'daughters of gentlemen' in Ashbourne. The journey to and from was a daunting one. Whatever the weather, and usually accompanied by one of her parents or her Auntie Annie, Muriel walked two miles over the hill and across the stiles to the Bletch. Here she continued her walk over the fields, crossing Bletch Brook down the valley before she ascended yet another steep hill. From here it was downhill across the fields to Tissington Station where she boarded the train for Ashbourne. In very heavy winters when the stiles and hedges were indistinguishable under the heavy snowdrifts, the going must have been extremely hard for an adult, let alone a child. Had she enjoyed her education, the journey might have been worth all the effort, but she didn't, so the effort must have been enormous.

Ann Vidler

I went to school in Parwich. I used to love it there, I wouldn't miss a day, but Ashbourne school I absolutely hated. I'm more interested in making things. I like to do things with my hands more than my head. I love cooking and sewing, dressmaking, that sort of thing.

Barbara Lowes

MISS WALKER'S CLASS circa 1936.
Back from left: Charles Twigge, Albert Wilson, Len Gibbs, Don Allsopp, Walter Wilson, Stan Weston.
Third row left: Aggie Atkinson, Nancy Hinton, Jessie Gibbs, Kath Ward, Audrey Dale, Margaret Edge.
Second row from left: Jessie Sims, Bella Wilson, Audrey Ratcliffe, Joyce Brownlee.
Front row left: Alfie Atkinson, Cyril Lowndes, Don Fearn, Percy Edge, Jack Allsopp

I went to Biggin School in 1941, when I was five. To get there I only needed to go across three fields into Cardlemere Lane. My dad took me on the carrier of his bicycle, with my gas mask and dinner bag. He would drop me off at Biggin Lane End at Mr. and Mrs. Watson's, who had two daughters, and they would take me the rest of the way to school and back. My dad would come with his bicycle and collect me. I would get on the carrier again and ride home, about three miles. It was very cold and frosty in winter. School transport started about the middle to late '40s.

When school meals began, we had them in Biggin village hall. After the war, when the prisoner of war camp was no longer needed, they transferred the meals from the village hall to the camp so they could use more up-to-date kitchens, about a quarter of a mile from school. The coal man, Terence, that comes to Parwich says I used to give him a piggy back ride up to dinner 'cause he was only tiny with these little legs! We had to walk, hail rain or sunshine. 103 pupils attended school in two classrooms. They had to use the chapel for another classroom, for three teachers. We had no bullying, no nothing and the teachers were very nice, yes, they were. I was very popular at school, though I say it myself, and I got up to Head Girl. I got on with everybody. We used to meet up with Hartington school and go by bus for swimming at Matlock. It was outdoor, and we had to go whether it was summer or winter! We also used to go by bus one day a week to Ashbourne for cookery and needlework. We had polio at Biggin school and were closed for a month. We'd three with polio, one very bad, ending up with callipers on her legs. One ended up lame in one leg, and the other one got it in her arm and shoulder. It was a bit scary, that.

Alan Oldfield's sister Peggy was a teacher at Biggin school when I was there and she went to school camp with us. School camp was our holiday. We went to Sutton on Sea from Monday to Friday. We used to have jobs to do every day and we had points. We had circle tents and we slept with our feet to the pole. Every morning we had to roll the side up and get all the clothes in the holdalls and put them to the middle of the pole, and we got so many points each for doing it. Some of us had to do the potatoes for the day. We used to have entertainment and play sports on the sands. On the Thursday before we came back on the Friday we could walk to Mablethorpe and go up on the sand and spend our pocket money. We went two years in succession. I think I was fourteen last time I went. Ada Birch was a pupil teacher when I first started school, while waiting to go to college. She says. "I can see you now coming with your little black gym slip and your long black stockings!" She came to Parwich after that. In those days you didn't go on to another school. You could go to grammar school if you paid. So we went to school till we were fifteen. I left school in 1951.

Mary Rawlins

Opposite: Gerald Lewis (in background) at Cambridge

At [Darley Abbey] Mr. Spencer [the tutor] appeared with a large bunch of nettles in one hand and a pill box in the other. The nettles were black with a multitude of caterpillars of the peacock butterfly, and he had an additional collection in the pill-box. He instructed us to put the nettles in water, and day by day to watch the interesting transformation of caterpillar into chrysalis, and of chrysalis into butterfly. He was not aware that caterpillars before they settle into chrysalides go through a wandering phase, and often crawl for great distances. Unhappily, those he had brought to us were just at that stage of their career, and next morning only two remained on the nettle, all the rest had walked away. Great was the outcry raised through the house by our mother and the maids. There were caterpillars everywhere, caterpillars in the bedrooms, caterpillars among the food being prepared in the kitchen, caterpillars going up and down stairs. I fear the bucket and the housemaid's brush quickly ended their lives...

Mrs. Curtis

T. H. Lord

July 1887

CORNER OF MARKET ST
MARKET PLACE CAMBRIDGE

Claud Lewis (right) and possibly one of his brothers.
While many left school for work at fourteen, the gentry left
public school bound for university.

We didn't go to the local school in the Channel Islands to start with because my mother, Ethel Hopkinson, was a bit concerned that the local children spoke French patois, old Norman French. This was in the early 1930s. She had been a teacher at Parwich school, and loved teaching so she started teaching us at home when we were five. It was all very official: she belonged to some organisation where you could teach children at home, and we had little desks and followed a proper school day and had exams, and only a half day off for our birthday, which made us twins very annoyed. My mother was fascinated by botany, and as a very young child, she started getting me interested in flowers. At seven we were sent locally to a private Froebel school. My

mother was very enlightened about education; in fact I think my poor father sometimes found this quite difficult, having been brought up a true Victorian. In his childhood children didn't speak unless spoken to, while she was all for explaining to you why you were doing things, which was extremely modern. But he always accepted anything she said. In our upbringing she was given a free hand, because he felt she knew more about children than he did; but it didn't go down very well when we later came to meet my father's brother, Rev. Claud Lewis. By that time he had sold the Parwich Estate and bought a house in Wales called Evancoyd..

Mary Whitechurch

They had wonderful concerts at Parwich School and I think I have been to all of them since David was at school, and he would be five and he is fifty-five now. At one time I knew every child in the village. Mind you it was because I worked at the school, I was caretaker for a little while, 1970s-80s, and they couldn't get anyone else so they came and asked me. Harry helped me and we did it between us, but it was more to be with the children than anything else. There was one girl, Sarah Lambert, a shy sort of girl I used to make a bit of a fuss of, and after she left school and went away, she went on sending me a Mothering Sunday card every year.

Ella Hopkinson

When we were in Parwich at Wakes time the Headmaster used to bring the children down at dinner time and pay for a ride for all the children in the school, then Father used to give them a free ride as well. Oh, I can see it now; you could hear kids on the dam wall shouting, hip, hip hooray, it's Sykey! It was a regular thing that was, and if any kids was missing out of school you'd always know where to come and find them because they used to come down to us and they'd to be either running round like heathens or saying, can I do this Mr Sykes, or can I help you Mr Sykes? Even though we were travelling round a lot it was easy to make friends because with you being a fair girl, if they made friends with you they'd get free rides, which is only natural isn't it?

Clara Evans

I went to school here in Parwich and I enjoyed it. The first Head Teacher I had was Mr Fearn and at that time he lived at The Fold with his first wife. When I first started school she used to take me there, and she was a lovely lady; but then she became ill with multiple sclerosis. When the new school house was built they lived there. After she died we had another lady called Mrs Weston who lived at Middle Moor Farm, and she taught me. Mr Fearn was very musical. He wrote a lot, and he put new tunes to hymns, and set poems to music. We always did lots of singing because that's what he loved.

At school we had an infant room then the juniors. At that time there were two junior rooms with a partition between them, so you'd have three years in one room and three years in another, because in those days if you didn't pass your eleven-plus you'd stay at Parwich school until you were thirteen. After that you could take your thirteen-plus. Later they altered it so you went to the County Secondary School at eleven and could take a thirteen-plus. I took my eleven-plus, passed, and went to Grammar School in Ashbourne. So when I left Parwich School there were two years above me still. Mr Fearn taught the last three years and Mrs Weston taught the first three juniors, and then a lady called Mrs Lousier, who came from Brassington, taught me; very nice she was, she was lovely. Yes, we enjoyed being at school. We all got on

together, and were happy, and there's still quite a few of us living here today. We played all kinds of things like hopscotch, and in those days the school had gardens which we used to do every week, digging and planting seeds. The garden was in the Square, where the lawn is, opposite the school. That was the boy's garden. The girls used to do the little gardens round the school.

I had friends to stay when I went to the Grammar School. They used to come for perhaps a week, because obviously it was nice for people who lived in towns to get out into the country, and I would go down and stay with them.

Valerie Kirkham

Valerie Kirkham
in her Grammar School uniform

Clara Evans

I lived in a caravan on the fairground. What was it like being brought up in that sort of environment? Well, when we became school age we used to go to a different school every week, but when we got to Calow, we'd be there for four months. I remember I had a new little blue velvet dress. It must have been Whitsuntide, and Dad started us at William Rhodes School in Chesterfield, a massive great school; petrified I was, and I'd only be about five, and this teacher was one of those snappy sort of people. She went round the classroom asking each child to read a paragraph. Well the others couldn't read properly but they made the effort, but when she asked me to read and I said I couldn't, she told me not to be stupid and read. I says, "I can't, I don't know how!" I remember whimpering and she got hold of me and shook me until my teeth rattled, and when she let go, I fled and ran home. My dad put me up

on his shoulder and we went to see the Headmaster, and when we walked into the classroom, the teacher went as white as a sheet and the Headmaster says,"I needn't ask any questions, I know she's telling the truth." Thereafter that woman was a different person again.

At the end of the travelling season, when we were back at Calow, Father went to see the Headmaster there and he says, "Why isn't the children improving?" And the Headmaster says the reason is too many different teachers trying to teach them the same thing, and each teaching in a different way. At one school we'd be learning joined up writing, and then at the next school they'd still be printing. The Headmaster said that going to school on a weekly basis wasn't doing anything for us, so we stopped going in the travelling months and went only during the winter.

I couldn't read until I was thirteen. In the end I decided that I had got to concentrate on one subject and I picked reading. I used to go in the corner and pinch Father's Westerns, and I remember sitting there hunched up. I started off putting two letters together and getting the sound, then onto three letters. For ages and ages I used to struggle with 'was'. I mean, it doesn't look like 'wos', does it? It didn't really make sense. Then I went from three letters to four letters, and eventually I could read a sentence and make sense of it. My mother couldn't read, so I couldn't ask her to help me. There was only Father with the education and if you asked him anything he didn't want to know. So every time I was missing, I'd got me head in this book. My mother used to say, haven't you got anything better to do? Come and get this done, or do that.

Parwich School Centenary 1861-1961

PARWICH SCHOOL CELEBRATES ITS CENTENARY 1861 - 1961

Back from left: Headmaster, Mr. Fearn, Mrs Ada Birch, Mrs Fearn, Mrs Hansford, Sir John Crompton-Inglefield, Lady Crompton-Inglefield, Mrs Braddock, Mrs Leedham, Mrs Dodds, Rev. Hansford. Fourth row from left: Janice Lees, Suzanne Wayne, Caroline Fearn, Barry Kirkham, ?, ?, David Wibberley, ?, Third from left: Barry Wibberley, Susan Lees, Ann Webster, Glenis ?, ?, Chris Lowndes. Second from left: ?, Freda Webster, Janet Shipley, ?, ?, Steve Hudson, William Webster, ?, Front left: ?, ?, Paul Allsopp, Kevin Goldstraw, Jane Twigge, Susan Webster, Susan Ridgard, Susan Johnson

At Secondary Modern school a girl asked me to jump in the long jump so I said, okay, 'cause I'd got long legs then, see. So she says, right, I want you down here every lunchtime to practise. Right, she says, you're in the team for the summer sports, and I says no, and she says yes, most definitely yes; and I say, most definitely no, and she says, why are you being like this? I say, for the simple reason I shan't be here, I shall be gone in March. We travel with the fairground all round Derbyshire. She says, why didn't you tell me this before? I says, because you never asked me; you was telling me.

Although we were travelling round with the fair, I did go to school in Parwich on two or three occasions because I can remember going with my little flowered cup for milk. In the infant classroom there used to be an open fire and they used to bring the crates of milk and stand it at side of fire, and it used to

PARWICH SHOP (left) AND THE SCHOOL.
"I don't know who the children are in this picture, but I expect most of them are little Allsops." A postcard to her daughter from Charlotte Halliday's mother, with original drawings.

get nice and warm and creamy; and if there was a chance of having extra I was there, because we never got milk unless we were in a place a fortnight and we could go to the farm for it.

Clara Evans

I went to Parwich School until I was thirteen. My brother, Tom Lees, who is one year older than me, walked with me from Ballidon. We had three routes over the fields, the top way, the middle way and the bottom way. We had no wellingtons in those days, and in the winter, come rain or snow, our feet used to get wet through. Mrs. Hampson, the Headmaster's mother, used to take us in, dry us, and give us a lovely orange, one of those big ones, so we didn't mind the rain! I

remember the lovely sunny days too. I remember the big cracks in the fields.

I went to Bradbourne School for one year because they wanted more scholars or they were going to close. I was thirteen then, and I left school at fourteen and I've worked hard ever since.

Catherine Elizabeth (Dolly) Wayne

My boys, David and John went to Parwich School, and then David got a scholarship to the grammar school and from there he went to Bristol, to university. It was a bit of a struggle but he went, and he wrote to me and he says, "Mum, although it's been a struggle, I'll try and make it up to you in time to come."

Ella Hopkinson

Grandparents

Roger and Peter Graham with their grandparents, Beatrice (wearing her gold chains) and Fred Graham.

My grandmother, Elizabeth, known as Beatrice Graham (née Coultman) was born in 1872. I have many personal memories of her which cover the period from approximately 1948 until her death in 1954. She was 69 when I was born and she was 72 when my brother, Peter, was born. I did not know at the time that we were the only grandchildren of my grandmother and her four sisters and one brother: the other five Coultmans did not have children).

My parents, my brother and I used to visit Parwich on a regular basis. We had an old pre-war Hillman car and the thirty-mile journey from Long Eaton to Parwich via Derby and Ashbourne took just over an hour. In 1948 my father had been a headmaster for 24 years and he was a very strict father. However, in the house of his mother, there was no doubt whatsoever who was in charge - his mother!

I remember many things about my grandmother; the Yorkshire puddings cooked by her and served in a large dish with rich gravy as a separate course. They were crispy and curled up at the edges - wow! I remember too the bottles of dark coloured liquid in the dairy, one bottle of which was given to my father to drink at lunchtime. I found out a few years later that this was beer. I never saw my father drink beer at any time in his life except in Parwich and then only until 1954 when my grandmother died. I remember my grandmother's cats and their food, steamed fish, on plates scattered around the house. At their peak there were twenty-one cats at one time, and because of this I developed a big dislike of cats at a very early age!

My grandmother always dressed in black, including black boots, and I never saw her wear any informal footwear. Her jewellery was elaborate, consisting of many gold necklaces and chains which she wore round her neck. She corresponded constantly with the local press. She used to answer puzzles and enter quizzes using my name and stating my age at the time. I remember her telling me on one occasion that I had been highly commended! The judges must have thought that the handwriting of a 6-11 year old was very mature, having in reality been written by a 75-80 year old! The loo arrangements were a further cause of distress: up the garden path at the back of the outbuildings. Pooooh!

When I became a chorister at St. John's Church, Long Eaton in 1953 I remember my grandmother coming to a service and telling me how proud she was of me BUT that I MUST hold my head up when processing through the Church.

Roger Graham

My grandfather was Alf Brownlee. I'm not sure where he was born. His dad lived on Lenscliffe, opposite the school playground, at Lilac Cottage. My great great granddad and he used to live there, and I remember he had this lovely grandfather clock with a sun and moon on it, and all these stuffed birds in cages, and when he died my granny smashed them all up, she said it was rubbish.

Barbara Lowes

Alf Brownlee
leaning on the corn merchant's classy motor

I don't have any memories of Gibbon's Bank: in fact it was only about four years ago that I walked right up to it. But it seemed a part of my childhood, because Mum would talk about it quite often and we had a postcard of it. One thing she told me was that in spite of all the children she had, Granny did washing for some of the farmers' wives. They would send her white bonnets to starch and then pleat with irons like curling tongs. Imagine all the work that went into that, heating the irons on the open fire, and looking after her family as well. The bonnets had to be laid very carefully in a basket, then Mum or one of her sisters would deliver them after school, walking probably a couple of miles each way. Mum told me how badly Granny was paid, and I can remember her saying,

"And none of them ever offered me so much as a drink of water when I'd walked all that way and had to walk all the way back!"

I suppose they'd have taken the laundered bonnets and brought back the dirty ones for laundering.

Betty Stone

Elizabeth (Bessy) Evans 1786-1880.
Women's lace caps and collars required laborious washing, starching and ironing.

Embrocation for Rheumatism and Lumbago

One ounce of oil of rosemary, one ounce oil of cloves, one ounce oil of oreganum, one ounce of spirits of Turpentine, one ounce of spirits of ammonia, once ounce Tincture of cantharides, one ounce alcohol. Mix in a light glass stopper bottle and shake up when used. Heat a saucer on embers, pour a little in the saucer and rub it on the part affected with the hand, previously warmed by the fire so as to encourage absorption, and keep the bowels opened with Claytons Restorative Pills. Two pills twice a day have a wonderful invigorating Effect.

Mary Emma Hopkinson

Grandpa was a roadman, so he didn't earn very much and I fear he drank far more than he should have done; they all seemed to in those days, it was a pattern of life. I used to think, how awful, that men could be so inconsiderate, but when you think they'd been working hard all day and they came back and there was probably baby washing and all sorts of things hanging about, and all the children, it isn't much wonder that they went out. It wouldn't do nowadays, would it?

There were some letters at home from my grandmother to my mother. I never read all of them, and I think they were disposed of; just a little bundle of letters as a mother would write to a daughter in service. But I do remember a particular one. Grandma was not at all well for the last few years of her life and she writes: "The parson came to see me last week and brought me a pot of Virol from the Charity, and I really think it's doing me good."

She must have had very little education but her writing was clear, and the grammar was right, the punctuation was right.

Betty Stone

Ada Willa (Granny) Flower leaning on the garden gate of Church Gates. Dam Farm is in the background.

Grandparents looked after you when you were young, and you looked after them when they got old. Girls were expected to look after their grandparents, as my mother looked after her grandma. The eldest seemed to be the one who did it. My aunt, my mother's sister, went into service, and my mum's younger sister went out to work, but my mum never did while she was young. Later on, she cycled to Ballidon, Hipley and Gorse Hill to deliver the post, as well as doing half of Parwich.

My mum also looked after her dad's mum, because she lived opposite us and I used to go there when Great Grandmother was living. We used to look after her when she was ill.

We had a rocking chair and Granny Flower used to sit in the living room at Dam Farm knitting, and the cat used to sit on her knee trying to chew the wool.

Valerie Kirkham

Weak Eyes

May be released by washing them in cold water or dissolve four grains of sugar of lead and crude sal ammonicas in eight ounces of water to which add a few drops of laudanum. With this mixture bathe the eyes night and morning. Rose water is good for the eyes.

Mary Emma Hopkinson

My grandmother, Beatrice Graham, was a founder member of the Parwich W.I. and a life member of the Mothers' Union. As an active member of the church, she was also on the Parochial Church Council and was a bell ringer on many occasions. She was a Sunday School superintendent and a member of the Nursing Association. The newspaper, in her obituary, went on to say that she "was a conscientious worker for all deserving causes and will be greatly missed in the village."

Roger Graham

Barbara Lowes' Great Grandmother and Great Grandfather Moorcroft with their grandson, Fred (son of Lily Brownlee, née Moorcroft)

My granny used to make all her own things; everything was home made, none of this ready stuff, she did it all, she wouldn't buy anything. They used to keep a pig in the shed, in what we called the 'ovel. Then they killed it, not that I agree with them killing animals, but I can see my granny now making black pudding with it. She used to get her hands in and mix it all up, oh it were 'orrible! She used to make cheese, and she used to bottle all the fruit. She had this big pine dresser full of all preserves and things. When you think how we live today, life's too easy now.

Barbara Lowes

Mary Anne Shaw (1843-1936) at Brentwood with her granddaughter, Muriel Brownson

At the age of ninety, when she gave a newspaper interview, Mary Anne Shaw could see to read without glasses. The press photograph shows her at that age to be stout in build, dressed in a formal dress with long sleeves and a high collar with a little ruffle above the collar. Her hair is white and pulled into a bun. Mary Anne said in the report that she had waltzed with her eldest daughter, Annie, a few months previously and still had six of her children alive.

At some time during the 1920's James Brownson, Muriel Brownson's grandfather, came to live in the Brownson household at Brentwood in Parwich. This proved to be an unfortunate move, for James was a somewhat difficult man, a widower, with Victorian values and a dictatorial manner towards women. After a strong disagreement between Muriel and her grandfather concerning the

way that James flaunted his wealth in order to get his own way, James left Brentwood and went to live in Stony Middleton. His son George's death, on January 27th 1927, must have been a heavy blow to George's wife, Esther, and James' own death a year after was an even worse blow, for he left nothing to Esther or Muriel. The cottage in which they had lived for nearly thirty years was bequeathed elsewhere.

Ann Vidler

My grandfather, Arthur Bembridge, used to bake and deliver bread from Hognaston to Parwich, at first by horse and cart, later by van. I loved my grandfather. He read from the Bible to us every Sunday after Sunday school, then took us for a walk. He'd say, "Now be quiet, children," and poke with his stick in the hedge to show us a robin's nest. He left each of his children a property.

Eileen Ellis

Eileen Ellis, née Steeples (right) with her Mother, Great Grandfather, Grandmother and sister, Joyce.

ALL THE FUN OF THE FAIR

Top left: Grandma Oadley's 'Aerial Flight': "Mum is on it, aged about 19, with an 18 inch waist." (Clara Evans).
Top right: Mrs Sykes (Clara's mother) in her caravan; centre: the Iron Maiden; below: Grandma's carousel.

My Grandma Oadley went round with her fairground all her life. She used to come to Parwich with the aerial flight. If you can imagine, it had three legs, with a coupling on the top and a cable coupled onto it, and it went the length of the Green and onto three more legs. There was a loop with a handle, and you hooked it onto a pulley, then you held onto the bar and let go. At the bottom end of the playing field there used to be a marsh, waterlogged all year round, so if you was lucky, you'd hit the bales of hay at the bottom with your feet and that was fine, but if you hit it with your belly it could knock you off and you'd fall in the water. So when folk had had a pint or two they didn't bother like, you know! And Grandma had the Noah's Ark; it went faster and was a much bigger thing than the dobby horses, and had all different animals.

The traction engine called "Kitchener", later changed to "The Iron Maiden", was Grandma's. It had been built in 1921 to haul stone from the stone quarries, but at the end of 1931 these engines were replaced by steam lorries. During the war, the government took it and the story goes that a German submarine sank on some coral reef, and with the Iron Maiden being higher off the ground, they took the fire box off, and put it higher up still, so that it could go further into the water. Another engine was coupled onto the front and probably another one again, and they got a cable onto the submarine and pulled it off the reef. There were supposed to be some very secret papers on board. I don't know where this was, or if it's true; it's a story what's been passed down. After this she was taken back to the Leeds workshops of Fowler's to be rebuilt into a "Little Lion" type of showman's engine. Much later, she starred in the film called "The Iron Maiden" and was renamed accordingly.

Before Grandma Oadley acquired the Iron Maiden, the waggons were pulled about by shire horses. She and my grandfather bought another engine from a quarry at Birchover but they couldn't drive it properly as it needed three people, a stoker, a blockman and a steersman. My mother used to have to stand with one foot on the footplate and one foot on part of the engine, and me dad said he didn't like that idea so he made a seat out of an old tractor seat and fastened it on so she could sit down and steer. These engines have the dynamo on the front to work the electricity. The present owners don't keep it like we used to. I don't think they know how to clean 'olivers', those lovely twisted brass rods.

Grandma also had the Winchester Rifles. I remember Mum telling us how she saved a man's life once when she was looking after it. There were these big targets and they used to shoot down a tube. Two men had been in the pub and were having a bet, and the bet was, whoever lost paid for the shooting. Mother was standing there loading the rifles for them, and for some unknown reason they had an argument, and one threatened to shoot the other, so Mother rammed her thumb between the trigger guard and the trigger, so he couldn't actually press the trigger. She never did get paid; you put that down to misadventure.

Clara Evans

Weakness of the knee joints
Rub your knees with your hands every night until you feel a glow and then rub them for about ten minutes with a mixture of soap liniment and laudanum equal parts (Label Poison)

Mary Emma Hopkinson

Pastimes

From right: Alf Brownlee with baby Fred; his wife, Lily (née Moorcroft) Grandma Moorcroft, and Lily's sister, Lucy Twigge and son, Reg.

A picnic in the country has always been the cheapest and most popular form of family relaxation, whether it be in the early part of the twentieth century (as above) or (below) a W.I picnic on Parwich Hill in more recent times. From back left: John Fuller-Sessions (who carried the picnic) Dorothy Littlewood. ? Marion Fuller Sessions, Rosemary Chambers, Pat Wright, Ann Brown, Ann McCabe. Front: Dorothy Foden, Ann Knight.

Pastimes

Leisure time at Brentwood in Parwich was spent mostly in the little living room, developing the skills which Esther and Annie's mother, Mary Anne, had taught them. Esther was a talented needlewoman: she could embroider and knit, crochet and dressmaker to a very high standard. Many of the things that she made for me are still in daily use, especially the crocheted mats which were worked in a fine yarn and followed an intricate pattern. Also in my possession is a long baby gown, finely inset with lace, which she must have made for her daughter, Muriel, over seventy-five years ago. It is beautifully stitched, for whatever she did, she did it well. Sadly, I do not have any of the intricate matinée coats that she knitted for her grandchildren. Esther was always an avid reader and was lost without a book at hand. She belonged to a library until her sight failed her. She and Annie liked Bridge and Whist, and spent many a happy evening with friends, playing cards in the sitting room.

Musical evenings were a favourite family pastime, and as Esther and Annie were both accomplished pianists and both could play the mandolin, they quickly became accepted into the circle of local farmers. Esther's special friend was the wife of Dr Twigge, and through her, introductions were made and a social circle formed.

An organisation which was to benefit from Esther's special brand of organising skills was the W.I. She was a founder member of the branch and I have still got her W.I. Badge. She took an active interest in all W.I. affairs, and exhibited her handicraft, her preserves and cakes at every opportunity. She and her sister entertained the members by performing musically for them and they represented their local branch at National gatherings of the W.I.

Ann Vidler

Baby Muriel Brownson wearing the gown her mother, Esther Brownson, made for her.

Mrs Dodds presided over the December meeting of the Parwich Women's Institute when they met last Thursday. Prior to the commencement of the business, thanks were tendered to Miss Fox for her valuable work in the Institute during the past 10 years when she held the office of president. Miss Fox suitably responded.

from 'The Parish Messenger'
Parwich, 1956

I've been in the W.I. fifty odd years. It was held in a wonderful old hall, with a coke boiler in the middle that often used to be red hot. While the new hall was being built we met at Hallcliffe, with Mrs. Dodds, who was President then, and at various people's places. I think I am the oldest member now. I've got a photograph of me from when the Memorial

FASHION IN LATE VICTORIAN TIMES

From the family albums of Mary Whitechurch. The baby is a boy, though wearing a dress. The women in the centre are Lucy, Alice and Susan Lewis, daughters of Susan (Carr) Lewis (seated middle right) with her sea cadet son, Frank. Their brother, Claud Lewis, in his clerical dress, is seated bottom left. Susan (Carr) Lewis, their mother, was widowed at the age of 53: she had nine children to raise, all of whom were adults by the time she inherited Parwich Hall in 1892.

Hall was inaugurated, and in front of me there's a glass of beer - well it's brown stuff - and everybody laughed and said, "Look at Aunty Ella with her glass of beer," because my strongest drink is lemonade! The lady sitting next to me was the farm manager's wife.

As a newcomer, it was a bit difficult to get to know people. I used to be very shy until I went nursing and then all the shyness was taken away from me. To me Parwich is a wonderful place and the villagers are wonderful people. Of course, Harry would go for a drink at the Sycamore, and got to know people through that; and when the children started school I met other parents.

Ella Hopkinson

"**D**own with Jam and Jelly: now W.I.s can talk about sex" ran the headline! In addition to singing Jerusalem at every meeting, the Womens' Institute had decided to haul itself into the twentieth century and allow its members to discuss religion, sex and politics. In 1971, at their Annual General Meeting in the Albert Hall, an overwhelming majority voted for the motion, though not without heated argument on the part of the more traditional members. Reporter Roland Young says that "The biggest cheer... went to Mrs. Rachel Wilde... who said that when she urged her daughter to join the Institute, she had replied, "Oh mother, jams and jellies!' The Institute had to get away from this image!"

Gillian Radcliffe

[I am indebted to a 1971 press cutting by **Roland Young,** source unidentified, found in the Parwich WI Scrapbook.]

In spite of the treacherous weather conditions there was a good attendance at the December meeting of the Parwich Women's

Sampling the Jam! Jill Simpson and Kathleen Allsopp

Institute on Thursday, December 20th. A demonstration of plucking and dressing poultry was given by Mrs. Prince, and much amusement was caused when Mrs. Prince produced a live bird for the demonstration and proceeded to show all the various stages of preparation until it was ready for the oven.

The Parish Magazine, 1957

One of the first electric radios in Parwich was in our home at Rock House, because the lines came over from Tissington, and the Sycamore Pub had the first juke box in the area, before they had one in Ashbourne.

Ken Wayne

In days gone by you'd sit at night and play Ludo or Dominoes. My mum and dad played with me. We didn't get a television until I was ten or eleven, so we'd sit and do puzzles, or my mum would teach me to knit. There was a lady who lived where the Lowes live, Mrs Twigge. She used to teach me at Sunday school, and she was friendly with my mum and gran, and she came across and taught me to embroider. Everybody taught the children to do things, and I think that is why we are all practical. I could knit, I could sew and cook, and I liked doing all those things because Mum did them with me.

THE CARR SISTERS DRESSED FOR RIDING.
Ellen, Elizabeth, Frances (Mrs Curtis) and Susan (Mrs Lewis)

The sister' parents, Rev. John Edmund Carr and Ellen Carr (née Evans) lived at Parwich Hall from 1822 - 1833.
Susan and Frances inherited the estate from Sir William Evans in 1892. This later passed to Rev. Claud Lewis,
Rev. John Edmund Carr's grandson.

She used to be there icing the Christmas cake and I'd be helping her, or she'd be baking and she'd let me help; or she'd say I could have a bit of pastry and I'd make something and give it the dog! I remember making a pastry pie. It was a layer of pastry and a layer of jam, and my mum cooked it, but I'd played with the pastry so much it was so hard the dog couldn't get his teeth into it. My Mum did the same with my youngest one. When she had him for the day he'd say, "Nan, are we baking today?" and they'd make some buns or whatever. He can still do it now, which is good.

Mrs Braddock had beatle drives at Flaxdale House to raise money for the church, and in those days everybody went to things like that. You'd keep moving around, and there would be so many tables in here and so many tables in there. They had whist drives as well, for the church. My mum would take me and teach me to play.

Valerie Kirkham

Miss Elsie Fox used to teach us the piano. She was a tiny lady who gave us lessons on the upright piano in the nursery on the top floor of the Hall. We had a canary whose chirping annoyed Miss Fox terribly, and she would throw a cloth over its cage to stop it tweeting. Miss Fox played the organ in Church. She played a wonderful Bach voluntary that we christened 'Over the sticks'. As the music got faster and faster, like a horse race, we had great trouble not laughing. My father had a most wonderful sense of humour.

Patricia Bagshawe

Miss Fox lived at Retlenden. We thought it very 'posh'. My sister Joyce and I used to go for music lessons. Miss Fox was a very tiny

person. She came to us for petrol but found it quite difficult to see over the steering wheel. If you looked through the windscreen you'd see these two little eyes peering above the dashboard. We used to call her Miss Trotter, I don't know why. Miss Fox had two beautiful golden labradors. One was called Lorna and the other was called Doon.

Eileen Ellis

On the swing, in the orchard at The Fold.

I did Guides and Brownies in Parwich for about six years with Miss Fox. I was Tawny Owl and Miss Fox was Brown Owl, and Eileen Steeples (no relation to Eileen Ellis) was the Lieutenant. We had to disband because there were so few children left. We held it in the Institute. We used to go out and make fires up Monsdale Lane and Dodds Hill. There was a little valley there, and we used to make a fire and fry sausages; and we made flour and water 'dampers' and had a little tea.

Dolly Wayne

I went to Brownies in Parwich until I joined the Brownies at the Grammar School in Ashbourne. I remember going to the District

IN THE GARDEN AT THE FOLD

Gardening has always been a popular pursuit for both sexes in Parwich. Here, Mrs Greatorex is seen enjoying the rose garden at the Fold with her nieces, the Misses Gadsby.

MAIN STREET, PARWICH.
The corrugated iron building on the right is the old Village Institute

Commissioner's house to take one of my tests, and having to knit a woolly hat for it, and her screaming that she were on fire and we had to roll her in this blanket to show that we knew what to do if someone was on fire! Great fun that was. In Parwich, Mrs Cundy and Betty Wayne did the Cubs.

Valerie Kirkham

We used to sit at night cutting up woolly skirts and coats and things to make peg rugs. Sunday was a day for a treat. I remember running out with a basin to get ice cream to eat with tinned fruit for Sunday tea. It was brought to the village by Mazza, an Italian man with a motorbike and sidecar. Then there was Wakes, and carnival. One year my sister and I dressed in grubby monk's robes and went as "Two Dirty Habits". We used to get

into some mischief! "Shall we go door knocking?" we used to say, for something to do in the evening. We'd tie cotton onto people's doorknockers and keep pulling it, letting it rattle. That was our evening entertainment.

Kathleen Allsopp

When we were at Aldwark, there was no post office, we'd no shop, no pub, we'd nothing. George Fox, the farmer I was brought up by, had a little motorbike and sidecar and we used to go tripping off on a Saturday night, and I was at the back in this little tiny sidecar. They were such happy times. We used to walk miles to a dance, from Ballidon to Parwich for instance. In those days you didn't have television, and there were such a lovely lot of dances.

Parwich women ahead of their time? Ladies Football Team. Back left: Evelyn Weston, Frank Steeples, Ivy Weston, Gladys Tipper, Joyce Twigge, ?, Minnie Webster, Kath Goldstraw. Front left: Kathleen Allsopp, ?, Wibberley, Elsie Webster, Betty Weston, Connie Edge.

The next generation, late 1940s, back left: Christine Weston, Shirley Gibbs, Jean Calladine, Brenda Brownlee, Mary Edge, Hazel Calladine, Veronica Twigge. Front left: Delia Wayne ?, Evelyn Chadwick, Carol Cooper, Phyllis Allsopp.

We used to all gather together on a Sunday night, walk up to Longcliffe and buy a little packet of biscuits with four biscuits in it, then we used to walk right down to the pub called the Lilies, on the Via Gellia, all the girls and boys, you know. They were lovely times. Now the young people go off abroad instead of walking off to Longcliffe! On Sunday I used to go to Chapel. I've always been a chapel person or a church person. I've always gone to a place of worship.

We came to Fernlea, in Parwich, and were there four or five years. I was in my teens then. It was lovely living in Parwich: but it didn't matter where I was, I was always happy! We knew everybody in those days, everybody. Now we know not half of them. Mind you, at ninety, things do change!

Catherine Elizabeth (Dolly) Wayne

In the old village hall on Saturdays there were films for the children and a ticket cost 6d. Wakes Week was something to look forward to. The brass band would parade round the village and the fair would be set up on the lower green.

Sara and Vere Dodds

Transport could be a bit of a problem for a teenager. There was a Thursday bus to Ashbourne, and two on Saturdays, including one to the pictures on Saturday nights, and to Derby on Fridays. There were no cars in those days. I remember cycling to "Gone with the Wind" at Ashbourne, and sitting almost four hours, and then cycling back again. There was a bus to the Elite Cinema, and the Empire.

Kathleen Allsopp

Ashbourne was a lot better than it is now. There was a greater variety of shops and less traffic. The market was better and we could go to the pictures. There used to be two cinemas there, one, the Elite, was in the market place where the arcade is, and the other, the Empire, was where they had the dancing down at the social club by Sainsbury's.

Mary Rawlins

In October 1927, The Empire Cinema in Ashbourne was showing two films said to be at the cutting edge of fashion and technology. It was noted in the Ashbourne Telegraph, on October 28th, that "The Blue Danube" would be "a special treat" and was a picture which had "caused quite a furore'" wherever it had been shown. The paper notes with excitement that to "add to the interest of this pleasing film a special orchestra has been engaged.... and Mr. Fred Grime, our popular baritone, will contribute vocal solos during the production of the picture".

Having catered to the tastes of the ladies and young romantics during the first half of the week, the second half promised more thrills from "that giant of all screen dramas, *Men of Steel* featuring the incomparable Milton Sills with Doris Kenyon." The picture was described as "intensely dramatic, and a drama that blazes with the white heat of molten steel - romance that gleams with the ruddy glow of love's dawning." Its photography was clearly revolutionary for the time, "particularly when a water tower falls, spilling its water on the hot metal, making it splash in all directions". The "powerful story of love and hate" was said to contain "magnificent thrills."

Gillian Radcliffe

AMATEUR DRAMATICS

Parwich has a long and still thriving tradition of putting on concerts and plays, many written by a Parwich woman, Evelyn Weston. This picture probably dates from the end of the First World War, which saw Mrs Adahlia Bower-Mabson (seated front right) widowed when her husband was reported missing in action. To her left is Elsie Brownlee, and behind (from left) are Clarice Brownlee, Billy Dakin and Lottie Allsopp.

A moonlit night was necessary for the success of the occasions, and concerts and dances organized by local people for local needs were greatly appreciated by large gatherings. The dances were of the old-time variety, and a goodly number of square dances such as Sir Roger de Coverley, the Country Dance, Lancers, Quadrilles, Spanish Waltz, and many more interested the happy gathering. The musicians appear to have been what was left of the orchestra of the old Normal Church, the violin, the flute and the cello, aided by the piano and the accordion.

The concerts rehearsed for months, were given by local people, and every item was appreciated by the crowded audiences. We heard many songs (which are still great favourites) for the first time in Parwich, for example, "Loves Old Sweet Song" and "My Grandfather's Clock."

H. Birkentall,

We've always put on concerts in Parwich. At the moment we're doing this play, [in 2002] *The Easter Bonnet*, and the lady who wrote it [Evelyn Weston] used to write an awful lot of sketches. Her daughter is the same age as me, so we're all friends together. When we were kids her mother used to write these sketches, and it was always about the family, and I don't know why, but I was always the boy with the cap and the trousers! Pam Slater's dad used to play the piano and we used to dance. We did these concerts when we were nine or ten. That was village life and everybody got together.

Valerie Kirkham

I can remember concerts at Parwich with Mrs. Steeples who organised them. There was

one in particular. We had a horrible thing in the old Institute, to heat it, a big stove in the middle of the room; and we had a game and somebody twizzelled me round and caught my leg on this stove, and I can remember Mrs. Steeples gathering me up and looking after me, and I thought, how lovely to have a mother like that, when you've lost your own mum as I had. We had lovely concerts: we used to sing and dance. All the family took part in the concerts.

Dolly Wayne

Ointment for Scalds and Burns
4 ozs of Olive oil, 1oz of red persipet, 1 ozs of white wax
dissolve the oil and wax together then add persipet.
[This recipe is repeated in a clearer hand, plus the comment, "is a good receipt."]

Mary Emma Hopkinson

When I took part in concerts at the Institute I used to have nerves, and my leg started wobbling, so Mrs. Steeples used to hold on to it to stop it. We were doing "Old Uncle Tom Cobbley and all", and I'd got old Mr. Rogers' knee breeches on, tied all up with string, and of course I was sat on this rocking horse thing, and the leg were going, and I was so relieved when it got to my turn. Then one time Eileen Ellis was singing, and Betty and I were dressed up in blackout material. We'd made little sort of leotards for ourselves, and we were acrobatting on either side, going over and tumbling, while Eileen was singing away, "You always hurt the one you love", a song that was much too old for her. Eh, we did think we were good! I remember some ostrich feathers - I loved these ostrich feathers but I can't remember what we did with them. I think it was a play, because I remember

The Concert Party. Beatrice Graham, back row, second from left. Esther and Annie Brownlee with their mandolins? (See Ann Vidler, *Pastimes,* p.106)

being first on stage and I sat there in this old fashioned dress with my bosoms up high, and long skirts, and I'd got this beautiful great big ostrich feather. Mrs.Cole, the vicar's wife, was on the piano. I can see the vicar and Henry standing on the stage singing "On Richmond Hill..." Oh it was hilarious!

Kathleen Allsopp

When I was about thirteen I started coming to dances at the Institute, the old Village Hall in Parwich. Of course, I was chaperoned: my mum came with me and people used to think we were sisters. Dad came sometimes. If it was late at night, Dad would fetch us. We used to have to bribe him. I wasn't one for walking in the dark though it was safer than it is now. We went to dances at Brassington Wakes, at Biggin of course, and to Parwich Wakes.

Mary Rawlins

We used to walk to dances. We traipsed to Tissington over the fields with our hair in curlers, and our wellingtons on, and when we got there we used to do our hair and put our dancing shoes on. The dances were held in the Village Hall in Tissington. I was only fourteen when I was walking to all these dances but there was no fear. You wouldn't let fourteen year olds do it now, they wouldn't be safe.

Kathleen Allsopp

When we went to Youth Club at the Institute, we used to sit round the stove. We'd go to dances in there and it was freezing, absolutely freezing, and the cloakrooms just had concrete floors. We danced to a lady called Mrs. Wain and her band. She wore this long dress and sat at the piano playing, while her husband played the drums. I can see her now in this blue dress with no sleeves, her arms wobbling. She had grey hair and could have been in her fifties, sixties sort of thing. The fellas used to wear bow ties and proper suits; you wouldn't see that now would you? All you see is a record deck and disco dancing, you don't see the old slow, slow, quick, quick, slow. We girls used to go along to learn how to dance. There were refreshments, two sandwiches and a cake and a cup of tea. I can't remember what we paid, not a lot. I also remember us going to dancing classes in Ashbourne to practise our

quicksteps and waltzes, but we didn't dance with fellas, we just danced with each other! It was quite funny that was. As I got older, my aunty and uncle were going to dances and they'd take me along. My mum's two brothers were good dancers, and one of them took me and my cousin as partners as his wife couldn't dance. That was great fun, it was.

Valerie Kirkham

When we came [*to the Sycamore Pub*] in 1936, no ladies were allowed in the bar. There was a bell at the front door, which the women would ring to have their jugs filled with beer.

Ken Wayne

When I was younger, but no longer had to be in bed by half past seven, and there was a dance on at the Institute, we would go and lean on the wall to listen to the band. We could hear it from the bedroom actually. That was quite exciting, something I hadn't experienced close at hand, because although we did have hops in our village school from time to time, I wasn't allowed to go until I was 15 or 16, by which time I could dance a bit as I had been allowed to go to one of these studios where a lass taught us ballroom dancing. I remember going this one time to a grown up dance at Parwich Institute. There were refreshments, tea and sandwiches, I suppose, but it wasn't as exciting as I'd imagined it to be. Fortunately I had enough boy cousins to dance with occasionally, because at most village hops as I remember, boys were there and girls were there, but always the same girls were left sitting, and all the tall boys chose the tiny little girls.

Betty Stone

CARS ON MAIN STREET, in the background, the War Memorial and St. Peter's Church
Mrs. Mabson was one of the first people to own a car in Parwich.

AUTUMN

September brought the mushrooms, which were gathered in the early morning before the insects could damage them. Soon the blackberries became ripe enough to pick for jams, jellies and pies. Sloes could be gathered from the blackthorn for making sloe gin for a treat at Christmas. Crab apples were picked, the basis for mint jelly. Damsons were a very popular Derbyshire fruit; most gardens would have a tree, and these were used for jam, jelly, and damson cheese - a type of purée about the consistency of lemon curd. The children could earn a few pennies by gathering acorns for feeding the pigs. Chestnuts were collected for roasting in the fire on cold winter evenings. Conkers of course, were collected and given secret treatments to harden them in the hope of producing a winner. Walnuts may have been picked too, as my Grandmother Hopkinson's "Receipt Book" 1887 - 1889, has a recipe for removing walnut stains from hands using methylated spirits of Calais sands [?]. Walnuts were often pickled. They were also used to rub on scratches in dark wood to re-stain it. September brought the Harvest Festival, and as the evenings drew in, dances and outings would be arranged at full moon, as there was no street lighting to see your way home. My mother often played the piano for these gatherings. She enjoyed this, but felt that she missed the chance to dance herself.

Mary Whitechurch

Making quince jelly.

To Preserve Eggs

5 Qts Water, 1 oz saltpetre, 1 lb salt
Boil ten minutes
When cold stir in 4 spoonfuls of Lime
In two days, fit for use

Mary Emma Hopkinson

Blackberry Wine

Take 1 pint of berries, add 1 pint of water; let it stand for 6 or 7 days, stirring each day. Then strain, and to every gallon of liquid add 3 lbs of lump sugar, 2 teaspoonfuls of ginger, and 1 teaspoon of cinnamon. Boil a few minutes then pour into vessel. When it is just warm add a small piece of yeast. When cold, bottle. Cork lightly to allow for working.

Mabel Fletcher

Days of Work

Our experience of Radical mill-owners, and of those who worked for them, was that they were most oppressive employers of labour. I mention one instance in detail, the particulars of which were peculiarly harsh. A young woman, far advanced in consumption, was ordered by her doctor to discontinue her work. She did so, and was at once told to return by her employers, the order being enforced by the threat that if she left the work, the whole of her family would be turned away. She returned to the mill, and remained as a worker until she died. In contrast to these mill-owners, we always had before us the object-lesson of the mills at Cromford, owned by the Arkwrights, excellent Conservative people, whose "hands" were cared for, and had no cause for complaint.

Mrs. Curtis

When I left Parwich school I went to Tatton's Mill at Mayfield. I was a warper for ten years, warping nylon and acetate for the parachutes. The war finished the day I should have started work, so I had a fortnight before I began. Warping was done by foot, on a massive warping machine. You stood, and you had a big creel with three hundred and something bobbins on, with all this yarn that you had to thread. Then it went in sections, onto the big loom, and you worked it with your foot, so you were standing awkwardly all day long, for ten hours a day. It made you ache but you got used to it, and it was interesting. And then just before I left we got onto the little German machines; they were very big but not high. (The others were higher than you were). It was hard work, piece work.

We used to travel to work on the bus, leaving at seven o'clock and getting back at a quarter to six. That was from when I was fourteen years old. I did that for ten years. I left when Paul was born, when I was twenty-four. It's now called Mayfield Yarns. Eileen Ellis went there when she first left school but then she went up to the Care Centre to be a Red Cross nurse. A lot of us went to the mill, the majority, because a bus went. The service was run by Eileen's dad, Mr. Steeples. We used to have a busload. Women worked in the mill or in service because you had no means of transport you see. You were seven miles to Ashbourne, and there were no cars or buses. You had to cycle if you went to work at Ashbourne. The bus to Mayfield was private, it went just to work and was paid by Tatton's, the mill owners."

Kathleen Allsopp

When my mother went to the Sycamore Pub, seating for 110 we had, and all new crockery, dinner service and terrines, gravy bowls, and all the knives and forks to lay it out, and we did all the catering ourselves in those days, bar cooking the meat - Peach, the butcher, used to do that: you had 20lb joints and they were carved upstairs; and we only charged the Odd Fellows £3 or £4 a year for the rent of the room. They had it all day and it took me a full day to scrub it all out on my hands and knees it did, a full day. So then I put the price up to about £6, £8 something like that, and they packed it in. All the work it took, they didn't realise. We had to have extra staff, and give them all something for helping out.

Ken Wayne

Miss Mary Graham, Postmistress of Parwich

When my grandmother, Beatrice Graham, first moved with my grandfather to Parwich she was probably employed as an assistant at the Post Office; then in 1915 the Post Office business became vacant and my grandmother was appointed Postmistress, with my Aunt Mary, her daughter, as official helper. On 6th March, 1916 the Post Office and adjoining land had been transferred from the Rev. Claud Edmund Lewis to Miss Lucy Ward Lewis, and on 24th March 1924 it was bought by my grandmother for £380. She was Postmistress from 1915 until her death in 1954, and my aunt held the same position from 1954 until her retirement due to ill health in 1984, by which time she was an astonishing 85 years old.

My aunt, Miss Mary Graham, worked for the Post Office in Parwich from 1915 until 1984, a total of 69 years. Prior to the First World War she worked as an assistant in many post offices throughout Derbyshire. I have her diary from 1926 in which she states the pay for the Post Office in fourteen different villages. She mostly earned 4/- per day, although she only earned 3/- a day in Youlgrave, Kirk Ireton and Alstonefield! Her

pay was very low compared to office workers in towns, and it was no surprise to me that the Post Office in Parwich ceased to operate shortly after her death in 1990.

My aunt's job was to deliver the letters on foot up the Dales, covering a distance of twelve miles. Sometimes, on arriving back home, she might have to set out again to deliver a telegram. After five months of this, Aunt Mary went on war duty to help out behind the counter at Ashbourne Post Office, in the Market Square. Before the war, this work had been done by nine men, but after they were called up, their duties were taken on by four women, including my aunt. Four years later, when the men were demobbed, she returned to Parwich, and started travelling around the area, covering for people on holiday or sick leave. Her only transport was her bicycle, and the one disposed of in the 1980s was definitely a pre-war model of the sit-up-and-beg variety. Villagers remember her jumping onto the saddle from the back, and pedalling off wearing dangerously long skirts.

Auntie Mary had a tremendous sense of duty to the Post Office. From 1954 she didn't take any holidays, and when in later years the Post

Outside the Post Office. Fred and Mary Graham?

Main Street. An early picture of Sunniside (right) which became the Post and Telegraph Office. Brentwood is to the left. Note the woman's old-fashioned cap and apron. The 'shed' is said to have been a saddler and cobbler's workshop.

Office insisted, she stayed at home and assisted her locum! In later years she sorted the mail for others to deliver, including Mrs. Esther Flower, who delivered to Ballidon and round about, Mrs. Ivy Brownlee who covered Whitecliffe and some of the village, and Mrs. Gladys Tipper, who did the rest of the village and Alsop en le Dale, together with Kath Goldstraw, who acted as official relief post woman, all friends of my Aunt. To the Ashbourne Telegraph reporter my Aunt said, "It's not that I'm a workaholic, but I have so enjoyed meeting people and everyone has always been so kind and helpful."

Roger Graham

In a short piece on Parwich Post Office published in the Derby Evening Telegraph, Thursday April 21, 1966, R. K. Forster notes that the village name has sometimes been mistaken for Harwich in Essex, causing the letters to go astray, and that "sometimes the village name is pronounced "Porridge", and "when that happens, strangers go astray!"

Gillian Radcliffe

My memories of Mary Graham go back to when I was almost five years old and she would be nearly twenty-two years old. Mary came to look after me when my sister was born. My parents got to know her while my father was working at Ashbourne Post Office *[where Mary also worked for a time]*. I recollect so well the happy times spent staying at Parwich during my childhood and while a teenager. Mary and I cycled miles to and from Ashbourne, delivering post and telegrams; I even rode Dolly, *[the horse]*, on some of those trips, which was heaven. We also walked to and from Alsop Station. The day Mary called on her way home to tell us of her brother Jack's death sticks vividly in my memory. I also remember that Mary always had a very strong will.

Dorothy Marsh

In the women's column called "Eve's Empire" in the Ashbourne Telegraph of October 28th, 1927, Stella Gardner noted that women "have always been labelled immodest when they have attacked the special preserves of men," but that "nowadays" women were entering the professions, because of those who dared to go, immodestly, beyond what was expected of them. The author says that nowadays "the doors of the doctor's consulting room, the aerodrome, the engineering workshop, and even the master mariner's cabin are open to capable women, thanks to the wonderful persistence of women pioneers." The President of the British Medical Association had recently deplored "the waste the world for so long has made of its women," yet the pioneer risked bringing down "on her pretty head the disapproval of the old-fashioned woman," especially the "shelter-loving Victorian" who would be "shocked by the modern girl's adventurous spirit." Nevertheless, today's modern girl was said to be "proving that a woman could hold her own with Mr. Man."

In the same column, however, Mrs. Mabel Hart extols the virtues of the traditional housewife, who should conduct her household affairs in a "business-like" way. Apart from being skilled in the arts of cookery, needlework and baby craft, she should "be able to lay out her housekeeping allowance to the best advantage." In this, according to the author, she often fails, spending thoughtlessly then grumbling to her husband "about inadequate housekeeping allowance", which is not fair. "After all, "he cannot give what he has not got."

Gillian Radcliffe

My father's elder sister, Lucy, a spinster, was a missionary in the Congo but became very ill and was invalided home. I can remember her being frail and getting malaria years later. My mother, Ethel Hopkinson, went out to what was then called Abyssinia, now Ethiopia. She had always wanted to travel. She used to say that one of the things she loved up at Parwich Hall were the big Atlases. When she was quite small, she used to take down the great heavy tomes and spread them out on the floor and tell herself stories about going to all the different places. In Parwich she kept house for her father, William Jackson Hopkinson, and when he died in 1919 she was independent at last, and free to leave, though she continued to teach at Parwich School for another two years. I don't quite know when she left the village, but at some point she started trying to earn a living, though all she could do was primary school teaching. She worked as a companion-help to various people, as ladies did in those days. She worked for Mrs. Wills, the tobacco heiress, and for another family somewhere in Sussex, and she always kept in touch with the children she had looked after. Then she answered an advertisement in The Times from a Mrs. Sandford, who was working in Addis Ababa and wanted a schoolteacher-companion. My mother went for the interview while Mrs. Sandford was in London for two weeks, and she liked my mother very much, so off my mother went. Mrs. Sandford had already gone back to Africa, so my mother did the journey on her own, which must have been quite an undertaking. She was about twenty-four at the time.

Mrs. Sandford and her husband were well connected, and there was a lot of social activity going on, dances, polo and so on, within the Legation compound. My mother used to tell us how she had been invited to dinner with Heilie Selassie, and eaten off gold plates which she was sure had been cleaned with Brasso and not washed properly! She stayed in Abyssinia for two years.

Mary Whitechurch

My mother came from the fairground; she was an Oadley, one of eleven children. She travelled with her mother, my Grandma Oadley, until she got married to my father, who was a Sykes; then they set up and travelled on their own, while Mrs. Oadley continued to travel on her own. My father belonged to a mining family from Temple Normanton. He left school at twelve and when he was fourteen he was leading the ponies down the pit. He was a settled down person, not a traveller. Fairground folk didn't like people marrying outside the travelling community because they thought a settled-down-person wouldn't stand it because it was such a hard life.

My mother was about thirty when she and Father got married and to start off with, they'd got nothing. They had a little caravan and she couldn't abide being idle at home. They hadn't got much money so what she did, she bought wood, a pole at a time, until she got enough to make a coconut stall. She had all the ironwork put on and then she set off. My father by then had left the mine and was working for a Mr. Parker, coal merchant. This was in the '30s. Father used to bring the lorry home from work at weekends, clean it out, take her to a place and help her build the coconut shy up, and she got the business

going like that. Eventually she was taking more money than what Dad was with the coal lorry. He was only getting about £2.50 a week - fifty bob. Dad didn't like the idea of giving up the coal lorry, but then he bought the swinging boats. There was a showman's paper called "The World's Fair" and it's like buying cars or houses: a certain person might say, oh I've had enough of this I'll buy something else. So that's how things got passed on round the travelling community. Then my parents bought the little roundabouts, the little horses. Next they made a little skittles stall, and the fair was just our family; we provided the whole fair wherever we went.

Clara Evans

Most of the members of my family were working on farms or in the quarries - those who stayed locally that is - which most of them did. That still amazes me, that people born and brought up in a village still want to stay there. I'm quite sure I would have wanted to get away as quickly as possible: in fact I did, from my own village. I thought it was awful everyone knowing everything about one another, and what they didn't know they made up!

Betty Stone

Aunty Mary Lees was brought up in Parwich and went to school there. She used to cycle to Ashbourne and back every day to work at Nestlés. Then she got lodgings in Ashbourne. Before that she worked for the Miss Twigges at Hartington, as a maid. Aunty Mary was my mum's sister and they lived at Church Gates. Quite a few people used to cycle to work in Ashbourne, then eventually there was Mr. Steeples' bus.

Sandra Chadfield

My mother was leaning over one of the vats in the Creamery in Parwich, up to her elbows, making the cheese. She was doing that, right, and she fell in! She were covered completely. My dad and some others got her out and washed her down and that, and they still sent the cheese to Parwich Dairy at Ashbourne, or on the train to London. They didn't chuck the milk away!

Ken Wayne

As a young girl, I used to go to Middle Moor when Mrs. Weston lived there. She was a teacher at Parwich School and I used to go and help her on a Saturday morning for half a crown. I used to go across the fields to look after her two boys.

I left school on the Friday and got a job on the Monday. I used to bike to Ashbourne to work at photography at Sandybrook Hall. They had a shop, Photo services, in Ashbourne, on Compton, and I used to develop and print the photographs. I'd glaze them and go in the dark room and do the spools, put them in the long tanks, and tint them. At the end of the day I cycled back to Upper Moor farm Parwich way, because I didn't like the big hills on the main road. I worked Monday to Friday, and Saturday mornings for £3.10 shillings. I wouldn't envy anybody cycling to work these days; it's not safe now. I used to set off and it was that foggy, misty or snowy and icy. I got snowed up two or three times with no buses running to Buxton, so I had to ring a friend up in Hognaston and say could I go there for the night?

When I got married and came down to live in Parwich, I went to work at the hospital. I was cook there from 1960 till I was pregnant with Judith in 1963. At that time it was a convalescent home where you got the young boys in with motorbike accidents, or people recuperating from operations. I used to start

at seven o'clock in the morning and cook for about thirty people, different diets and all, diabetics, salt free or fat free and so on. It was heavy going but worth it.

Then I worked at Parwich School for seventeen years. I cooked for eleven years while my children were going there and never had a day off. Then I started to suffer a bit with vertigo, and the doctor said he thought I was doing too much and I'd got to cut down. I was looking after my mother-in-law as well as a friend down the village, going there every day until she died. So then I left, but they asked me to go back part time. I was supposed to be relief cook but I was there most of the time. Then I went and did midday supervising for about six years. The children I cooked meals for are now sending their children to school and I see them when I'm meeting my grandchildren. Looking after them keeps me in community, and involved. I've always supported the school, one way and another, ever since I came here.

Mary Rawlins

At five year old, my first job at the fairground was putting records on. By this time we'd got an AEC bus and I'd be in the back, where they made me a bed out of spare canvas sheets. I used to lie there and put these records on, and every four records, you had to change the needle; that was my job. And when they turned out of the pub they used to come and say, can you put such and such a record on? Well I hadn't the foggiest idea what it were. Then they said one time, "It's time you was in bed", so they got hold of me, lifted me out and said, "Go on, off to bed, off to bed!" But I said, "I can't go to bed", and clambered back in't box, and was lifted out again; and father came and said, "What's going off?" And this bloke says, "It's time this child was in bed!"

"Oh she's alright, leave her, she's got a job to do."

So I'd get to bed at twelve, one, or two, depending how business was going. We waited for folk to turn out of the pub so that you got a last hour with the coconut stall.

Next I was promoted to the Roll a Penny stall. I could change a pound when I was six but I couldn't read. I learnt on the job, I learnt what I needed and I didn't need reading then. Having gone to bed late, what time did I get up in the morning? Well, they used to call me 'ten o'clock queen'. I used to like me lie in but they used to turf me out. Yes, it was a tough life and I don't miss it now.

Clara's mum, Mrs Sykes, on the autodrome with Kay, her granddaughter.

It was in Parwich that I nearly blew up the autodrome. Father says to me, "Just nip over there and put those wires on." In the middle of the autodrome there was an armature, and three brass rings that were black green and red, live neutral and earth. But there were no colours on the actual armatures, so I just put them on and did the wing nuts up and said, right, and father switched on (because you always tested them before the start) and all this pretty blue smoke and sparks come out and me dad said, "Oh you dozy looking little.... get over there again and don't come back until you get 'em right!" So I did and it got to be a regular job. On the side of the engine was a bar and you had to push these valves in to get compression, and when they were turning the handle at the front, you had to catch the compression at just the right moment and push the bar down so that made the engine fire, see. We used to have to do that several times to get it to start. I got it to perfection and that became a regular job as well. I must have been about ten or eleven when I learnt how to do that.

Once when we were winching the big waggon up onto level ground on the Green in Parwich, it started going over on two wheels and Don Lowndes came running out of the pub and jumped and put his weight in the door and brought it back on its four wheels again. He was a lad but a lovable one. One time he'd got some jackdaws and we were in the trailer, and every morning at six o'clock these blooming things would be running up and down the roof, and me mother says, "Do something about them birds will you?" So father puts his hand up with a stick. When you've been up all night you can't stand it, so I went and got one of those pellet guns, but the devils knew and they never came back! They settled down on top of the swinging boats and I took aim. But then I thought, I can't do this; yes I can- they're keeping me awake, yes I can! But every time I'd decided I was going to shoot, they flew away.

Don had everything, he had monkeys, parrots, you name it. To me he was a big, frightening man because he had a black moustache and dark hair and dark eyes. He used to have the Smithy. I can remember him making shoes for horses, pumping the bellows, the sparks flying. He always had

Clara Evans' mother, Mrs. Sykes had this caravan made to replace the old 'gypsy' caravan.

something different; either a donkey or a pony or dogs or ducks. It was like coming back to a zoo, it was that interesting to see what Don had got this year. When you're children you look forward to that sort of thing, it's an event. A few years later I bought Smoky off him, a Labrador Alsatian with a funny ear, that would fight anything. When I first had him he was absolutely lousy and he'd got all sores. When I'd bathed him and brushed him I cut an old sleeve off a jumper and put him inside it to keep him warm. I paid five shilling for him, a fortune in those days!

In Parwich the coconut shy used to be on top of the bank beyond the dam wall. Well, when folk came out of the pub they used to sit on the wall. Now, when people were throwing at the coconuts, they'd take a flying run at them, and at the back of the stall there were some iron plates to stop the balls from going through the canvas. Well, punters used to hit the plates and the balls would fly back and knock the men off the wall, and they'd end up in the dam! They used to come the next day with black eyes and all sorts of things, and they couldn't remember what had happened.

In those days the dam wasn't cleared out, it was all mucky from the cows from Dam Farm. Mother used to frighten us and say, "Now don't go in there, there's no bottom to it!"

Clara Evans

I notice a lot of change from when I was young - more cars, people moving in and out of the village. There are a few of the old families still left, but as my mum often says, at one time she could have named each family in each house; and obviously the village has grown over the years. Of course, having said that there wasn't as much traffic, we had the lorries coming through the village from Ballidon Quarry, whereas now there is a weight restriction which prevents them. It was quite busy really, but you just accepted it; it was work for the men of the village. A lot would have worked there.

Sandra Chadfield

Clara Evans (left) with her sister in law, Maureen.

128

Courtship and Marriage

[**T**he girl] had been this way before: the first time soon after her birth, the second when she had seen ten summers; once on her mother's back, once on foot for her initiation. Three more years had passed since then. This time she came as one of the company of adults....

Heating slowly in the pot, the resin grew heavy. She lifted the leather cover to test the brew, dipping a twig into the darkness... The timing had to be just right, or the brew would set too well and there would not be time to work... She called to her uncle and her mother, the tone of her voice a signal that it was time. The resin would hold the men's costumes when they danced but it was also for her. In two days, she would marry, taking her line into the valleys that ran down the far side of the hills. It was a good match. There had been no arguments, and the distant cousin who would be her husband seemed happy at the prospect of sharing her hearth. Besides, he would bring many cattle when he came, meat for the winter and for gatherings in the years to come.

Mark Edmonds.
"Ancestral Geographies of the Neolithic"

After her move to Parwich, childhood days in Lockwood were often recalled by Esther Brownson - the maids about their business; a groom called Thomas; the game room where the pheasants hung until they were ripe with maggots; skating on the ice in winter and the moors in summer; ploys to avoid unpleasant jobs by contriving to be busy arranging flowers. Like her sisters before her, Esther was tutored in the gentle skills of needlecraft, music and art, for like all Victorian parents with the time and money available, these accomplishments were never over-looked and were regarded as an essential preparation for marriage.

Ann Vidler

9th April 1897
Dear Miss Coultman,
Your letter duly to hand. To explain my case briefly. I am 28 years of age. Tall. Dark. Not stout. Good enough looking for a man. Been well educated and moved in good society. Also been abroad a little. I am of affectionate and cheerful disposition, and temperate habits. I think I could make a wife happy. I am fond of home life. My place is in the country. Durham. My income is one way and another about £150 a year. Could you send photo please. I will do same if you wish. I may say that our correspondence will be respected by me. Please excuse hurried note, but I am called away. I will be pleased to give further information if desired. I remain yrs sincerely

F.J.Graham
P.S. Please write soon if convenient.

My grandmother, Miss Elizabeth Coultman, later Mrs. Beatrice (Beatie) Graham, Postmistress at Sunniside, Parwich, met my grandfather, Frederick Graham, on what amounted to a 'blind date'. She had replied to an advertisement he had placed in a newspaper in March or April 1897, requesting friendship which would lead to marriage. My grandfather's letter of 9th April 1897, written in response to my grandmother's reply, was the first of 110

Miss Elizabeth (Beatrice) Coultman

letters the couple wrote to each other up until their marriage on 27th April, 1898. This unusual form of courtship was for Fred, my grandfather, an eventual triumph over 'disappointment', a word used as a constant refrain by Beatie as she tried to decide whether or not to meet him, or was prevented from doing so by circumstances beyond her control.

Fred was one of nine children of Mr and Mrs John Graham of Sunniside House, Sunniside, near Crook, Co. Durham. My grandmother was born in 1872, the sixth and youngest child of Mr and Mrs William Coultman, farmers, of Pickering and Thorpe Bassett in Yorkshire.

Fred Graham had worked in America and Canada, and according to his letter of 31 August 1897, the idea of an advertisement came to him whilst he was over there. He told Beatie that advertisements of that nature were common in that country! He also told her that

he wished to marry in order to have a home life of his own. It appears that he had recently returned from abroad to his parents' house and that his brothers and sisters had already left home.

In their early letters the couple exchanged information about Christian names, occupations, brothers and sisters, birthdays, and interests which included music, dancing, riding and driving horses, and church. There was a strong religious background to many of the comments made in the letters, and Beatie stressed the happiness of her home life: "No one wants a better home than I have for both Father and Mother always are so affectionate and kind to us all and especially me. I think it is with being the youngest. Whatever I want, I only have to ask, I don't care what it is." (23rd July, 1897) She had left her home and was living in Terrington, near Malton, where she was working (apparently unpaid) as a companion-help for a family friend with young children. Fred pushed very hard for a meeting with her, and on 12th June 1897 she replied saying that she would like to go to the Yorkshire Show or to Scarborough for a day or two: but on the 22nd of July she wrote:

I am writing to tell you of my great disappoint[ment]. I am unable to come to the Show. I have got influenza and the doctor says it is not fit for me to go out. The weather is so changeable. I am afraid you will think it is all an excuse dear, but it is not as I have been looking forward to coming so long. It generally is the case if I look forward to going anyway I am nearly always prevented by some thing!

There was further pressure from Fred, and then on the 27th August she wrote:

I am going for my holiday week after next most likely and then I will meet you at

Whitby as I have some good apartments there, that is if you intend staying a few days. I am pleased you chose Whitby, it is such a long time since I was there.

To which he replied:

Will you really go to Whitby? I should be awfully pleased if you would. We could have quite a time of it, and get well acquainted with each other. Do you mean next week, say about the 12th or sooner? Let me know and I will arrange for a day or two. I think I can manage. I will try very hard at least. Just name the most convenient time to yourself. I should prefer between the 10th and 13th but make it exactly to suit yourself. Now like a dear girl don't disappoint me this time. I so much long to see you Dear. To see the girl I have written to so often and thought so much about. I am nearly disheartened but still hope on.

On the 11th September she told him she couldn't go to Whitby after all because the friend with whom she was staying was very nervous of being alone when her husband was away! She had intended staying only for a few weeks "and I am here yet", but that "when she gets someone and I go home for a holiday, then we will go to Whitby. I should like it."

By this time Fred must have been feeling somewhat exasperated and wrote as follows:

I was rather disappointed you could not go to Whitby, you see Dear, I have waited so long. Are you a fairy Princess guarded by a cruel giantess or to be practical, a close prisoner? Are you acting as companion to your friend for the meantime? It must be very hard on you to be so tired. Can't you really manage a day or so? I am almost disheartened of ever seeing you. It is a long time since we fixed a meeting. Tell me the exact truth Darling and I will try to be patient over my misfortune.

On the 23rd of September, having received no letter from Beatie after the 15th, he "pleaded" with her and suggested the 1st of October at Whitby, and she replied giving him the date of the 21st or 22nd.

In Fred's letter of 23rd September, he raised the subject of an engagement. They had not actually met each other at the time, though not for want of trying as far as my Grandfather was concerned! "You see," he said, "we have written so much to each other and used such endearing terms, we ought to be engaged." The reply from Beatie (28th September) referred to God's will. "We shall see each other if God has chosen us to live together to make a blessing to each other."

At the end of September, after seven months of letter writing, Fred sent Beatie a "small present with my best wishes", and she thanked him, saying, "I am awfully fond of scent .You must know what I like." (The subject of scent had not been mentioned in any previous correspondence.) Later in the letter she suggested a meeting in Whitby around October the 9th, to which he eagerly replied that he would be "delighted" to meet her there "if you have no objection to that please. I think I should like to spend a few days when we are there if you can." Train times were discussed, and how they would recognise one another: "I don't expect that will be difficult. We can each wait round till the crowd moves then it is all easy enough." (Fred)

Alas, on 7th October, she told him:

I am not able to go to Whitby on Saturday. I am sorry to disappoint you love. I am anything but well and have a face about twice the size it should be with neuralgia. I got cold with going to Auntie's last week and then to Church on Sunday. I am so sorry Fred dear but I know you won't be cross will you? I will go next week for sure, either Thursday or Friday. I shall be able to stay a few days, say three or four. I will write about apartments for you, if you like, as I know some people there, in fact they are friends of ours, it is where I intend staying. Of course if you would like staying at a hotel, I am agreeable. I shall go alone, at least, I think so, am not quite sure.

She talks briefly about the possibility of bringing a friend, presumably as a chaperone, but adds: "She is a nice girl, perhaps you will fall in love with her, instead of me. Meanwhile Fred writes once more to express his 'disappointment', and undoubted irritation.

> I am very sorry to hear you are so unwell. However I hope you will soon be all right again. I was very much disappointed you could not go this time. You see Dear you suggested yourself this time. So I felt sure it would be right. Well I am about used to it by now. Will you go next week for certain? If so I will be patient. Write and tell me if you really will go. Let me know by Weds at latest. Time, Day and all the rest. (8th October 1897)

Two letters followed, one from each of them, and included in the envelope of Beatie's (14th October, 1897, the last letter before their first meeting) was a piece of paper in her own handwriting, presumably copied from a book, consisting of questions to ask a possible suitor, such as: 'Are you in love? How old is he? How many eyes has he? What is his income?' and so on, an *aide mémoire* from 1897!

At last the long awaited meeting and holiday were due to take place. Fred's train arrived first and so he arranged to meet Beatie off hers, relying on the photographs and brief description she had provided. The holiday appears to have been a success, and the first post-holiday letter was from Fred who said, "I am sure it was the happiest week I have ever spent." (25th October 1897). Two days later she wrote to say that, "I have told mother at last"

In late December 1897 Fred sent Beatie a ring, having guessed the size of her finger, and she agreed to go to Sunniside for a few days to meet his family, provided he would meet her at York station and accompany her the rest of the way. This was to be from 5th January, 1898. Fred duly went to York station on the appointed day but Beatie was not on the train! He eventually discovered that she was at her parents' home in Thorpe-Bassett, Yorkshire, having received that very morning a wire from her brother to say that her father was seriously ill. He died two days later. She wrote to him again on 14th February to say that she and her sister "have some business to see to next Saturday in Molton", and suggested they all meet there, then she and Fred could journey on to Sunniside while her sister returned home. Tucked into the envelope with Beatie's letter was one from her sister Betsy, who wrote, somewhat obliquely:

> Dear Mr. Graham,
> I had hoped to have had the pleasure of making yr. Acquaintance this week but am afraid there is a disappointment in store for me on that point. The "mater's" health is not all that we could desire but we must hope for the best and trust to seeing you at a not very distant date. When you get my sister up into Durham don't keep her too

Beatrice and Fred Graham with baby, Mary.

long. There are a thousand and one things for her to do here, every one of which will be left until her return.
With kind regards, believe me to remain yrs. faithfully,
B. Coultman

The visit to Sunniside was rearranged for 19th February 1898 (not earlier as Fred had requested) and the couple met at Malton prior to the journey. It appears that Beatie stayed a few days, and a wedding date of 27th April 1898 was fixed, subject to Fred making appropriate arrangements relating to living accommodation after their marriage. They were not to see each other again until the evening before the wedding. In her first letter of 8th March 1898, after her visit to

Sunniside, Beatie wrote:

My dearest Fred,
I arrived safely... Ethel was at the station expecting me... I am getting it strong, almost first words, have you got married and where is the gentleman? I of course had them for mugs. I turned the dear little ring round and they actually said it was a nice one and believed it until somehow it slipped a little way round again and they discovered it!

Things had progressed to the point where it was clear to Beatie's family and friends that there could be no going back. All the arrangements for the wedding were made by Beatie with a little help (through correspondence) from Fred, and on 10th

March, he told her, "I think we are alright." That was on Thursday but on Monday he informed her that they were <u>not</u> alright!

Fred's father was a wealthy architect and property owner. After returning to England, Fred had worked on a farm owned by his father and he was expecting some financial help from him when he married. However, such help was not forthcoming and Fred told Beatie that it would be better for both of them if he found a position elsewhere, that offered a house as part of the package (14th March 1898). The question of returning to their respective parental homes after the wedding was discussed, and even the postponement of the wedding was raised several times in correspondence, but both had the strong belief that 'God would find a way'. So it was agreed not to change their wedding plans and the Banns were read the first time on the 10th April, 1898. Two days later, Beatie told Fred: "The Banns were published on Sunday, so now people are wondering on all sides who you are and how I got to know you so far away," and he wrote back saying, the "whole show came out on Sunday". He applied for many positions and on the 18th of April, only <u>nine days</u> before the wedding, he told her that he thought he had secured a "place" in "Derbyshire. He then addressed a few practicalities concerning the wedding:

> Tell me what time you would like the ceremony and I will write to the parson. Another thing Dear, can we afford to go to Edinbro? It will be an expensive journey and as I said money is very scarce. I will try to raise a fiver to get us through.

In his next letter of the 21st April, he told her:

> I am trying to seek up a little money to put us on till I start. We should have £5 to get us nicely over this business. Well I will do my best. I can do no more, can I, love? Send me the size of your finger Darling. I mustn't forget that part.

His earlier letters were full of the sentiments that God would provide for them and his confidence was justified. On Friday 22nd April, five days before the wedding, the offer of the position near Derby was confirmed, and included a house. On the 25th April he wrote to her:

> My dearest Beatie,
> Just a few lines to say all is complete. At least as far as possible. I will come to your place sometime on Tuesday. Just for a little talk. I will just turn up. Probably alone. Have all your things packed ready. After the wedding we will proceed to York. If we have time, go to Derby that day. When we reach Derby take apparts. till we fix up our house. We may as well take <u>all</u> our things at first. Don't you think this will do? Then we have time to make the house a little comfortable before we move in. I think that is all Dearie. If you have a better plan we can do <u>your</u> way after all. I am sorry your mother is unwell but hope she won't be worse on Weds. Take care of your dear self, and be at your very best. I will soon see you so believe me,
>   your ever loving
>   Fred xxx

They were married on the 27th April, 1898, in Thorpe Bassett Church. She was twenty-five years old and he was twenty-nine. Eventually, after many different jobs and many moves, they came to live in Parwich, where Fred raised pigs and cows, and Beatie ran the post office and became a member of the Mothers' Union. The full circumstances surrounding

A PARWICH WEDDING. Miss Elsie Brownlee of Flatts Stile, Parwich, walks home from her wedding with her new husband, Mr.Joseph W. Dakin of Slate House, Parwich.

their meeting were not known to their children during their lifetime. My mother told me that her parents in law had met by chance whilst on holiday in Whitby!
Roger Graham

Dear Miss H,
Will you meet me @ the 5/- hotel ? prompt.
Yours Truly,
1/6

Scrawled inside the front cover of the
Receipt Book of **Mary Emma Hopkinson**

I remember one Sunday in Parwich when Iris, my brother Jack's wife, lost her engagement ring. She used to look after the hot dog stall. She remembered peeling the onions and taking the ring off and putting it to one side, so we thought she'd chucked it out with the water she'd washed the onions in. We was on our hands and knees going through all the grass for this engagement ring; we even got in the brook and shifted the stones about. Well we never found it until two years later: she'd put it in her handbag for safe keeping, hadn't she! And of course Jack had been saying, "If you think I'm buying you another engagement ring you've got another think coming!"

Clara Evans

Heartbreak

Ladies, fasten a safety pin behind lapel of coat or in a handbag. If washing in the toilet while travelling away from home, slip rings and wristwatch on the pin and re-fasten to your coat or bag. Result: No heartbreak and no lost jewellery.

Take a Tip

There was a difference of twenty years in age between my father, Gerald Lewis, and my mother, Ethel Hopkinson. I have been told recently that at one time my mother's father William Jackson Hopkinson lived on the Green, about two doors away from Hallcliffe. If that was so, my father, who lived at Hallcliffe, would have been a near neighbour. If he came to live in Parwich in 1892 at the age of twenty, and my mother was born in 1892, he must have watched her growing up. Presumably they got to know each other during that time, but there was such an enormous gap in age I don't think anyone could ever have thought of them as a partnership.

I think my father must have admired my mother: I think she was quite bright. She used to go to the Hall and read all the books there, so it's interesting to speculate on whether my father got involved in educating her. Of course, both my parents were involved in the church, where he was choirmaster and she played the organ. When Booth Hampson died very suddenly, I understand my mother played for his funeral as there was no one else at that time who was playing the organ in the village. I remember her saying how she found it a great strain, as he had been a very good organist and she was only learning, and she was only a young girl.

Eventually, my father went to live in the Channel Islands. He had visited there on a cycling holiday and fallen in love with it, and wanting a change, returned to build a house there. Perhaps he wanted to put a distance between himself and his brother, the Rev. Claud Lewis, who had made himself so unpopular with everyone in Parwich. He took his elder sister, Lucy, with him. She was a spinster, and they had been living together at Hallcliffe.

During the time my mother was in Abyssinia, she corresponded with my father and sent him some photographs, so presumably she'd also been corresponding before that. I've never seen the actual letters, only the photographs. Eventually he wrote to her and asked her to come back and marry him. She told me she found it very difficult to decide whether to accept, as she was having such a wonderful time in Abyssinia, a place which was challenging and very interesting.

My parents got married in 1928. My mother must have come home to Parwich, to her sister Lois's home, but then she departed to get married in Worcester. My father had two unmarried sisters, Lucy, who lived with him at Hallcliffe, and Susan, who lived in Worcestershire. He always did Susan's accounts and they were very close. She was a little older than him; he was the second youngest of the nine children, and I think she must have offered her house for the wedding, because my mother had no living parents, and no home.

Mary Whitechurch

The isolated nature of All Saint's Church, Ballidon, may even have been an advantage. In 1635 a William Alsop, an ordained priest, was named as 'officiant in clandestine marriages' at Ballidon. Perhaps it was

Muriel Brownson marries William George Vidler.

secluded and hidden enough to escape to for couples on the run from disapproving parents, a sort of local Gretna Green. The outcome of this was that William Alsop was declared 'a man unfit for the ministry and scandalous'.

Rob Francis

On April 1st, 1929, a few months after her father's death, Muriel Brownson married William George Vidler of Crouch End, London, in St Peter's Church, Parwich after a heavily chaperoned courtship. The couple met through a mutual friend, on a blind date. At the time both men were qualified engineers working in Derby at BTH (British Thompson Houston). Photos of the bride and groom show her to be slim and prettily dressed in a fashionable lace dress. Her veil was attached to a skullcap worn close to the head. Soon after the marriage, the couple moved to London.

Ann Vidler

I'd met Harry at Lord Rothschild's. He was the gardener. The Rothschilds never stayed anywhere very long, and one time we went to Northamptonshire, to Lord Rothschild's mother and we stayed there for quite a while. There was a governess and me, and we took it in turns: if anybody wanted to go for a walk, the other one would be there for the nursery. And each evening I just used to go for a walk in the gardens, and that was where I heard somebody singing away in the greenhouse, and I walked past and of course Harry spoke to me.

The children had a pony and a goat and geese, and wherever we went (though not in London of course) they had to come with us, and the groom had to leave his family and come with us as well. We used to go riding in the pony and trap and apparently Harry had seen me in it and said to the groom, "Who's that nice looking lass there?" and the groom said, "Well she's the children's nanny." And he asked the groom, had I got a boyfriend and he said, "Well, I don't know." That's how we met. One time, we were going to Peterborough to see Judy Garland in "The Wizard of Oz" and I'd arranged for time off, but Lady Rothschild came into the nursery and said, "Tomorrow we're off to London. Just pack the things up", and this is how they were. So of course I never did go to see "The Wizard of Oz", and it would be another year before I'd see Harry again.

We eventually married when Harry was in the Royal Marines and I was nursing. We'd see each other once a year if we were lucky. I don't think I would have been allowed to get married and still be a Nannie, and you couldn't be a nurse and be married. Really I've no regrets. When I look back I think, well, what a wonderful life I've had and I had a husband who I loved and he loved me. We were friends.

When we first came to Parwich we lived in the little cottage on the side of Hallcliffe. I was expecting a baby, and the church was here, the shop was here and the school was here, so we decided to settle, and apart from an absence of six months, we've been here ever since. We married in 1943, and David was born in 1946 and John in 1948. Harry, my husband, was the gardener at Parwich Hall for Sir John Crompton-Inglefield. To start with he had two helpers, but for sixteen years he did the gardens on his own until he got a bit of a heart problem. To begin with, there was a head gardener and an under gardener, and up at the house there was the butler, and the cook, a kitchen maid and two housemaids.

Harry loved Parwich Hall garden. He always worked Saturday mornings, but he'd go up on a Sunday morning as well to do his watering at about nine o'clock, and he'd not come down till about quarter to twelve and I'd say, "Harry, what have you been doing? It's Sunday!" and he'd say, well I just took a cutting of this or a cutting of that. But you see it was his life, and Caroline, the youngest Inglefield, always called it Hoppie's garden, because he just loved it. He spent hours doing it, and it showed.

He was greatly appreciated at the Hall. Then Lady Inglefield became ill, and they thought it would be much better getting nurses in London for her, so they decided to give up Parwich Hall. The Hall had already been given to the eldest daughter, and of course we were all made redundant. Sir John had everybody in: of course everybody lived in tied houses and they were told they could live in them for two years and then get out or buy them. When Harry went in Sir John said, "The house, Hopkinson, is for you for your lifetime, and for Mrs. Hopkinson's lifetime."

So I can be in the house and not pay rent, and the Crompton-Inglefield girls still come to see me. When they got married, no matter where the house was, in London, or wherever, we were always invited. We went to all the weddings, and the christenings.

Ella Hopkinson

I married Eric Allsopp in 1952. We met when I was about seventeen. I remember going to his 21st party. He took me to Blackpool Illuminations and there's a photograph of us with my friend Eileen on a motorbike and sidecar, taken in the photographer's studio of course. We went by bus. Eric worked in Quality Control at Rolls Royce.

Kathleen Allsopp

Father was very big friends with Frank Steeples and he used to have one of those little old fashioned Morris 8s. Well, I mean, they was two big men, weren't they, and they used to squash into this little tiny car and go to the Miner's Standard at the top of Winster. Well when they've had one or two pints coming back they don't know where they're driving do they? On the back lane as you're going to Pikehall there's a dip and the car went upside down on its roof. So these two strapping great men struggled out of this little tiny car, picked it up, turned it over, put it back on its wheels, climbed back in and raced home! And me mum never found out until years later. Since father used to drive the lorries, if he'd lost his license or we'd lost him we'd have been well and truly down the Swanee!

Clara Evans

I 'snaffled up' my husband, Arthur Wayne. He was a Parwich man. I went to school with him but I could never remember him there at all. I was thirty-two when we got married.

ORCHARD FARM. THE MARRIAGE OF ANNIE SEALS TO JOHN FENTEM.
William Jackson Hopkinson is on the left, second row from the back.

139

Of course, I was a long time in the Forces. When I first met him he was working at the quarry at Alsop Moor. Then they closed that, and he went to Ballidon. He was a well driller. He was very lucky, Arthur was, because he said to me,

"Now I'm telling you this: if anything happens, tell them that I told you it was dangerous."

It was a big thing he worked, and the next morning it was down in the bottom of the quarry, it had dropped in the night. Had he been working on it that would have been it.

I'm ninety and I still get about and do all my own housework, and I read a lot. I've never been a worrier, I don't get any tension. I take things in me stride and I've always been happy. I've never been smacked or anything like that in my life, ever, so therefore I've never been hurt: it makes a lot of difference. Circumstances alter cases don't they?

Dolly Wayne

I met John on a blind date. Some friends of mine used to go out on a Saturday night and took me along with them and he came along as well, he was a friend of theirs, so that's how we got together. He lived at Pikehall. I started going out with him when I was eighteen and married him when I was twenty-two.

In Parwich there are a lot of connections between families. Well, villages are like this, everyone's related to everyone else it seems. Someone said in the shop the other day how you can't say anything because everyone's related to everyone else, but we're not really!

Valerie Kirkham

I remember whenever there was a wedding at the parish church, lots and lots of villagers went to see it and wish the bride and groom well, and rice was thrown at them - very uncomfortable, but at least the birds cleared it up! The bride and groom would get silver horseshoes and silver boots, and a wooden spoon: I had one and I'm probably still using it.

Betty Stone

I was married in June 1951 in Parwich. It was a beautiful day. We had a marquee on the lawn. The eight bridesmaids wore delphinium blue dresses and carried red roses, and I wore creamy pink brocade, the family veil and the family tiara. My mother and Harry Hopkinson had decorated the church and we had a Yeomanry guard of honour outside the church. It was a lovely country wedding.

Patricia Bagshawe

The garden at Hallcliffe was created by our mother with the help of Mr Spencer, the stonemason. We loved watching him making the stone balls which were set on pins on the pillars and walls which divided the garden. Our mother was passionate on the subject of improving the soil. At Isma Crompton-Inglefield's wedding in London, Colonel Crompton-Inglefield's cowman, "Badger" (George Twigge), approached my mother in the Hyde Park Hotel, in his best blue suit and face shining from the unaccustomed surroundings, and said the best thing he could think of: "Eee, Mrs Dodds, I've a load of muck for you in 't morning". She was thrilled.

Sara and Vere Dodds

THE MARRIAGE OF KATHLEEN BROWNLEE AND ERIC ALLSOPP
at St. Peter's Church, Parwich. Left: Eileen Storer and June Steeples, Mary Ellen Allsopp, Doug
Allsopp and Frank Steeples. Right: Beatrice and Alf Brownlee, Mollie and Sheila Brownlee.

After the war, when we became decontrolled and there was ease of movement as you might say, I met Ray. Ray was in the army from 1944. He is from Ashbourne originally, so when he was demobbed he came back to Parwich and then went to study art at the Slade in London. I met him just before the war ended, after V.E. day but before the Far East. He came back from India in 1945, and we met at Ashbourne hospital, where I was working. The staff nurse there had known Ray casually before the war, and they met quite by chance on a bus coming back from Derby.

It was the hospital dance coming up, a fund raising event, and she invited him and he came along with his brother. I didn't see him for quite some time afterwards. He will tell you that I chased after him but it wasn't quite like that. When we first met he said, quite literally, "Don't fall in love with me. I don't need a woman, I'm married to Art." I thought, how arrogant, to think I might have designs on him! So he disappeared and went off to the Slade, but then a short while later he was ringing me up saying, come and take this Nanny's job down in London. Well, although he was so happy to be back in Art it was a pretty lonely time in London, living in a bedsit with only a student grant. In the meantime, my brother had married and had brought his wife to live temporarily at my home in Darley Abbey, turfing me out of my very nice bedroom into the spare single room, so I was looking for another residence and I took the job.

After Ray's second year at the Slade finished, he came back to Derbyshire and I left the doctor with the three little boys I had been looking after because he had now come out of the air force and they were moving to Bristol. I came back home without a job. Looking back over the years, I had an awful lot of jobs in about ten years, but they were all connected in one way or another. In September 1948 Ray was appointed to Sheffield College of Art and we were married in the November. He was thirty-one by this time and we had no money, oh anything but. We lived midway between Sheffield and Chesterfield in what had been a village but had gradually been built on and built on, and just got busier and busier.

We came back to Parwich in 1982. Ray had retired at 60 in 1977, and we took about five years deciding where we were wanted to live. I don't know how many properties we looked at, and then we rediscovered Parwich.

Betty Stone

I met my husband, Denis, on the village green in Parwich. He was a Parwich man. At least, I think he came to Parwich when he was a tiny baby. We was open and Denis came shooting at the shooting stall, and he won this mug and it had got a crinoline lady on, and he says, "Here you are, that's for you!" So I thought, how weird! I must have been twenty-four. Then he came back and said, "I don't think you'd want to go out with me,

would you?" So I said, "Why not?" I mean, I'd never been interested in boys. "Oh," he says, "I'll pick you up Sunday then." Well I got all ready and waiting and he never turned up! I says to his sister, "I have never been stood up before in my life." (I'd never been out with anybody either)! So she went down and told him, and he came back on the following Saturday night and went and apologised to my mother and says, "Do you think I could take Clara out this Sunday?" So my mother says, "Well you better not ask me, go and ask her yourself." So he says, "I don't think I've got another chance, have I?" So I says, "Well, you turn up on Sunday and see." The previous Sunday he'd got cold feet.

He turned up in a brand new Hillman car and I thought, phew! We went to the pictures at Derby and coming back, we called at a funny little pub. You went in and sat down in the kitchen and the landlord came out with the beer in an enamel jug. So Denis says to me, "What would you like to drink?" I says, "Well, I'll have a medium dry sherry please", but he got a sweet one. When we got back home Denis says, "Can I see you again?" And I says, "Well you'd better, hadn't you, now you've started this off like?" After that Denis used to come and help us with the fair. By this time I'd got the shooting stall and darts of my own. That was when when I was nineteen.

We settled in Parwich after I was married in 1967. When we were travelling round I says to Denis, "Is there any chance of us building a bungalow in Parwich? Where we've got the bungalow now was an allotment which belonged to his father. So for us to be able to build on it Denis had to pay his father a turnover fee. We started digging the footings out at weekends.

Clara Evans

Outings and Red Letter Days

Villagers on the Green in Parwich.

The Sunday School outing to Roystone Rocks

Outings
And 'Red Letter' Days

It must have been about the year 1847 that for the last time I saw our beloved Queen Victoria. She honoured Derby with a visit, staying for one night at the Midland Hotel on her way home from Scotland, and Derby did its best to give her a loyal welcome when she arrived at the railway station. We went, of course, to join in the welcome. The station was a festive scene, with floral decorations, and on each side of a broad gangway up which the royal party were intended to walk, tiers of seats sloping upwards were arranged. These were filled by ladies in brilliant costumes. Up and down the gangway paraded superb-looking men in full dress uniform. I shall never forget the splendour of those uniforms, nor the beauty of the men who wore them. The effect of the whole scene was dazzling.

Punctual to the moment the train arrived, the door of the Royal carriage just opposite the gangway. Out stepped the Royal party, the Queen first, leading the Prince of Wales by the hand. Dear woman and most honoured Queen! She appeared in a "drawn" white silk bonnet, much soiled and the worse for wear, and her small figure was wholly enveloped in a Scotch plaid shawl worn point downwards, as was the fashion in those days. But, wholly unconscious of any deficiencies in her toilette, she walked between our ranks, smiling and bowing with gracious dignity, every inch a Queen, and I think the more honoured for her contempt of externals, while retaining all the true dignity of her Royal station. The Prince of Wales, a pale, inconspicuous-looking little boy, wore a much tumbled brown holland frock, which showed evident signs of the experiences of the journey. The Prince Consort followed, with two or three other children in brown holland. He wore a tweed waterproof, and stooped a good deal. The children had evidently travelled under the care of their parents, no nurses being in charge to take the trouble of them, or "put them tidy" at their journey's end. When the Royal Party had passed on, a footman appeared with a large green baize bag; this was filled with toys which were handed to him out of the carriage. These homely details brought before us the simplicity and domestic habits of Her who reigned over us, and whose manner of life was a model for that of every wife and mother in the land. After the footman and the toys I remember nothing further concerning the Queen's visit, except hearing afterwards that when she sat down to the magnificent luncheon prepared for her at the Midland Hotel, she asked for a rice pudding for the children.

Mrs. Curtis

Despite being so off the beaten track, Parwich had long been a tourist destination, largely due to the railway which came to Alsop en le Dale.

Some local people would go further afield on holiday from Alsop Station and we also had visitors from elsewhere coming to stay at the New Inns Hotel and at Parwich Lees. For some years in the 1930s we had a "Camp Coach" in the sidings at Alsop, convenient for access to the station toilets. Camp Coaches were old railway carriages containing 2 berths in each of 3 compartments, a dining room (converted from 2 former compartments) and a utility room for cooking and washing. Paraffin was provided for cooking, heating and lighting. Equipment included crockery, cutlery, glasses and bedding, all of which had to be checked each

A SPLENDID VEHICLE, COMPLETE WITH CHAUFFEUR, OUTSIDE THE POST OFFICE IN PARWICH

145

A VICTORIAN PICNIC.
The Evans family of Darley Abbey

Sunday with the change of visitors. Bed linen arrived in a hamper from Derby Midland Station. The rental was £6 per week. I remember parties coming from London, Birmingham and Bristol. We had a gallon can of water ready for the visitors, together with any groceries they had ordered, and had a kettle boiling when they arrived.

Charles Allen
From Recollections of Alsop en le Dale Station, compiled by Stewart Williams.

As a young woman, my husband's great grandmother, Mary Anne Shaw, was handsome. She was above average height and stately in build. A silhouette that we have of her shows her to be wearing an elaborate hat. Her hair was swept up on top of her head and her collar is up-standing. It may well be that she purchased these clothes in Paris. Esther, Granny Brownson, remembered hearing about her parents travels and the preparations which took place before they departed. Clothes were packed into trunks, portmanteaus and hat-boxes and taken with the couple as they travelled first by horse drawn carriage, then train and afterwards packet steamer to France. The last stage of the journey overland was by coach.

Ann Vidler

Our summer holidays in 1840 were spent at Boulogne-sur-Mer. The boat which conveyed us from London to Boulogne was unseaworthy, and barely survived the terrific storm in which we crossed the Channel. The *Emerald* never went to sea again, and it is a marvel that we escaped with our lives. We were hurled over the "bar" into Boulogne harbour on the crest of an enormous wave."

Mrs. Curtis

THE EDWARDIAN PICNIC.

A grand affair. This may be a house party of the Lewis family in the fir plantation mentioned by Frances Curtis up behind Parwich Hall? The picture may include Alice and Susan Lewis (wearing straw boaters)

The Great Exhibition, held in the first Crystal Palace, was the result of suggestions from the Prince Consort, and carried out under his directions. The idea was new and the realisation of it an immense success. The attendances were enormous; during its last days it was almost impossible to obtain standing room. Ten thousand people were once inside the building, with the thermometer at 90°. What we enjoyed most were the more expensive Wednesdays, when the Palace was used as a meeting place for London Society, and became a promenade for its gayest members, including many of the most noted beauties of the day. Their beauty was chiefly in the Amy Robsart style (the fashion of that year), with large blue eyes and level eyebrows below a broad forehead; a short face tapering to the chin, with exquisitely cut features. Their dresses were of "Organdie-muslin", of soft flowery patterns. Crinolines were not yet invented, nor high-heeled shoes, and the lovely maidens walked with a grace that these later inventions would have made impossible. These girls were of medium height, (tall stature was not then regarded as a perfection), and viewed through the haze of distant long years, they seem to me the loveliest representations of womanhood.

Mrs. Curtis

When I worked at Parwich Hall, Colonel Inglefield had a Ford shooting brake, and every Tuesday night, any of the staff could go to the last house at the Elite picture house in Ashbourne, girls and boys. We used to come out of the pictures at twelve o'clock at night in those days. We all used to cram into this little shooting brake coming back, lads and lasses. There were about twelve staff in the house, six gardeners and two grooms, two chauffeurs, all that sort of thing.

Ken Wayne

John and I got married in '68 and we took my Grandma to Cornwall for two weeks in '69, and that was the first time she had ever had a seaside holiday or any holiday in her life, and by then she was probably seventy. I think she'd been to the sea with us for days out, but she'd never been to stay, and we took her for two weeks to Looe and Bude. It was so hot; it was a beautiful fortnight and I think she loved every minute of it. I don't think I went to the seaside until I was five, and that was only a day trip, Liverpool to New Brighton on the ferry with Mum and Dad. I was absolutely petrified on this ferry. We stayed there for the day and came back; first time I'd had my feet in the sea I think. I was eleven or twelve the first time we went away on holiday to stay. We went to Southport with my aunt and uncle.

Valerie Kirkham

We had a day out one day: four of us walked to Dovedale. My elder cousin was 14 at the time and she'd just left school, Kenneth and I were about the same age, and my brother two years younger than me. We walked up to Alsop Station, across the road, down into Milldale, all the way through Dovedale and back to Thorpe. I was not in the least impressed with Dovedale. It was pointed out to me, this cave and that, and Lovers' Leap, but it was so hot and very tiring, and a long, long way when you are only 9 or 10! We went into Thorpe and got a train to Tissington, then walked back over the fields from there. We took sandwiches to eat, cheese, a very nice Chiltern cheese which was a spreading cheese, and probably tomatoes, separately, not in the sandwiches, and home-made fruit cake; and instead of carrying drinks, we took a raw jelly in the packet. I think we had two different flavours.

Betty Stone

A TRIP TO BLACKPOOL.
Eric Allsopp, Kathleen Brownlee, and Eileen Steeples.

Take the girl next door; everything had to be shining new, with nothing out of place. She had two girls and I still keep in touch with them. I used to say to David and John, "Come on, we'll go down to Bradbourne Mill and have a picnic!" We'd go on a day when the buses ran and we'd walk down but come back on the bus, because the children had played about and they'd got tired. And I remember the little girl saying to me, "Aunty, can I come?" and my saying, "Yes, if you want to. Ask Mummy if you can come", and I said to her mother, "Oh, why don't you come too?" but she said "Oh no, I've got too much work to do and I haven't got any food ready," so I said, "Well, I've got plenty, and I've got a bottle of lemonade and some fruit", and so off we went.

Ella Hopkinson

As a child I had several holidays staying with my grandfather and Aunt Thirza in Parwich. My grandfather still had his slaughterhouse where the Royal British Legion now stands and I have watched him slaughtering pigs there. At that time he and Aunt Thirza lived in a small cottage, which was the last in a small row just past the slaughterhouse, going towards Alsop en le Dale, and built close to sheer rocks at the back of the cottage. That cottage still stands today. I have a great affection for Parwich and when in the area, still like to go back and re-live old memories.

David Webster

I remember going on a school outing to Llandudno once, with pupils and parents. We went by train from Buxton and that was a great experience 'cause we were then in the juniors. Mr Fearn used to say "We're not going on an outing unless we make it something to do with school", so we each used to write what we'd seen and he put it into a book, like a scrapbook. I remember I did the one when we went to Llandudno; what we'd seen on the journey and the rest of it, and that was only the second time I had ever been to the seaside. We had a lovely day there and we paddled in the sea. We didn't have an awful lot of outings, but that's the one that sticks in my mind.

We used to have Sunday school outings but we didn't go very far, only to the park at Bakewell, or somewhere in Darley Dale and have tea, and spend the day on the swings and things because that was a novelty to us all; we had nothing here when we were little, no swings or sea-saws. We used to go down to the playing field from school to play rounders every week, and the boys played football. But as for any other playground, we hadn't got it. You made your own entertainment really. I suppose we played tennis on the roads, because there wasn't the traffic there is now.

Valerie Kirkham

We went on a coach outing to Blackpool Illuminations, Betty Weston, Shirley Bradbury, Connie Edge and me. Connie was clutching a big teddy bear she'd bought early in the morning for her grandchildren. "Well," I says, "you're not going to carry that great thing all day around Blackpool are you? Why don't we come back later?"

So the man says, "Well, if you buy it now you get a free seagull."

So when she's paid him, she says, "Here, where's my seagull?"

And he says, "Well, you've got to catch the *** first!"

Mary Rawlins

READY FOR THE PICNIC

Ella Hopkinson, who loves children as much as they love her, frequently set off on picnics with them to Bradbourne Mill.
From left: Reg Twigge, John Appleby, Eric Allsopp, Ella with son John, Phyllis Allsopp, Gill Ridgard and David Hopkinson.

The Annual Garden Fête at Parwich Hall.

In Parwich we had both Chapel and Church, the British Legion Hall, the Mothers' Union, and the Women's Institute; the Garden Fête each summer, a cricket pitch, a village sports day for the children, Wakes Week when the fair came to the Lower Green for a week each year; there were Cubs and Brownies – and all this in a village which, together with Alsop en le Dale and the surrounding farms, numbered only a few hundred people.

Angela Dodds

Celebrations

Of social events, both grave and gay, there were many. Of the happier memories one is reminded forcibly by a programme of the celebration of the restoration of peace after the Crimean War. The event took place on June 5th, 1858.

The celebration was almost exactly like those of the 1887 Jubilee and the 1897 Jubilee of Queen Victoria, and of the Coronation of Edward VII. In the Peace celebration there was a procession which included every phase of the village folk. Starting from the School Green, they marched to church with flags attached to each section, also a band, and a banner preceding the Odd-Fellows, to finish what must have been a very colourful, impressive sight. Lunch and tea followed, and as everyone was asked to bring a knife and fork, one can guess the good cheer there was.

The later celebrations were followed by a huge bonfire on the top of the hill, and it was a wonderful sight to see the fires all being lit up on the surrounding hills in the same way. As the fires died down, torches were thrust into the dying embers, and a chain of fire winding and curving down the hill-side could plainly be seen by those waiting on the

A FAVOURITE PASTIME.
<u>Pictured above:</u> Miss Mary Graham (right) on a picnic with her family.
<u>Below:</u> Miss Graham (left) on a picnic with a friend, in the 1970's.

Green to begin the firework display which brought a happy day to a close.

The last night of the old century was another happy occasion. The church choir gathered and went round the village singing appropriate hymns to astonished people who volubly protested that they had already had the carol singers. The reply given to this protest was "A Happy New Century" to you. England was at war with the Boers, and with the wonderful optimism of English people, we all thought that the end of that war was the finish of all wars.

Helena Birkentall

Dear George,
Perhaps it may be a treat for you to hear A little of our proceedings in Parwich since your absence. You know we were going to rejoice and show some Loyal tricks when you left us? Our subscription raised A purse of a little more than £45 which enabled us to purchase 3cwt weight of Beef & 10 stone of Flour, with Eggs Fruit &cc Which was made into Plumb pudding, the puddings were made at different Farm Houses, and when collected together were Drawn down the Street in a Large Waggon with Musick Men riding in the waggon & playing God Save the King- about 100lbs of Beef and as much of the pudding was Distributed to poor Families with each Head one penny rool of Bread - this was a very fine treat to the poor children and the Inhabitants and was on the evening before the rejoicing day.

The morning being favourable we began to Arrange Tables, seats &c to the length about 60 yards in front of the Hall and a most Excellent Dinner was set out: of the Old English Fare, Roast Beef & plumb pudding with Sauce, & Bread &c. But being a little detained as usual with the parson before we could go into the church; and a little when we

was in, that our dinner was wet & starving on the Table before we could get back - this was a hurrying time, indeed we were obliged to carry our victuals into the Hall & Tables &c and I suppose there sat as many as 200 people at different times at a very plentiful Dinner - This being over Tea was then ordered for the Ladies and A great provision of hot cake and Butter with cold Bread and Butter, cream strong Tea & well Suggared, and a little Rum to their Tea, the old ladies swil'd in this Novelty till they were satisfyed - and about 100 women young and old were rais'd from the Tea Table by the help of these and other pours.

The evening approached and the parties assembled to a Dance the first was led down by J G Johnson Esq of Bradburn and Miss Edensor of Manchester and about 60 cupple Danced that evening. After the Dance Mr. Johnson & Mr Edensor gave many Loyal Toasts which were drank with three times three: and evening was spent with singing and Dancing, and to finish the week the two following evenings were held up by the Young Ladies and Gentlemen of the village with Music & Dancing. You will burn this letter when you have read it.
I remain Dear Geo
Your Truly
John Alsop

This letter was sent to 'The Reliquary' 1874/75, by the 'late Mr. S. Swindell', perhaps the one who farmed Flaxdale for much of the nineteenth century. Julie Bunting in the 1992 Peak Advertiser, suggests the celebrations were part of nation-wide rejoicings at the exile of Napoleon to the island of Elba in 1814. The parson mentioned would have been the Rev. Carr, whose wife was once thought to have been responsible for planting the cross-shaped wood on Parwich Hill.

Edwardian or fake? Are these ladies celebrating something, or dressing up? When did tea cost 6d?
Mrs. Beatrice Graham is on the front row, left.

For King George VI's coronation we had a bonfire on the top of Parwich Hill and it poured with rain. We got access by Hill Top Farm, but by the mere there was terrible slipping and sliding, as we struggled with my youngest sister's pram. My sister Cline [Caroline, now Mrs. Kilner] also remembers a bonfire which I think must have been for the coronation of Elizabeth II.

Patricia Bagshawe

To celebrate the Queen's coronation there was a flurry of tree planting in the village with the W.I. giving each member a flowering cherry. The avenue of horse chestnut trees at Nether Green was planted, along with the copper beech on the Green. The beech and the chestnuts have flourished, but only three of the cherry trees remain: one in the garden of Nether Green house, one behind Walnut Cottage, and one on the Green in front of Hallcliffe House. Also there were four other events in 1952 that will be remembered by villagers. There were four weddings: Eric Allsopp to Kathleen Brownlee, Abel Shipley to Elizabeth, Ambrose Wilton to Irene Lees, and Don Ellis to Eileen Steeples.

Peter Trewhitt

Wakes Fair, Parwich

THE 'JUVENILE' AT WAKES FAIR.
"Father remade it with boats after its old fashioned cars were beyond repair." (Clara Evans)

Parwich Wakes used to be a 'red letter' day. It started on a Monday and I can remember coming to Parwich and there was a big turnout at the bottom there, roundabouts, and these things you hit and a thing goes up; and gas lights, I can remember them. If we hadn't have come to Parwich Wakes we should have been heartbroken. We all had new frocks.

Dolly Wayne

We set up the fair in Parwich opposite the Sycamore Pub on the Green and it was like coming home. Even when I was a little girl of about five we used to come here, and I always said that if I had to settle down, the place I could settle in was Parwich. With staying here a fortnight, we got to know everybody and everybody was so kind. We'd got the swinging boats which used to stand at the

right of the top end. (It's a garage now); and then there was the lorry with the generator for driving the lights, and the autodrome. The autodrome was a machine with motorcars what went up and down and round. There were only three autodromes built by Lake's and apparently we've got the last surviving one. We've still got the coconut shy, the skittles, the roll a penny, the slot machine, and the swingboats, but my brother Jack sold the little Juvenile (the little horses). It was down Matlock for many a while. Dad bought a bit of land at Calow and built a shed out of railway sleepers to house our things in.

To begin with you didn't need a license and the [fairground] rides weren't insured like they are today, though we had to insure the lorries, and you had to have a license to tow your trailer. We charged threepence and sixpence for a ride, or seven shots for a shilling, and folks got that crafty they used to save the seventh one, so that by the end, when they'd spent their money they'd got about six free shots, and it was practically a prize every time.

At Wakes they used to have these parties up in the Village Hall. It was a corrugated iron place then. You used to have to take a plate and a cup and a spoon and they'd have jelly and trifle and cakes and sandwiches and pop; and I used to say to Mum, can I go to the party, Mum? And she'd say, not unless you've got some clean socks. So I used to go in't caravan but I couldn't find no clean socks, so I used to take my shoes off and turn my socks inside out and say, "I've got some clean socks on Mum, look!" "Oh right, she says, but be back here for five o'clock", which was opening time see.

Parwich Wakes was one of those times when everybody let go. They saved up all year and because there wasn't the holidays then like there are today, all the children used to save their pennies too, and it was 'the thing' because there was the carnival, sports day, there was something going off every day. At one time they used to have motorbike races up on Parson's Croft.

Clare Evans

On Dolly Wayne's 90th birthday I rang in to Radio Derby for a request, but they got the name wrong and called her 'Wally Wayne'. Her real name is Katherine Elizabeth, by the way. I was sat having my breakfast one morning listening to Radio Derby when I heard:

"I've got a letter here from a.... looks like Ethel," he says, "and it's for.... looks like Wally of Parwich." Oh, I jumped up quick and put the tape on, and I got it, the song, and when I got her a card, I put inside, "To Wally,

from another Wally (Walter)." Then I made the address on the front, 'Mrs. Wally Wayne'. We had a good laugh when I saw her.

Ken Wayne

DRESSED FOR THE CARNIVAL.
Lizzie Webster and Ethel Hopkinson

Mrs Sykes's coconut shy.

FASHION IN THE 1920'S AND THE 1940'S

Top left, the wedding of Mr. and Mrs. Robert Steeples (note the bridesmaid, right). The two central portraits belong to Clara Evans' family. The pretty girl on the right is her Aunt Alice. Below them (left) is the wartime wedding of Esther (née Lees) and Samuel Flower. Lower left, shoes typical of the period. Right, a beaded dress owned by Dorothy Littlewood, and a similar dress in a painting by Edouard Vuillard of Madame Laroche. Ella Hopkinson owns a similar style dress.

WINTER

The coming of winter meant short days and long winter evenings with candles and oil lamps for lighting. Oil lamps were particularly time consuming in their upkeep. The shades and chimneys had to be washed daily, the reservoirs refilled and the wicks trimmed. There were fires to clear and lay. If anyone was ill, a fire in the bedroom was sometimes allowed. My mother, as a child, loved the patterns that the firelight made in the dimly lit room. Winter coughs and colds and particularly whooping cough, measles and scarlet fever were real problems. The school attendance levels would drop if these illnesses increased in the villages. With cases of diphtheria there was often a ruling that the neighbours of infected children should not attend in the hope of controlling the spread of infection. Homemade cough mixtures and embrocations were prepared, these being much cheaper and often more effective than the proprietary medicines available. The unsurfaced roads made travelling and even visiting difficult during periods of bad weather. Heavy snow and severe frosts came every year and brought with them the problem of icy surfaces and frozen village pumps. Sticks and logs for fires needed to be stored somewhere dry. The Christmas puddings were cooked in November. Dried fruit had to be washed, checked for sticks etcetera, and dried before use. If the sugar was in block form it would need crushing with a rolling pin. When the ingredients were mixed the family gathered in the kitchen to take their turn at stirring and making a wish. Each pudding was wrapped in a cloth and tied with string to make a sphere. If several were to be cooked they might be boiled in the copper (but not on a Monday, which was the day the washing was done.) Four to five hours cooking can make a lot of steam. Before Christmas, came the carol singing rewarded with wassail, a spiced wine, and mince pies. A Yule log was brought home with holly, ivy and mistletoe for decorating the house. I do not know how soon the fashion for Christmas trees, introduced by Prince Albert, would have reached Derbyshire villages.

One of my personal early memories, aged about three years, in the early thirties, was of a Christmas tree which had among its decorations three opaque glass birds with spun glass coronets and tails which could well have been Victorian. I wonder if these could have been used at Hallcliffe or the Hall, or perhaps at Bradbourne Hall, where my Grandmother also lived? This tree was lit with real candles in small metal clip-on holders. These candles had to be placed level, and also so that they did not ignite the branches above. There was always a bucket of damp sand placed nearby in case a fire started. The candles only lasted a few minutes, but I remember the effect of the flickering light being quite magical.

Mary Whitechurch

Winter trees in the croft at Flaxdale House, Parwich.

160

Smithy Lane, Winter 1947.

For a Cough

½lb Treacle, 1 gill vinegar, 1d sweet nitre, 1d Eather, 1d Laudanum, 1d oil of Peppermint

Mary Emma Hopkinson

Stormy Weather

In 1846 there was a disastrous flood in Parwich following a cloud-burst on Alsop Moor. The raging waters swept down the back of Cross-Low, through the Middle Hills, and along the Alsop road to the Meadows. Cattle, pigs, fowls, outhouses, and the good top soil of the Moor were swept away. The occupier of Staines Cottage was desirous of saving both himself and his Christmas pig, so he sat on the back of the pig and rode triumphantly to safety.

H. Birkentall

Whooping Cough

2d oil of amber, 1d spirits of hartshorn to rub down the back bone with a feather.

For Whooping Cough

Dissolve a scruple of Salt of Tartar in a quarter pint of water and add to it 10 grains of cochineal. Sweeten it with sugar. Give to an infant a fourth part of a tablespoonful four times a day; two year olds, halfspoonful; from four years old, a spoonful

Mary Emma Hopkinson

Sluice gates were used to flood the warm spring water from Ball Croft over the Meadows, and the youth of the writer's generation skated and slid over the ice under the shadow of Gorse Hill.

H. Birkentall

Everyone knows what a hard winter that one of '39/'40 was in every sort of way, but to a small child it was magical - deep snow and tobogganing, then snowdrops in the orchard and playing, daily, up at the Hall with my friend Caroline Crompton-Inglefield, a few months my junior.

Charlotte Halliday

Mother used to make her own bread and oatcakes, and in the winter time we used to have churns with flour in them and get all catered up for the snow. It was hard living at Upper Moor farm in the winter because we'd no mains water until the mid '40s, and no electricity. We had a well and a pump. It was 1946 when they started to put the water on,

Charlotte Halliday and her brother Stephen, playing in snow at The Fold, March 1940.

and they built a reservoir at the top, at 1300 feet above sea level, the highest point. Course, then the 1947 snow came and that curtailed it for a while, so we'd no water at all. We had to melt snow in the boiler next to the range and ladle it out and put it in the kettle and boil it to make drinks. The snow was white but the tea used to be black. Yes, we've roughed it.

Mary Rawlins

Snow Proof and Water proof
India rubber, 1oz in small pieces
Boiled oil, 1 pt

Dissolve by heat, then add 1 pt hot boiled oil, stir well and cool

Mary Emma Hopkinson

In 1883 or thereabouts, a terrible storm struck the village. The windows of the ground floor rooms of the school house were blocked up by a snowdrift, and as in all such storms, Parwich was completely cut off from the rest of the world. For a few days before the storm the usual warnings had gone out - the falling temperature, the ominous pointers of the weatherglass, the terrified flight of birds against the background of a dark, forbidding sky, and above all, the huddled gathering of

Parwich Hall in deep snow.

horses and sheep under the south side of the stone walls, from which they had to be forcibly driven to a safer place. These were the warnings, and they were promptly acted upon by the villagers. Fuel was stored in every available space indoors, ample supplies of food were secured, and the big farms had three months emergency rations for man and beast gathered in the autumn in readiness to meet any such storms which might come. On that day, nearly seventy years ago, we were snug, warm and well-fed.

At the farms the making of butter and cheese went on as usual. During this snow storm, Sanson [*Samson?*] Copestake, the village postman, who walked to and fro from Ashbourne to Parwich by way of Tissington, was snowed up. Search parties went out and found him buried in the snow in the Bletches.

In spite of several happenings of this kind he reached a ripe old age.

Another terrible storm took place at the beginning of the present century. A villager was found buried in the snow up the Alsop Road. His friend carried him home shoulder high. He, too, lived on for many years and died only a few years ago.

The railway extension from Ashbourne to Buxton had just been opened, and Ashbourne Grammar School boys travelling home by the school-train found the line blocked up. They report that they had a good time. In 1933 another severe blizzard struck Parwich, but there was food and fuel in plenty, so all was well.

In 1947 a 15 ft. snow-drift blocked up the entrance to the village in Thorn's Lane.

163

Wright Greatorex, a familiar figure, the local carrier, seen here on a winter's morning outside The Fold

Severe rationing was still going on, and fuel was so scarce that trees were felled and distributed. Of food there was one week's meagre ration in hand, and the plight of the farmers, who could not use their milk and could not send it away all because transport was completely at a standstill, was deplorable. Some scrubbed out rain-water tanks and filled them with the rapidly accumulating milk. The centuries-old self-supporting village was, for better or worse at an end.

Helena Birkentall

We threw gallons of milk down the drain in the snow, when they couldn't get through. Nothing else you could do with it. We used to have big snows then. We used to go down to Cromford with the milk, but of course, you couldn't get. We made cheese, but you could only make so much.

Catherine Elizabeth (Dolly) Wayne

When it was snowy, Harry and I used to take the children up to Bell's Yard and we'd have sledges. Bell's Yard is the little field between the Care Centre and Parwich Hall gardens; and that was steep enough for children to slide on. We couldn't go far because there was no petrol and apart from that, just after the war, everybody was in the same boat, and nobody had got very much money.

Ella Hopkinson

164

The winters, it seems, were always cold with plenty of snow. We had a wonderful time tobogganing on the Bletches, and when the roads became impassable, we would take the toboggans a couple of miles to the lane-end where the groceries from Howell and Marsden in Ashbourne would have been left for us.

Zelda Kent-Lemon

In winter we used to toboggan down Kiln Lane. Before the war, there was hardly any traffic. The Hospital was a lying in hospital then for women, so it was very quiet. There was a mere on Parwich Hill and one hard winter I remember my sister Isma and I going up to slide on the ice (*Isma, now Mrs. Lutyens*).

Patricia Bagshawe

Harry and I came to Parwich in 1946, just after the War, just ready for the 1947 winter! In Suffolk when I was a child, if it snowed at night time you'd think, oh, lovely, we can get up and play snow balls, but by nine, ten o'clock the snow would all be gone. There used to be a little shop in Parwich, Miss Northcliffe's, and the day it snowed I went down there and everything was covered with snow. Well, to me it was like fairyland. I went in the shop and there were so many people in there, and I said, "Oh, doesn't everywhere look lovely!" and nobody answered. They must have thought I was crackers! Harry was ever so good: for weeks we weren't allowed to go up round the top because it was dangerous, but he'd take me for a walk because he knew I loved the snow. I can

remember going over one little wall up near Hilltop and we went almost up to the waist in snow; and as we got round, the snow was so high I can remember looking down and seeing a bird's nest in a tree, which just shows how deep it was. Somebody would say, "Harry, there's coal at the lane end, and that would be the lane end onto the Bakewell road, and off they'd go, and he'd no sooner got back than somebody said "Harry, there's bread at the lane end," and off they'd go again; and I said, "Oh Harry, all that way," and he said "We don't go by the road, we go over hedges and it's much quicker."

There was no milk went for weeks. The farmers just had to throw the milk down the drain because lorries couldn't get. Nowadays it wouldn't be like that because there are so many implements to clear the roads. Then, men had to go shovelling the snow by hand. It started in March and it was May before it went.

Ella Hopkinson

Delivering coal in Creamery Lane. The woman on the right is thought to be Eric Allsopp's grandmother.

Birth, Sickness, Mortality

Birth

Ann Webster (née Alsop) a Parwich woman, was the village midwife. She was married to my great grandfather, James Webster. James was the eldest son of my great great grandparents, William Webster and his wife, Lucy who, according to the census of 1841, were living with their six children at the Mount in Parwich. William was a butcher, and on his death the business passed to James. Unfortunately, James died when he was only forty-two years old, leaving his wife, Ann, to bring up five children on her own. The census of 1861 lists Ann as widowed, though it does not record where she and the children were living. She was probably at the Green, where James had built a cottage which, I am told, still had earth floors. In 1861 my grandfather would have been only three years old, so he would not really have known his father. Whether midwifery was something Ann took up after her husband's death to support her own family, or whether she had been a midwife before that I don't know.

David Webster

[The 1901 Census lists Ann Webster, a widow born in Brassington, as a midwife in Parwich. She was then 80 years old.]

I had my first baby, John, in the hospital in Leicester, because it was just after wartime and it was so difficult to get in anywhere. I got to Leicester from Parwich by taxi, when I was already in labour. We went with Mr. Steeples (who used to drive the taxi). You didn't go until you really were in labour. I was new to the area and I remember looking out at the hills and thinking, wherever am I going to, because it was all new to me. I stayed in Leicester a couple of weeks. We were so thrilled because I was a children's nurse and I badly wanted a family. I had David, my second, in Belper.

Ella Hopkinson

Mrs. Blackwell was my great grandmother and she used to do midwifery in Parwich as well as laying out the deceased. We called her Grandma Blackwell, and she was Dolly Wayne's Aunty Polly. (Dolly is my mum's, cousin.) This would be in the 1920s-30s I think. She lived at Church Cottage with Uncle George. She'd been married twice and my granddad was the first child of the first marriage, but he was brought up by his granny and granddad, up on Gibbons Bank. Granny and Granddad Blackwell were married in 1914.

Grandma Blackwell started practising midwifery during her second marriage, and I know she delivered my granny's children. Mrs. Wayne, who used to live next door to us at School View, had twins, Betty and Mary, and she wasn't too well after she'd had them, and I think one of the twins was poorly: so Grandma Blackwell took them down home with her for a while. They were only about three pounds each when they were born, which nowadays would mean they'd be in an incubator. She kept them in a drawer, which is what they used to do in those days, lining it with cotton wool and so on. They grew up to be healthy children and adults. Mrs. Wayne

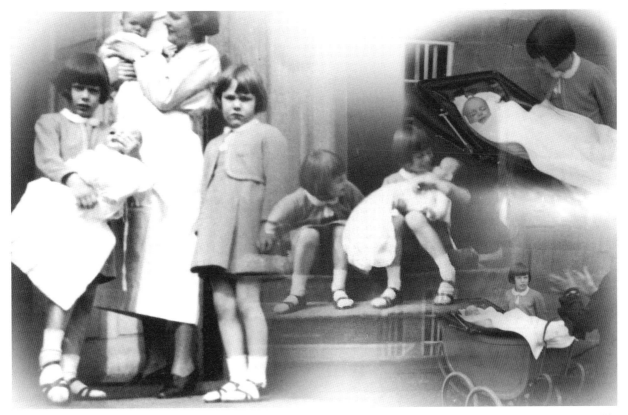

THE NEW ARRIVAL: Patricia Crompton-Inglefield and her sister Isma look dubiously at the camera while their Nanny holds their new baby sister, Caroline. The life-sized doll, it seems, is much more interesting.

herself lived to be ninety. She became Dolly Wayne's mother in law when Dolly married Arthur Wayne. The twins Grandma Blackwell had nurtured were Arthur's sisters. As Grandma Blackwell got older, Dolly Wayne used to go round and help her, and she continued doing the same for Uncle George after Grandma Blackwell died. I can only just remember Grandma Blackwell. She was quite a small lady, rather plump, with a round face, and she wore dark clothes.

The Miss Evans at Orchard Farm also did laying out, and Mrs. Hopkinson [Ella] also helped sometimes. In fact I think she and my mum actually laid out Grandma Blackwell. Then when Mrs. Graham died, I think Mrs. Hopkinson said she helped lay her out, and one of the Miss Evans came as well. I remember that when there was a funeral and it was coming up the village, we always used to draw the curtains, and everyone along the street to the church did, as a mark of respect. It didn't matter whose funeral it was, whether it was a relative or someone else.

Sandra Chadfield

When we lived up at Daisy Bank, there was no transport by road, so when my mother went into labour she had to walk either to Ballidon Lane End, or to Brassington along the railway line. Only the fittest survived in those days; that's why I'm so fit now!

Kathleen Allsopp

167

MOTHERHOOD. Kathleen and Eric Allsopp and Eric's mother, Mary Ellen Allsopp with baby, Paul.
Centre: Kathleen as a baby.

Sickness

In the 1920s, when my mother, Ethel Hopkinson, was working in Abyssinia, the family left Addis Ababa during the hot season and went up into the hills to a plantation. Mrs. Sandford, her employer, had for some time run a medical clinic up there, and people used to come to it each morning. There was no other medical provision, so she did everything she could. On one occasion Mrs. Sandford had to go back to Addis Ababa, leaving my mother up in the hills with the children and the ayah and various other people. Unfortunately a man broke his leg and she had to set it, getting two or three

people to hang on the end and pull it straight. There were no anaesthetics of course. She'd seen this done before but she'd never had to try and do it herself. She only dared to attempt it because she knew that if she didn't, he might never walk again.

Mary Whitechurch

For Gathering

Marsh Mallow leaf

Soak in Water; put underside to draw then topside to heel.

(Gathering refers to any area where pus was collecting and it brought it to a head)

Mary Emma Hopkinson

168

I remember my great grandmother wrapping my septic finger in a bread poultice. I think she also used herbs. To my relief, the finger healed up perfectly. This was during the war, when antibiotics were available for the troops but not for the general public. My great grandmother was at pains to heal me since her adopted son, who had survived action in the Great War, had died of septicaemia some time after it.

Gillian Radcliffe

The July Memoranda of the Ashbourne Cottage Hospital (in the Ashbourne Telegraph, 28th October 1927) notes that the Matron's expenditure for that month was £54/4s. Fourteen patients were admitted, fifteen were discharged and nine were still in hospital.

(In old money, the dash '/' divides pounds from shillings and shillings from pence)

When I had shingles I went to Dr Bradbury and he asked me what other things I'd had and I said, "I've had everything - measles, mumps, even diphtheria and scarlet fever", and he said, "Well in those days you could have died with scarlet fever". So then I told him about the black, horse-drawn van that came to fetch you in Suffolk if you had something like that. It was always called 'the fever van', and the man sat on the front to drive it, and if ever you saw the fever cart you thought, oh dear, who's got it now?

When I had scarlet fever I was taken to a place that used to be an old gaol. I hated porridge and my mother knew that, so she sent enough eggs for me to have eggs every day, but they still brought porridge to me and I said, "I can't eat it"; and I know this sounds dreadful, but they made me, and when I brought it back they made me eat what I'd brought back! I've never forgotten it. I hate a hot bath. I'd much rather have a cold bath and they put me in a really hot bath and I was red when I came out. So they were not kind. I stayed there about two months.

Afterwards they burned your toys and everything. When I was a nanny, the little girl got scarlet fever and it was wartime and I said to the doctor, "I will stay with her. I have had scarlet fever so it makes no difference to me", and he said "Well you'll have to be isolated. You won't have any time off", and I said, "I don't mind that." She'd got an old piece of shawl she called Cuddles, and they said that would have to be burnt and I said no, it was everything to her. So I said, "I'll wash it, and when the room is fumigated I'll put it in there." Our food was put on the bottom of the nursery steps. That went on for about seven weeks.

Ella Hopkinson

My idea in going to work at the photographers was to escape from the farm, rather than doing nothing with my life, but in 1953 I had to come home because my mum was very ill. Grandfather had got T.B. and both Mum and I were looking after him, so we all had to go for check ups, but we were immune to it. Then Mum got pneumonia and they didn't expect her to live. She was in the D.R.I. at Derby and Grandfather was in the Derwent hospital which was a sanatorium just out of Derby. From Derby, I had to catch another bus to get there. I'd get a bit of tea in Derby, in the bus station café on the upper deck, then I'd come back on the bus, walk up the lane and cook a meal for my father and brother. It was a heavy life then. My mum was in hospital for six months, and my grandfather for twelve months, and I was only seventeen, running the farmhouse, (Dad and his helpers were doing the milking) and going to hospital, running up to the main road to catch the bus to Derby and back. I think it's made me tough. The bus went every two hours so it was a long wait if you missed one.

Coming back late at night, I'd have to start and do all the washing I'd brought back from hospital, with no washer, no nothing, and get them dry and take another lot the next day. I was looking after my brother as well, because he was six years younger than me. He'd laugh and call me a cruel devil because I used to look in his ears and pull his hair and brush it (very tight curls he had) and send him to school a clean boy. It was eleven o'clock or midnight before I got to bed, then up again next morning about six. I just got through it and that was it. I had eighteen months of that.

Mary Rawlins

I had two children, Jonathan and Belinda, and I had Jonathan first. He wouldn't feed properly, and when we took him to the hospital they said he had a blockage in his throat but it turned out he hadn't, he was just stupid at feeding.

Barbara Lowes

In November 1904, Esther Shaw left home for the first time to marry George Francis Carrington Brownson at St Thomas' Church, Huddersfield. At the time the bride was twenty-two and her groom was thirty-one and in poor health. George and Esther moved to Leeds after their marriage and Annie, Esther's sister, came to live with them. Failing health had affected George's prospects and it was decided that the three should go into partnership in the art business. George was to frame the pictures that Annie painted for Esther to sell in the shop. In 1905, eleven months after their marriage, a daughter was born on October 27th. The birth of this child brought with it attendant problems because the child was delicate. She suffered from a chest complaint induced by living in a smoky city. A solution had to be found to the problem and it lay in the removal of the family and Annie from Leeds to Parwich, home of the Brownsons. So when Muriel was two the family moved to 'Brentwood', a cottage in the heart of Parwich with a shop attached. This they rented from James Brownson, George's father. Here Annie and Esther were to run the village shop for over forty years. George was to continue his craft as a frame maker in a workshop behind the shop and Muriel was to live there until she left to get married twenty-one years later.

Ann Vidler

Brandy and Egg Mixture
for the stomach)
Take the whites and yolks of three eggs and beat them up in five ounces of plain water. Add slowly three ounces of Brandy with a little sugar and nutmeg. Given in cases of great prostration. If the stomach is very irratable take a tablespoonful of cream, heat it up well with the white of new laid egg and add slowly to frothy mixture. Add one tablespoonful Brandy and dissolve a bit of lump sugar.

Mary Emma Hopkinson

My mother-in-law had worked at the Hall. She lived in Smithy Lane, then behind the shop. When she couldn't work any more I looked after her for seventeen years, bathed her, decorated for her. She broke one hip twice and then broke the other one. We managed to keep her at home but it was hard going.

Mary Rawlins

An item in the Ashbourne Telegraph of 28th October, 1927, carries the headline "Piles Cannot Resist this Healing Balm." Treatment recommended was an antiseptic called "Man Zan" which "draws the fiery pain out of the sore part", promoting accelerated healing. Tubes of the ointment were available from Thomas Plant, Chemist, Ashbourne. "It costs 3/- or for 3/2 a tube will be sent to you in a plain wrapper, post free. No need to mention your ailment - just say Man Zan."

Gillian Radcliffe

Our mother (Mrs Rose Dodds) took turns to push a trolley round the Parwich hospital wards for the W.V.S. It sold soap, toothpaste and sweets. She was friendly with the matron and once, when my parents went away, we were sent to stay at the hospital. I was homesick and rather frightened, and the only thing that I liked was being allowed to immerse my arm into a large vat of green gelatinous liquid which adhered to the skin.

Zelda Kent-Lemon (née Dodds)

Mr. Moorcroft, gardener at Parwich Hospital

For cramp in the Stomach

Bathe the feet in hot water; rub the stomach with the hand and give a dose of strong peppermint tea or a tablespoon of sal volatile in warm water. Great attention should be paid to the bowels.

Mary Emma Hopkinson

David had to go into hospital with osteomyelitis for three months, and he was in the Children's Hospital in Derby, and I was so worried because I knew he was being moved, and I didn't know where. The day before, the vicar said to Harry, "Harry," he says, "I've been pulling a few strings and David is coming to Parwich Hospital", and so of course we were delighted. But when I got to the Children's Hospital and asked if he was going to Parwich they said, Parwich? Of course he isn't, he's under this certain doctor and Parwich has never been mentioned. So I said, "Well, where is David going?" and they said, Bretby and I had no idea where Bretby was. Well, it's near Burton on Trent and the ambulance men said to me, "Now, you do

realise that we can take you there but we can't bring you back again?" I thought, well if that's it, I'm going. So I went to Bretby, and saw that David was comfy. He was only thirteen. I left around six o'clock at night. I had to walk down a long drive to get onto the main road and I didn't really know what side of the road to stand on to get the bus, and in the meantime Harry was getting worried and rang the hospital in Derby to see where I was. They asked David what time I'd left him, and then of course he was worried. I got home about half past nine at night.

They said that David could have an operation but I'd heard that it really wasn't a success, and it was best that people didn't have it, and I was torn in two. I knew they wouldn't operate on David without asking us, but I got so worked up about it. The vicar came again and said, "I've been in to see David and they're going to operate," and I felt dreadful; but when I got through to the hospital, they said they'd decided not to operate, and oh, I was so thankful.

Ella Hopkinson

In the 1920's Esther Shaw had a mastectomy in Leeds Infirmary. In those days before the discovery of antibiotics, improvements in anaesthesia and high technology in surgery, such radical surgery was very dangerous. Happily she survived the ordeal and hardly suffered a day's illness during the remaining sixty years of her life. Her husband, George, had grown to accept his disability and Esther had learned to live with the constant fear of his attacks; and with the move to Parwich, their daughter's health had improved.

Ann Vidler

I used to get ill with blind quinzies that went abscessed, and one time I was in Chesterfield Royal Hospital and I couldn't see a thing. They burst sometimes (I used to get them regular) and the doctor came and lanced them. You know when you blow a balloon up you get that white stuff inside? On this occasion they think that I'd swallowed some of that and it had poisoned the quinzie and affected either the nerve or a tube or something, and I was totally blind. After three weeks and three days I lied the best way I could to get out, and eventually they did let me out. I must have been about eight. In the end they said I would have to have my tonsils out, so I went to Abercrombie Street hospital in Chesterfield, a private nursing home, because the waiting list for tonsils was that long. So my parents had to pay for that.

Clara Evans

Quinsy

Any of the astringent gargles may be used after quinsy, but none perhaps, answers better or is more accessible to the poor, than the decoction of oak bark… Further, all unnecessary muffling, either by fur or otherwise, about the neck, should be avoided, for there is no more fertile source of a sore throat.

Things Everyone Wants to Know

When I was very little I used to have warts on my fingers and this old lady told me to get some raw meat and rub it on the warts and then bury it, and as the meat rotted the warts would disappear. Well I did that but the dog must have followed me round to the back of the shooting stall, because I discovered him digging up the meat and eating it, and I thought, well you rotter, that was half my lunch; and I'd still got the warts, hadn't I?

Clara Evans

Wart Killer

To clear warts, boil some potatoes, and with the water in which they are boiled, bathe the warts. At the end of a week they will have nearly, if not quite gone.

Take a Tip

Spider's web (cobweb)

The cobweb of cellars, barns and stables, has been reputed from time immemorial of value for arresting superficial haemorrhages. Dr. Graham says it is a valuable remedy for ague; and it also allays diseased irritability, both of body and mind, in a surprising manner. Under its influence, the pulse, when quick, frequent, irregular, and excited, becomes slow, calm, and regular. It will often thus tranquillize much better than opium and henbane; and its soothing properties point it out as a valuable palliative in the advanced stage of consumption, in asthma, in chronic hysterics, and in other spasmodic complaints.

Things Everyone Wants to Know

My Aunt, Miss Mary Graham, Postmistress of Parwich, had always been a very hard working lady and totally devoted to her parents. After her mother died in 1954, we continued to visit her regularly. Her mother had kept up to 21 cats, but now their numbers had declined and their food consisted of tinned Kitty Kat and the like, distinctly preferable to the palate of her "townie nephews" than the home cooked fish, liver and lites had been. In later life she gave up her cats altogether, and enjoyed feeding the wild birds that came to her garden. During one winter a robin regularly came into the house and flew after her from room to room.

My memory of my Aunt, from when I was a child, is of a very kind, quiet, tall, good-looking lady. My memories as an adult are the same, but with the addition of the words "very stubborn". I clearly recall trying to get her to buy a fridge and a TV: she refused. I also recall telling her that I was going to buy her a fridge: she retorted that she couldn't stop me but she wouldn't put anything in it! She had a spell in a nursing home in Ashbourne in the mid 1980s, but she craved to return to her home so, a few months later, when she had recovered her strength, she returned to Parwich. In April 1989, she was ill once again and I had to persuade her that she needed full-time professional care in a nursing home. She refused, so we spent the next hour negotiating - my 47 years against her 89 years. Eventually she agreed, but she wanted to wait a month until her 90th birthday. More negotiations ensued and we eventually settled on a few days grace for her 'to get her things together' after which she went to live in Dove House, Ashbourne, for the last 18 months of her life.

I used to visit her regularly in Dove House and told her she was much better off there:

total disagreement! She told me that she loved every nook and cranny of her home and she wanted to return as soon as possible; after all, she had lived there for 74 years.

I have very fond memories of both my grandmother and my aunt. Both were very strong ladies; the former was a matriarch, the latter had a softer nature but was very determined and equally resolute.

Roger Graham

MISS GRAHAM'S 90TH BIRTHDAY
in Dove House, Ashbourne, with her nephew,
Roger Graham (left)

While compiling this book, I have been told many stories about the eccentric women who have lived in Parwich. Miss Roberts' behaviour at the village pump was a case in point. Apart from cursing the water, she had been known to enter the churchyard at night to stab her mother's grave. Miss Norcliffe, who kept the shop on Church Walk, sometimes appeared at night looking like a ghost in the churchyard. Eveline Shaw tells the story of how her brother and his friends, all aged about nine or ten years old, went into the shop to buy a packet of sweets. Miss Norcliffe always wore a big leather pinny, but when she turned round to fetch the sweets off the shelf, it was revealed that she was wearing nothing underneath! The boys fled in terror!

Sadly, though funny, such stories tell us much about the unenlightened attitude to senility and mental illness of the time. As Eveline says, you just had to get on with it. But pride was also part of the problem. Eveline tells how an aunt of hers, who lived in Parwich, refused all offers of help. When she became so ill that something had to be done, she was found to have a mouse's nest in her bed!

Gillian Radcliffe

Mortality

Will of Agnes Allsopp
(widow of William Allsopp) 1571
In the name of God Amen the 28th daye of Januarye the yeare of our lorde 1570 I Agnes Allsopp late wyffe of William Allsopp disesses of parwiche widow sicke in body but whole in mynde and memorye make my will and testement in forme and manner following
first I bequeth unto Allmighty god my maker and Redeemer my soule and my bodye to be buryed within the churche of parwich aforesed
Also I bequethe towardes the Repayring of the aforesed church 3s and 4d
Also I bequethe unto George Alsopp my sonne one peare of yron bond whyles
Also I bequethe unto Henry Allsop my eldest sonne one strike of barlyee Allso I bequethe unto gregorie my sonne one strike of pees.
Allso I bequethe unto Raphe Alsopp my sonne one mare three sheep one coppe yoke one cutler and one harow with one paire shiettes one peare of blankettes and one couerlyd
Also I bequethe to Raph my sonne aforesed and elizabeth my youngest Daughter all My corne and hey
Also I bequeth unto elizabeth aforesed all the Rest of my Goodes discharging and paying all dettes bequethes and several expences
Allso I make the aforsed Raph and elizabeth my lawffull executtors of this My will and henrye Allsop my eldest sonne Robert Myllenton my son in law and gregorye Allsop my sonne the overseers of this my will Aforesed These beying wittnesse Robert Myllenton Thomas Allsopp George Twecrosse George Alsopp and Henrye Burttone Clarke with others

[In the name of God, Amen, on the 28th January 1570, I Agnes Allsopp widow of William Allsopp of Parwich, deceased, being sick in body but whole in mind and memory make my will and testament. Firstly I bequeath unto God Almighty my Maker and Redeemer my soul, and order my body to be buried in the Church of Parwich. I bequeath towards the repair of Parwich Church 3 shillings and 4 pence.

I bequeath:

To my son George one pair of iron bound wheels

To my eldest son Henry one bushel of barley

To my son Gregory one bushel of peas

To my son Ralph one mare, three sheep one 'coppe' yoke, one coulter, one harrow, one pair of sheets, one pair of blankets and one coverlet

To Ralph my son and Elizabeth my youngest daughter all my corn and hay

To Elizabeth aforesaid all the rest of my goods, paying my debts and expenses.

I make Ralph and Elizabeth my executors and appoint Henry, Robert Myllenton my son-in-law and Gregory Allsopp, my son, overseers of this will.

The following are witness Robert Myllenton, Thomas Allsopp, George Twecrosse, George Allsopp and Henry Burttone (clerk) with others]

Courtesy of, and transcribed by
George Henry Allsop

My grandmother, Elizabeth Lees, died before I was born in 1916, but when we came here in 1982 I was speaking to Mrs Webster, Ron Webster's wife, who was quite a lot older than me, and she remembered my Grandmother's funeral. Her sons, four of them, carried her coffin from high up there on Gibbons Bank down to the church. The villagers put out their stout kitchen tables and carried them to various points along the route so the bearers could rest. There wouldn't have been many houses on the way at the time so they must have carried those tables quite a distance. I also remember my mother talking about carrying the coffin of an infant on more or less the same route. She and another schoolgirl carried this little child's coffin. There were white ribbons on it or maybe cord, and she and the other little girl were crying long before they got to the church because of the pain in their hands. A very thoughtless thing to expect really wasn't it?

Betty Stone

176

This is the last will and Testament of I, Jeanetta K. Allsopp

I give the big Clock & the Bible to Sampie* the large Table & Dad's box the White bed with Flock Bed & all complete I give to Victor Pillows & Blankets, one Bed complete with Feather Bed Mattress pillows & Bed Clothes as in Ordinary use The Sewing Machine tea service given to me by Jack I give to Rosie, 2 old Plates to Jack I give the remainder of the Beds Bed linen all my Clothes Dinner Service tea service to be equally divided Between Fanny Lily & Rosie, I give the remaining Furniture & other articles to be divided between Sampie Fanny Lily Victor & Rosie - I owe £30 to Fanny lent to help buy the House but I sent Fanny occasionally £1 while she was paying off Miss Goodman I owe £8 to Victor £3 to Rosie If Sampie will repay these amounts also pay Fanny £10 Sampie £15 Victor £15 Rosie £15 I give the House to Sampie because of the help given to me over many years I do not want any quarrelling Sampie I know will try to be fair to each of you all, Sampie will erect a suitable stone in the Churchyard for Dad myself & Violet The Funeral expenses will be paid out of my Insurance Co-Operative Stores Odd-Fellows Club & any Money left over be divided.

Jeanetta K Allsopp

November 9th 1937

Witnesses to the signature of Jeanetta K. Alsopp and signed in the presence of each other.

Francis J. Brownlee. Alfred E. Brownlee

*Sampie was Jeanetta's eldest son, Sampson Edward.

Will courtesy of Violet Oldfield

JEANETTA ALLSOPP
Centre: Jeanetta (right) and her daughter, Lily. Top left: Jeanetta with Lily and baby Daisy. Top right: the four Allsopp sisters, Lily, Violet, Fanny and Rose (Rosie). Bottom left: Jeanetta's daughters, Violet and Rosie. Bottom right: Lily with her husband, Walter Schofield, and Daisy.

The first member of the [Alsop] family is mentioned in the old registers of 1639. The last of her line was Miss Anna Alsop, who died at the Close in 1912. At her death, the beautiful and valuable heirlooms of the Alsops were sent to Christies of London to be sold. They included a spinet; a tallboy; a fine dinner service of pewter on an old oak dresser; fine china and carved high-backed chairs of great beauty. Two of these fine chairs are now in the Chancel of Alsop Church: a gift from Miss Alsop.

Helena Birkentall

The following prisoners took their trials at our Assizes which concluded on Thursday at noon: William Webster the unhappy person who was convicted of poisoning Mrs Dakin and Miss Roe of Parwich, near Ashbourne, in this County. Suffered the dreadful sentence of the law on Friday last. The evening before he was executed he persisted his innocence in the most solemn manner, and said he would address the people in his last moments, and declared himself not guilty. The next morning however, previous to his receiving the Holy Sacrament he acknowledged (to the Chaplain and three other gentlemen) having put poison into the ale with intent to poison Mr Dakin, and that he, and he only, caused the death of the two women. On being asked, at the place of execution, if he had anything to say to the people, he replied, "no, I cannot speak" I AM GUILTY.

Derby Mercury, Thursday 26th March 1807

One compares the simple mourning customs of today with those of a century or so ago, nodding plumes on hearses, heavy "mourning" of crepe which hung in long streamers from the widow's bonnet, and also long hat bands flowing from the men's hats. For each man invited there was a pair of black kid gloves, and the funeral tea which followed was a scrumptious feast. A woman I know wished to be "buried with ham tea", and to be conveyed in a hearse drawn by six black horses with black loin clothes.

Helena Birkentall

My grandparents' younger son Jack Graham died on Thursday 20th October 1927 at the age of eighteen. He had been a pupil at Ashbourne Grammar School and had just passed his final matriculation exam. He was teaching for a year at Parwich School and was planning to go to University in September 1928. He was taken ill suddenly and died a few days later in Ashbourne Cottage Hospital from a pneumonia type illness. Although I have not seen the death certificate, I have his diary for 1927, the last entry being made on Monday 10th October. He was a keen athlete, a member of both the school cricket and football teams, and a member of the school Cadet corps. For a time he was also a member of the choir of St. Peter's Church in Parwich. The entry in his diary on Saturday 8th October indicated that he had been digging up potatoes in the morning, cycled to Carsington in the afternoon to play football (won 4-1), cycled back to Ashbourne to see his girlfriend and then cycled back to Parwich in the evening. He was a sociable and well liked young man whose death plunged the village in gloom and must have devastated my grandparents.

Roger Graham

Last month Len Gibbs asked for information about his ancestors and their 'funeral biscuit' making business. I now have it on good authority that the Ironmongers used to live in a cottage in the area we now know as 'the Quarry'... Mrs. Ironmonger died about 60 years ago and her husband ten or so years later. The house has long since been demolished.

The practice of making funeral biscuits is in fact a Staffordshire custom and (*they were*) long thin finger biscuits. The custom was to give the men a clay pipe and half an ounce of tobacco and the ladies a funeral biscuit. In these days of being politically correct (Saints preserve us!) no doubt the ladies would be puffing on their clay pipes and the men would be munching the biscuits.

Funeral biscuits were particularly common around the Warslow area. Obviously Parwich is almost on the border of Staffordshire and it is hardly surprising that the biscuits had at least part of their home in Parwich. Crumbs!

Rev. Jack Cooper

This interesting account is not strictly accurate. The Ironmongers were not related to Len Gibbs and funeral biscuits were more than just a Staffordshire custom.

Funeral Biscuits

12 oz flour, ½ teaspoon baking powder
10 oz butter, ½ teaspoon caraway seeds
9 oz sugar

Sift flour and baking powder, add sugar and caraway, and rub in butter.
Press out the mixture, stamp with a wooden mould and bake 30 minutes at
300 F, Mark 2.

When it was my great aunt's funeral, I remember my great uncles coming to Dam Farm, and all these old ladies in long black coats, boots and black hats. I wasn't very old, I was at school but only just, and so to come round the corner onto Dam Farm front and see all these people outside was a bit of a surprise! We had trestle tables from the pub, and long forms for them to sit on because the rooms were quite big. We also had long tables, which we used to wind open, and then put leaves in the middle of them. It was always funeral teas at Dam Farm if it was any relative of ours. Funerals were a big event. You always had fruit loaves. Currant bread was a funeral thing, and it always reminds me of funerals. Granny used to make seed cake with caraway seeds, and my grandma, my dad's mum, used to make super currant bread; it was the best I've tasted. Mum could never make it like that, Grandma was just so good at it.

Valerie Kirkham

To Wash Black Dresses

Make a lather of 8oz soap, 1 oz oxgall in a pan of warm water. Wash the merino in this and then wring out. Dissolve a small piece of alum in cold water; rinse the merino in it and hang out to dry. Iron or maybe when nearly dry.

Mary Emma Hopkinson

I lost my mother when I was thirteen, and I was billeted out. I lived on the farm next door with friends, George and Nellie Fox. I was brought up by them as part of their family. Then the family broke up and the daughter went to live at Aldwark and I went with her. They weren't related to me but they were kindness itself. I don't know where we would all have landed without them. They took Tommy and me but not my brother John. I know it's a silly thing really, but I can remember my aunty saying, "I'll have the two, I'll have John and Nancy, but I'll not have Dolly." Well, it still sticks. I was only thirteen and I thought, whatever is Dolly going to do? She'd a big family and she was marvellous to take any of us on. You see, we were four little children, all school age, and father couldn't cope. I was lucky really. I left school at fourteen but I didn't go out to work: I was part of my adopted family.

Dolly Wayne

In the nineteenth and early twentieth centuries the death of young children, through poverty, sickness, malnutrition or inadequate medical care, must have been one of the most heart breaking things for people to bear. Apart from epidemics, another frequent cause of death was childbirth.

Gillian Radcliffe

Death in young children
"I remember," says Dr. J. B. Harrison, in his "Medical Aspects of Death," a little child, who had her handkerchief in her hand, which she spread out repeatedly with apparent care and in a fantastic manner that would have been amusing, but for its fatal import." The picking of bedclothes, and catching of the hands as if at imaginary objects, are well known as indications [of death].
Things Everyone Wants to Know

Funeral card of Heneretta Rosa Degg
The beloved Wife of John Degg,
And the beloved and affectionate daughter
of Edward and Mary Ann Brownlee,
Who departed this life February 1, 1892,
aged 22 years, and was interred at St. Peter's
Church, Parwich.

A light is from our household gone,
A voice we loved is stilled;
A place is vacant at our hearth,
Which never can be filled.

We saw her sinking head,
We saw her dying eye,
Yet joyed to think her spirit fled
To yonder happy sky.

My mum was saying that she could remember when stillborn babies were buried at night, round the back of the church. I think they were just buried, without any service. We had a stillborn baby, but times have changed: Charlotte had a proper burial in the churchyard, and we had a little service for her. In the past it was quite a taboo subject; people didn't talk about it. I remember saying at the time, it must have been terrible for the parents, especially the mother, if everyone ignored what had happened, because it does help to talk about these things.

Sandra Chadfield

FUNERAL OF SUSAN LEWIS

The Lewis family gather outside the summer house at Parwich Hall after the funeral of Susan Lewis who died there in 1914.
Back row left: Rev. Edward Harcombe (who officiated) and Susan's sons and daughters: Ernest Carr Lewis, Susan Evelyn Lewis (spinster) Arthur Lewis
(together with his wife Margaret) Gerald Lewis (Mary Whitechurch's father) and Frank Lewis (a sea captain).
Front left: Elizabeth married to Rev. Claud Lewis (vicar of Parwich from 1904), Lucy Lewis and Alice Harcombe (née Lewis).

William Samuel infant son of
William and Elizabeth Dale
Who died April 5th 1859
Aged 11 months.
Weep not my Father and Mother
My Brothers, and my Sisters dear
Weep not for I am blest.
For I am where the weary are at rest.
O come to me.

Affectionate Remembrance of
the late James Twigge
who died July 27th 1870
aged 63 years.
Also William, son of the above
who died 8th April 1849
aged 12 years
Also Edward, son of the above
who died Oct 8th 1859 aged 10 years
Also two who died in their infancy.
Also Mary Ann, wife of the above
Who died Nov 4th 1892
aged 85 years

My mother lived in Canada part of the time when she was growing up. Her mother was taken ill with T.B. and died, leaving my mum, aged four, and a little sister six months old. My grandfather had had to pay to try and make her better and it took all the money he had, so he sold up and went to Canada. She used to say that in Canada they skated more or less before they could walk. While she was growing up she used to come back to England by ship, three weeks at a time. She went to school in Canada till she was sixteen, then the family came back to Sheen in Staffordshire and I don't know whether they farmed again or not, but I think they did. Then my mother got married and came to live at Upper Moor Farm, Parwich, in 1937. My mother had a good memory for things, right up to her dying day, even at eighty-four.

My great grandfather got killed under the old railway bridge where the trail is now, as you come out onto the main road at Alsop en le Dale. It was something to do with a horse I think. Of course, my grandfather lived with us and was as much father to me as my own father.

Mary Rawlins

Milk Flour and Steel

Beat up carefully one tablespoonful of flour, one raw egg and twenty grains of saccarated Carbonate of Iron with half a pint of new milk. Flavour with nutmeg and white sugar: to be taken for Lunch. strongly recommended by Dr Broadbent in the early stages of Consumption

Mary Emma Hopkinson

When we got married we lived with Aunty Annie for a while, at a farm just coming into Parwich village. She had five children but she lost every one. She used to call me 'my little ray of sunshine'. Oh she did, I loved Aunty Annie. She and David both died together, within two days of one another, and were buried together on the same day. She always said, "When David goes I want to go as well", and she did.

Dolly Wayne

My aunty was brought up by my great aunty, my granddad's sister, with her being only six months old when her mother died.

Mary Rawlins

I was quite close to my cousin Theresa who lived in Ashbourne, but sadly she died when she was 18. We were more like sisters. I used to go down there and stay, and I did go on holiday with them once or twice. She was an epileptic and she died of an epileptic fit. She was the one who was closest to me; there was only eighteen months between us. My aunty used to come to Grandma's for the day every week, so we used to play together. When we were little we weren't very friendly, we used to fight like mad, but as we got older we became great friends. It was nice having somebody like a sister, it was nice, it was nice.

Valerie Kirkham

Valerie Kirkham with her cousin, Theresa.

On May 8th, 1936, Mary Anne Shaw died peacefully in Parwich at the age of ninety four. During her life time remarkable changes had taken place. She saw the introduction of the plane, the car and the bicycle; the invention of the fridge, the electric cleaner and the gas stove as well as the power that worked them; she witnessed the birth of radio communications, the telephone, Music Halls and jazz. She read of the annexation of India to the British Crown and its disasters such as the Indian Mutiny. Florence Nightingale was one of the women whom Mary Anne might have admired - Mrs Pankhurst was perhaps disliked by her. We do not know. She lived through the First World War and yet followed the progress of the Crimean War and its famous battle, 'The Charge of the Light Brigade'. Slavery in America was abolished after she had married, and the American Civil War fought and won by a Republican army, presided over by Abraham Lincoln. It seems incredible to me that my husband, John, should not only have sat on the lap of Mary Anne but also have a memory of a lady in her rocking chair who had seen so much history made during her long life.

Ann Vidler

Eveline Chadwick aged 2, with her brother, Len, and their grown up sister, Joan.

There is a gap of thirteen years between Eveline and her sister. In between, twins had been born prematurely, but because it was a home delivery, and there had been no means of getting to a hospital quickly, it was not possible to save them.

Attending to the Dead in Neolithic Times

It had been two years since her death. Two years since they had built the frame on which her body was carried to the tomb. A day's walk and a season from the hearth that fed her in her last days... Her husband gave food for the funeral. It lasted three nights. On the last, according to custom, she was placed on the threshold, at the entrance to the house of the old ones.

She was between worlds. A quilt of stones was placed across her body to encourage her to stay and, once this was done, there was the handing on of all she possessed... death came as she slept. She had seen over thirty summers... From then until her funeral, her shade stood by the river, waiting for her kin to arrive...The shaman had spoken to her but she did not reply.... Now... it was time to raise her body, to clean her bones and place them with the others... Many would come and that meant many mouths to feed.... The shaman faced the living... He began with the invocation of names, the chain of generations... As the shadows deepened, he ducked into the tomb... The older woman]...picked up the skull and the longer bones and carried them into the tomb.

Mark Edmonds
"Ancestral Geographies of the Neolithic"

184

Wartime

The Civil War of 1642-9 does not seem to have affected Parwich very much, except that farmers going to Ashbourne Market complained to Cromwell that the Royalist troops proceeding from Tissington Hall to Ashbourne were blocking the roads. A chase of the offenders ended in a brisk encounter at Sharplow, then the practical women went about their business.

Helena Birkentall

The year 1853 is chiefly remembered by me as having been overshadowed by the Crimean War. For more than the life-time of one generation England had taken no part in any European war, and that she should continue to remain at peace with her neighbours, keeping clear of their quarrels and complications, seemed in every way desirable. But by a series of diplomatic blunders it became inevitable that war would be forced upon us. The English people, as a whole, could not understand the cause of the quarrel, and thought that, by political discretion, peace could be maintained. This, I believe, was the opinion of Queen Victoria and her Consort. But it was not to be. War was God's judgment on an ungodly nation, and war was declared.....

The Crimean War, with all its attendant horrors, is a matter of history, and these records only concern my personal memories of this sad season. We foregathered with our young friends each day to spend hours in making "comforts" for the soldiers. which probably, through vile mismanagement of those responsible, never reached them. No other subject or employment seemed at that time worthy of our attention. The mission of Florence Nightingale was of intense interest to us. With her we had a tie of kindred, her father being second cousin to our mother, and my relatives being closely intimate with her family. I never knew her personally as she was a good deal older than I, and before I was grown up she had withdrawn from her own family circle to devote herself to hospital work. "A craze" this was pronounced at the time, and her action was severely criticised by her friends and relations. I remember the sarcastic remark of a young man cousin when she was the centre of national admiration, "Oh, yes, we are all going to be proud of Florence now."

Mrs. Curtis

Of old scholars of Parwich School who went out into the world, one thinks first of the little band of volunteers who went in 1899 to fight in the Boxer War. Most of them are dead now, but one who sent greetings to his folk in Parwich this last Christmas, fought in both World Wars as well as in the Boxer War.

Helena Birkentall

Keep the home-flag flying;"
that's the cry we hear today,
While our gallant lads in blue
and khaki are away,
Housewife, do your bit as well,
and fight against expense,
As bravely as the menfolk give
their all in our defence.

From: *The Best Way Cookbook No. 3,*
A Practical Guide for the Housewife.
(World War One)

Most of those who went from the village to the First World War were natives and schoolboys of Parwich. Eight did not return, and the cross erected by the people in memory of these sons of Parwich bears the familiar names of people who have lived for generations in the village. The carillon of bells erected by a lord of the manor is rung every Sunday, and should remind us that it rings in memory of these gallant men of ours who gave their lives for all that Parwich meant to them. As the years passed by one saw the terrible effect on the anxious and bereaved parents and relatives of the long years of war. Most of these people were themselves scholars of the school and had sent one, two, three, and even four sons from the village overseas. They were never the same again.

Helena Birkentall

The Parwich War memorial is a Limestone Celtic Cross which stands beside the church gate, bearing this inscription:

**To the glory of God
this cross is placed here by the
people of Parwich in honoured
memory of the men who fought and died
in the Great War AD 1914 - 1919**

Pte Albert Roberts, *The Sherwood Foresters*
Pte Leonard Twigge, *The Sherwood Foresters*
Pte Thomas Twigge *The Sherwood Foresters*
Pte Thomas Hadfield, *Lincolnshire Regt.*
Sgt Fred Moorcroft, *The Sherwood Foresters*
Pte Arthur Calladine, *Rifle Brigade*

1939 – 1945

Pte Ronald Cotteril, *R.A.S.C*
Sgt Brunskill Lowes, *Lancashire Fusiliers*
Grdsn William Mace, *Grenadier Guards*
Tpr Robin Philips, *Royal Armoured Corps*
Pte Jack Steeples, *The Sherwood Foresters*

These were the brothers, husbands and sons of Parwich women. Other service men and women were more fortunate: they survived to tell the tale, returning home to their grateful families. There are photographs in existence of Parwich men in uniform stretching over 85 years, from Fred Moorcroft, who never returned from the First World War, through to Alan Hickmott who joined the army in 2002.

Places where people have been posted range from Nottingham to Germany, Cyprus, Singapore, Burma, India, Bosnia, Ireland, Iceland, Norway, the Arctic and Antarctic. There were those who cooked, those who tended the wounded, those who drove, those who defused bombs, those who operated wirelesses, climbed mountains, who had been evacuated from Dunkirk, raced over the deserts after Rommel and landed on the beaches at Normandy.

Florence (Flo) Harris

I knew you in this dark; for so you frowned
Yesterday through me as you jabbed and killed.
I parried; but my hands were loath and cold.
Let us sleep now…'

Wilfred Owen

1. Fred Moorcroft, pictured here, and with his men, was killed on 3rd January, 1918. He served as a Sergeant in the Sherwood Foresters.

2. Kathleen Allsopp holds a cumbersome World War 1 gas mask.

"Whatever hope is yours,
Was my life also; I went hunting wild
After the beauty in the world…"

Wilfred Owen.

There are soldiers of the ploughshare as well as soldiers of the sword, said Ruskin. There are soldiers in the little homes all over England as well as soldiers in the trenches - housewife-soldiers, with no deadlier weapon than frying-pan and saucepan, yet with the true, brave spirit, can help their country by saving every penny and making war-time meals as appetising as in times of peace, at half the cost.

Pickled Pig's Cheek

This can be served with roast potatoes, haricot beans, and parsley sauce. If you buy half a pig's head, the cheek can be used for this dish, and the rougher parts-the ear, nose, and half the tongue (and buy a trotter as well) - can be made into a collared head for another day.

To pickle the cheek, put it in a bread crock, and put over it one ounce of salt-petre, one ounce of bay salt, half a pound of black treacle, and a quarter of a pound of brown sugar. The cheek should be left for a fortnight in this pickle, and turned every day. To cook, put in cold water and add a tablespoon of black treacle, a tablespoonful of vinegar, and a bunch of herbs; half a lemon stuck with cloves can be used instead of vinegar. Simmer till done, peel off the skin, and shake brown breadcrumbs on the top.

Economical Sausages

When cooking sausages, put them in water and bring to the boil; then skin them, roll in flour, and fry in hot fat. Cooked in this way they will not shrink.

A Milk Preservative

A simple and effective way to prevent milk turning sour is to drop a small piece of clean horseradish into it when new. This will keep the milk fresh for several days.

Cheap Pastry

Are you fond of pastry? It is expensive if made with butter. Make potato pastry for pies that are to be eaten hot. Take equal quantities of boiled potatoes and flour, mash the potatoes with a little milk and salt, then rub them gently into the flour, adding a little baking powder. Then, with cold water, mix the whole to a stiff dough, roll out quickly, and use and bake at once.

Extracts, including the first paragraph, on this page are taken from:
The Best Way Cookbook No 3

MRS ADAHLIA BOWER-MABSON photographed with her husband before he left for the Front.
He never came home, having been reported missing in action. It is said that each evening she walked
to her garden gate and looked along the road, as though believing that one day he would return.

World War II

During the Second World War, Esther Brownson gave much of her time to organising the local branch of the Red Cross. She had boundless energy and enthusiasm and efficiently organised women into making knitted garments for the troops. After the war the Duchess of Devonshire was formally introduced to Esther and she was given a citation for her efforts. She was invited to become the Regional Commandant, a great honour in those days, but turned down the offer.

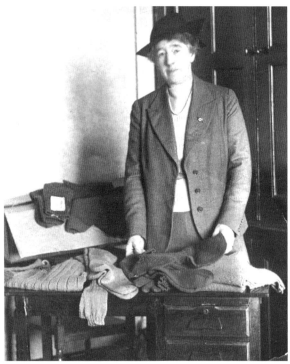

Mrs. Esther Brownson with garments knitted by Parwich women for the troops

The first air raid alert was an experience that Granny Brownson was often to laugh about many years later. Apparently, the village policeman cycled furiously through the village blowing his whistle. Believing the whole might of the German air force to be directed straight at them, they waited in the living room for the worst to happen. Blankets were doused in a zinc bucket to protect grandson Peter should gas be dropped; gas masks were nervously clutched in readiness and all ears were strained for the dreaded sound of enemy aircraft overhead. After some hours of anticipation and a slight relaxation of precautions, a telephone call was made to the policeman to enquire for news only to find that he had been awakened from his sleep by the 'phone ringing! Apparently he had forgotten to notify the public of the 'ALL CLEAR'. One wonders if his whistle was ever taken seriously again!

Ann Vidler

It was hard living at Upper Moor farm during the war, but living on a farm we were better off than some people. We had our produce to eat, chickens and geese and so on. Oh we took no harm, no harm at all. We sort of just accepted it - we knew no different.

Mary Rawlins

I was born in 1940, and while the war was on, we used to go into Chesterfield Queen's Park for all six weeks of the August holidays and also for the Whitsun holidays, what they used to call the 'stay at home' holidays. I can remember us leaving Chesterfield Queen's Park and coming to Wakes in Parwich.

Clara Evans

In *The Housewife's Guide to Making and Mending,* written to help hard-pressed housewives during World War II, it is suggested that it would be a good idea to make "a pair of knickers from an old jersey". No doubt the resulting garment was warm but also extremely itchy! The method was recommended as being particularly good with "a girl's woven jersey when the sleeves wear out or the jersey is outgrown." Boys fared better with "Pyjamas from Daddy's".

A PAIR OF KNICKERS FROM AN OLD JERSEY

Wrong Side

As a small child I remember being taken to a dressmaker by my grandmother to have some rather splendid dresses cut down to size. Unfortunately the material was far too grand to be comfortable and I resented bitterly the fact that I was being clothed in somebody's cast offs!

Gillian Radcliffe

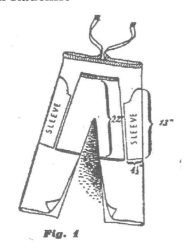

Fig. 1

Pyjama's from Daddy's

I remember when bread was on ration. It was evening time and Harry had had his tea and this was later on, when he often used to have bread and cheese; and I said, "You can't have bread, Harry. I've run out of bread until we get our ration tomorrow," and he said alright love, I'll have toast!"

Ella Hopkinson

When I worked at the Cottage Hospital in Ashbourne during the war all the doctors used to go on the rook shoot and bring these horrible things to the hospital to make rook pie! Only the breast was cooked. Cook used to go mad, she absolutely loathed it, chopping the beastly things up and then stewing them in a slow cooker with onions, to make a casserole in pastry. We had to eat it once a year, the staff as well as the patients. If we hadn't known what it was we'd have taken it to be some beast like chicken or stringy game.

Betty Stone

Peter Rawlins: I can just about remember them burning lime at that quarry that's overgrown up Parwich Dale, back down Whitecliffe.

Ambrose Wilton: I remember during wartime old Mrs. Webster at the farm, very timid and frightened she was when the German planes were over, and you could always see a nick of flame on top o't kiln as it were burning; and she used to create at beast door and say, "They'll be blowing us up", and he'd say, "Well, I'll tell you what, Mrs. Webster, if one drops I'll come and tell ya, and never did nothing about it!"

191

Charlotte Halliday at the Fold with her father, Edward Halliday

It was to Parwich we came when war was imminent. A friend advised us to get out of London on the evening of September 1st, and my parents packed up the car and drove through the night. I think I remember standing round a radio hearing Mr. Chamberlain on September 3rd. This was two days before my fourth birthday! After living in London, Parwich was a revelation of what life could really be like. I remember feeling that everything was different and exciting, even the beds we slept in!

Our parents had met the Crompton-Inglefields in the mid 1930s and had become lifelong friends. My father, Edward Halliday,

an artist, must have painted every member of the family - Sir John (Colonel as we first knew him) when he was High Sheriff of Derbyshire, Sir John and his wife on horseback, the two elder girls with their rocking horse on the lawn, and so on. A portrait of Sir John by my father still hangs in the Memorial Hall in Parwich. And thus my parents came to rent The Fold, a lovely old house in the centre of Parwich where Sir John built a studio for my father. It was a very long way from our London home so it was not a weekend cottage, but we continued to spend holidays there, once or twice a year, then, a lot later on, we stayed as guests at the Hall.

Around '39/40, Father did a painting of the state rooms at Chatsworth which was being used as a dormitory by its 'evacuees' (a girls' school, Penhros College) which visitors see there to this day. But he was also busy helping to form L.D.V. (Local Defence Volunteers) in Parwich, and my brother remembers that his experiences of the wrong supplies - from uniforms to ammunition - as well as trying to get his squad to drill, were far more extraordinary than anything "Dad's Army" could later invent. Soon they were renamed the Home Guard, and acquired khaki and proper rifles, but at the outset they simply had armbands and whatever weapons (including pitchforks!) they could lay their hands on. They made an old caravan into a lookout post on Parwich Hill and set up roadblocks which my brother, then six, remembers would not have stopped a bicycle. His drilling must have borne fruit, because they mounted a smart Guard of Honour which the Princess Royal inspected when she paid an official visit to the Military Convalescent Home.

The soldiers at the hospital in their sky blue suits and scarlet ties were a familiar sight about the village. Later in 1940 my father volunteered for the RAF, and my poor mother

The Parwich Home Guard reviewed by Princess Alice, the Princess Royal.

The Duchess of Kent visits the Rathborne Hospital, Parwich.

had to be given a crash course in driving. Our little Ford was very unreliable and to coax it across Derbyshire, along unsignposted roads, and with limited petrol, was <u>not</u> amusing. And somebody still had to fetch our drinking water from the village pump until the arrival of mains water, through the great Stanton pipes which we had long seen lying ready for installation beside the road.

By 1942 father had been seconded to a part of SOE, (Special Operations Executive) and was setting up a communications unit on the edge of Woburn Park, so we moved to Bedfordshire, and after that made only occasional visits to Derbyshire.

Charlotte Halliday

At the age of sixteen I went to work at Parwich Hospital as a Red Cross V.A.D. (Voluntary Aid Detachment). It had changed to a hospital when war was declared in 1939; before then it was a convalescent home for gentle ladies. The nurses were mostly well-to-do women, who didn't want to join the Forces and could afford to buy their own uniforms. I was determined to make something of my life, and was delighted when the matron agreed to take me on. My father was not so keen on the idea: perhaps he'd heard that V.A.D. stood not only for Voluntary Aid Detachment, but was jokingly known as 'Virgins Awaiting Destruction'. I nursed there for three years, suffering no calamity other than a chipped tooth, acquired while walking down Kiln Lane with a bedpan, pursued by my friend Iris brandishing a stinging nettle!

The hospital was staffed with a matron, two sisters, a physiotherapist, and V.A.Ds. We had a female ambulance driver, and a land army girl looked after the gardens. There were also

Eileen Ellis, Red Cross V.A.D.

two Sergeant Majors dealing with administration. Dr. Hollick from Ashbourne visited most days or when needed. Mr. Pulfertaft (a top orthopaedic surgeon based at Derby Royal Infirmary) visited when required, as he was the person who had performed most of the operations.

The patients were all members of the Armed Forces suffering mainly from orthopaedic injuries, which meant most of them were in plasters of some kind. When they were mobile, they all had to wear saxe blue suits, white shirts, and red ties. V.A.Ds had to buy their own uniform, and received fifteen shillings per month. At staff meals we had to stand behind our chairs until matron or sister walked in. After she had sat down, we could sit. I remember she made me drink a glass of

194

CHRISTMAS AT PARWICH HOSPITAL. Front row from left: Sheila Brownlee, Peggy Fearn, Jessie Gibbs, Eileen Ellis (née Steeples) Edna Dennis, ?, Irene Wilton (née Lees) Mollie Brownlee. The 'devil' is Godfrey Brownson.

STAFF AND CONVALESCENTS AT THE RATHBORNE HOSPITAL, PARWICH

milk stout every day because she thought I looked anaemic! Off duty in the afternoons, we would take some of the patients, who would be on crutches, legs in plaster, over the Bletches to Tissington, where we would have a boiled egg tea at one of the farms. We would always be rushing back to get on duty at 5 p.m. - a minute late and we would be in trouble!

Most evening we had some kind of entertainment, ENSA concerts, or cine films, or we would play cards or dominoes. At Christmas we put on staff Pantomimes. They were great times and I made lots of friends. I am still in contact with three of them and visit them at least once a year.

We had great fun but we also had to work very hard. Our shifts started at 7 a.m. and went on to 2 p.m.. We had three hours off, then back on duty from 5 p.m. until 8.30 p.m. That was called a split shift, otherwise it was from 7 a.m. until 5 p.m. Night duty was from 8.30 p.m. until 7 a.m.

Three years later I decided there was a big wide world outside of Parwich and I had to see some of it. I was now nineteen years old, so I decided to join the nursing service in the 'Wrens' (W.R.N.S.) and was on H.M.S. Mercury, a training ship for radar, but that is another story. I married Don Ellis and went to live in Wales, and returned to Parwich only 3 years ago.

Eileen Ellis

Housekeeping for the housewife was difficult in wartime. I was in the army, came home on leave for a week. Saturday night, after we'd shut the pub at 11 o'clock, me dad says, "We're going up to Knob Hall at 12 o'clock." That was ration days, you know.

RON BIRCH, ROYAL ARTILLERY 1945 – 1951.
A driver, mechanic who served in Germany. One of a number of gallant Parwich men and women in the Services.

He had a Hillman Minx which he'd bought for £30, and we drove to Knob Hall at 12 o'clock and cut half a pig up, brought it down to the Sycamore and put it on the thrall. It was the same with the 7 tons of coal me dad used to get. My brother and me'd come back after doing some building work and find at the back, where the cellar is now, a lot of coal tipped out. One of these miners had come in't pub. So we got it in quick. They used to come rabbiting round our fields and we got to know them well, and that's how we got 7 ton loads of coal during rationing.

Ken Wayne

We were eleven when war broke out, and my twin brother had already gone on to the boy's school in Guernsey while I was still at the Froebel school. We were evacuated as a school from Guernsey and came over in boats that had been to Dunkirk. Aunt Susan (née Lewis), my father's sister, was living in Worcester, and took my brother and me on during the war and the occupation of the Channel Isles. It was five or six years before we saw our parents again.

Liberation Day was the 8th May 1945, but it took three months to get official permission to return. When my brother and I went back to Guernsey after the war, we were sixteen years old. One of the first things we had to do was to take our English Identity Cards down into the town and have them stamped to say we were allowed to be on the island and had a reason for being there. My father, Gerald Lewis, took us down. We went into an office, and I remember there was a man behind the counter who wanted to stamp my card: it said something about a scar on my wrist, and he wanted to see it, and I was being quite pleasant and chatting away, but could feel my father shifting from one foot to the other, and I thought, oh dear, perhaps I'm talking too much, as you do when you're sixteen and a bit nervous. Then when we came out, my father said, "You shouldn't have been speaking to him!" So I said, "Oh, I'm sorry," because of course I didn't know my father, I hadn't seen him for five or six years, and I'd been eleven when I'd last seen him; and I remember all these feelings, of surprise and nervousness. My father said, "You musn't speak to that man or have any doings again with him. Only answer what he asks. He's a collaborator."

That was in August 1945. Of course, some people had made vast amounts of money out of the war. Some felt it was right to make money out of the Germans. Others felt that was wrong, because you were selling food to the Germans that could have been keeping the population alive. Others felt that everybody should be looking after themselves, and the devil take the hindmost. One of my father's greatest friends, a very intellectual man, used to play chess with a German who was also very intellectual and well read, and my father thought this was terrible. They used to play chess in the evenings after the curfew, because the Germans were allowed to move around, but the indigenous people were not.

Mary Whitechurch

Freda Kinder once told me about a trip she made from Parwich to the Channel Islands in the early 1950s. While she has no connection with Germany, her name has a Germanic connotation, and she was treated, as she said, like dirt. She'd never been so unhappy in all her life and she couldn't wait to get home!

Michael Radcliffe

Every night during the Second World War, Lord Haw Haw tried to guide the German bombers to Derby using the cross of trees on Parwich Hill as a landmark. Their target was Rolls Royce in Derby. The city suffered heavy bombing. and I remember sitting at the door of the bungalow watching the bombing and the searchlights.

The arrival of the evacuees from Leigh-on-Sea in Essex was a great excitement for us. I used to go sledging with them. A lot of the evacuees must have been frightened. They'd been taken away from home, and even maltreated. Some poor things came with head lice, and one child yelled for weeks because there was no fish and chip shop in the village. I remember how cruel the schoolmaster was that came with them, and how often he used to beat the boys. They spent half a day in the Institute and the afternoons in school. We used to have to go on nature walks in the

197

Evacuees at Fernlea

afternoon, or work in the allotments in the Square. It was quite an interesting time of life. We had these gas masks that had to be carried to school every day. The siren would go, and we were all supposed to go down in the coal hole which had got a flat, concrete roof, but we three sisters used to run home. We lived going out of the village, and by the time we got home, it would be the All Clear, so we were running backwards and forwards all day with these gas masks. We were definitely not going to die in the coke hole!

Kathleen Allsopp

In 1940 the evacuees arrived from Leigh-on-Sea in Essex. They brought their own teacher with them, and they used the Village Institute for most of their classes. We found it great fun having all these new boys in the village. I

was thirteen, and I formed a friendship with a fourteen year old boy called Joe, and we have kept in touch for some sixty years. He has five children and sixteen grandchildren. Thank goodness I didn't marry him!

A strange thing happened in connection with the evacuees. We were with Gill Radcliffe at Flaxdale House and had been talking about the war, and I had just said, "Of course, we haven't mentioned the evacuees who came to Parwich," when the phone rang and it was an evacuee, Derek Fill, ringing completely out of the blue. He had seen the website of Flaxdale House and wanted to know whether the owners were related to Jack Ratcliffe; (They are not, by the way). It was an uncanny moment. He used to live two doors away from me and went to school in Bradbourne. He lives at Trelawn Gardens, Leigh on Sea, and was Chief Accountant with C.T.Bowering.

Eileen Ellis

- I remember when the evacuees came and I made friends with one of them. She came from a very big family.
- They fetched them back home you know; they were frightened of what they would say. Their grandma had IRA men in her cellar. She lived in Manchester. Little Mary said, "Grandma's got IRA men down in her cellar."
- She told me about child abuse and all kinds of things I'd never heard of.
- They didn't know where milk came from, or beans or anything that grew in the garden. You couldn't believe it. I wonder what they lived on; fish and chips I imagine? They were very poor. We used to put Mary on a chair to sing: she was a lovely little singer.
- The evacuees weren't all treated fairly. There was a lot that didn't want them, but were

forced to have them because they'd got the room for them to sleep. I know one or two in Parwich where they weren't good to them.

-They used them, didn't they, and made them work?

-I remember one girl that came to a person in Parwich. She'd only got one daughter and naturally this child come, and she'd got nits, and she wouldn't have her nowhere near. They sat at a different table and in the finish they took her off.

- Well, we was very kind with them. They were happy enough with us, you know

-My friend never wanted to go home. She was very happy.

Coffee morning in Parwich

I can remember the war breaking out when I was three, and all the kerfuffle, and putting the curtains up for the blackout. I was sitting on the settle (an old fashioned one with a wooden back and wooden arms and a box seat). And I remember my father being in the Home Guard. I remember walking out in the fields when they bombed Sheffield and you could see it all ablaze from Upper Moor.

My dad had German prisoners of war from the camp at Biggin to work on the farm. They used to come up the lane and all they had was half a loaf of dry bread with a little hole poked out in the middle with a cooked sausage in it, and that was their dinner. I used to go and look and I said, "What's that?" I think we had two prisoners at a time. They worked well, I never heard any complaints and they were very nice people. They used to make all kinds of things, like cigarette lighters out of metal, and they made an aeroplane, and then they made a bat, with strings through and a weight at the bottom and chickens on the top that pecked, and they'd sort of burnt the wood in patterns. They brought me and my brother one each.

At Biggin school during the war we used to hang our gas masks on the back of those little tiny infant chairs, and every so often we had to have a rehearsal type thing. My brother had a gas mask that the whole baby went into: a piece came up between the legs and just the legs stuck out. It was a frightening looking thing, that was. I remember crying the first time I saw it because I thought, where the heck's he going? I don't think we ever had to use it.

Mary Rawlins

In 1938 my brother Jack was born and in 1940 I came along. By this time the war was breaking out and Father was sent to work at Markham's, a munitions factory in Chesterfield, but he was later moved to Grantham. We went with him and Mother continued opening up the fairground while father was doing his bit for the war, until a bomb landed in the nearby mere and shot muck over the van and the fairground. After that, Mother begged Father to take us back to Derbyshire.

Clara Evans

We came to Parwich just before the war started and I was away for six years till the war finished. When it started I was called up and sent to Bliss's, an American firm making twelve pounders, shells. The factory was just outside Derby and I was billeted in Derby. In the village where I came from you knew everyone, but there I never saw the next door neighbours. I was used to being on the farm in the open air and Derby wasn't nice at all. I had to work at Chester Green and I lived a good way from there, up Babbington Lane. I used to walk because that was the only fresh air we got. And then a soldier followed me one night. Well that did it; I was terrified. I could see him behind me all the time. So then I got a bicycle and cycled to work.

At Bliss's during the bombing we had to go down in the 'dungeon', a cellar underneath the building. Not far from where I was billeted my cousin got under the table during an air raid but she was caught and she died. There were four hundred working at the factory. We had to work a fortnight without a break, and then we had a day off and started again on Monday night at seven o'clock and worked until seven the next morning. Bliss's was dreadful. I suffered a lot with stomach trouble then. Just looking up at the lights, you could see all the brass floating around. You had to handle three thousand shell cases a night or day, whichever shift you were on. Each shell weighed about six pound. There were great big furnaces and the work absolutely ruined my hands. We had to keep putting them in this stuff like soap when it's gone like jelly. There was a big punch that used to go up and down, up and down, and the brass kept coming on conveyor belts and you'd got to be careful. The girl I worked for had her thumb taken off because she was holding the thing wrongly. The brass came in round, like a plate, and it kept going through the machines until it was tall enough. It went through different furnaces. It was so hot they used to have to take us outside to cool off. We went out every morning and had toast and dripping. It was a nightmare but I made lots of good friends there.

Then I was moved from Bliss's into Ashbourne, to Royce's where we made parts for Merlin engines. It had been a corset factory for years. In Ashbourne we worked from seven o'clock in the morning till seven at night. I had a good job as a turner, working on the Capstan lathe. It was a lot better than Bliss's. It was hard but we were happy: it was the same even at Bliss's; we were so happy there.

I used to cycle to work from Parwich to Ashbourne and I was frightened to death because it was dark and in the winter it was awful. I was absolutely petrified at times. Coming home from Ashbourne, Bradbourne brook runs towards the Dove and I remember cycling and looking down, and I could see a man who'd drowned himself. So I cycled on as fast as I could! He was a Parwich man, but I can't remember his name. Another time, I was frightened by such a terrible noise that seemed to be following me, but next day I found out it was only an old shed with a loose piece of corrugated iron. It was a wonder I didn't get a heart attack! I cycled on my own: nobody else in Parwich was called up, I think.

Dolly Wayne

When I came to Parwich I discovered that some of the young people had never seen the sea or even been out of the village, and I used to think to myself, what do they think about all day long, because I'd got so many memories, especially from my time with the Rothschild family? My parents couldn't afford to send me to college, so I said that I would start at the bottom, though my mother really didn't want me to. I think she thought I was going into private service, and she didn't want that. But I've always loved

Ella Hopkinson's young charges in their carriage

Ella and Harry Hopkinson

children and I still do, so I started as a nurserymaid for thirteen pound a year! My mother and dad had to buy my uniform and have my shoes mended because taking the prams out, we had a lot of walking to do.

At night time I had to clean the prams. Though the children never ate food in them they still had to be wiped out. They were the big wheeled prams. I don't regret my nursery days. I didn't have a lot of money but then nobody did. We stayed at Claridge's for three months once, and we had room service. I mean, in ordinary life I wouldn't have had that, would I? It was a wonderful life. I was with them about two years, but then the war came along and they said looking after children wasn't important, so of course I left, but I'm always glad I had that experience. I was just getting to the stage where I was getting good money and then it was all taken away.

When the war came, I went to a nursery school, and there were two hundred and fifty children there. This was in the country because in wartime the children had to come out of London; and they asked me what age group I wanted to see after, and I said over two but under five. I had twenty-five children to see after, and that was only for about a pound a week. Then I was ill: I think I was trying to see after every child and it got me down, and the doctor said, "You're not to go back there," and I said," Well what do I do? And he said, "Do hospital nursing." So I joined Civil Defence and nursed at Addenbrooks Hospital for the rest of the war and I loved every minute of it. My mother used to say to me, "Ella, you'll have some horrible things to do," and I said, "Well I can try." And I thought of her many a time when the blackouts were up and I had lots of horrible jobs to do; but no, I loved every minute of it. That was for a pound a week, four pounds a month, and you had to pay half a crown out of that for your laundry, as well as your National Insurance; and it all had to come out of that one pound. When we came here, Hallcliffe was a nurses' home, because there were lots of soldiers up at the hospital then.

Ella Hopkinson

I started nursing at Bretby Hall Orthopaedic Hospital. I went there because they accepted probationers at 17 instead of 18 years of age. Of course, in those days there was a lot of tuberculosis, so we got all the tuberculosis bone cases, some of whom might well be in the hospital for 2-3 years, maybe even longer than that. I was due to start there in the same month that the war began, and the week before, the hospital was almost evacuated. Everyone who could possibly be sent home was, because there was a big panic on and everyone expected dreadful air raids overnight. Of course, nothing happened, and gradually the regular patients came back. Then we were to take servicemen; great excitement; men who could actually walk about; but to my amazement most of them were in for varicose veins, hammer toes, flat feet, and various other things to do with their feet. They either couldn't get their boots on, or they couldn't walk far enough! The other cases we got were ones mishandled elsewhere, like shattered bones. Yes, it was quite exciting to see people coming in and going out within three weeks, and different faces coming in.

At Bretby there were people who came in to entertain. There would be a music hall from a group of amateur performers, and sometimes classical music, solo violins, small groups. We used to take as many beds as we could into the biggest ward and pack them in for the performance.

I didn't complete my training; I got sidetracked into looking after children. I worked in a hostel for evacuees in Duffield, and they were all the unbilletable children, all had problems. It was a lovely job. I worked there for four years and then gradually the children were taken back home and the hostels closed. There was a hostel in Ashbourne at the time, and when Duffield closed I remember bringing two of the children to the one there. After that I was sent (as we were still war conscripts) to the Ashbourne Cottage Hospital for about 18 months. It wasn't actually touched by the war, just non-acute cases and a bit of surgery, appendicitis and that sort of thing. It was a nice little hospital and it was very useful because the patients' own G.P.s came in and ordered their treatment and visited them, but of course those little units became uneconomical and they are nearly all closed now.

Betty Stone

At the start of the War my sister and I were weekly boarders at St. Ronan's but my youngest sister was still at home. In the orchard we kept two goats, Gert and Daisy, for milk. This was used to make cream cheese. We had a lovely Scottish nanny, who would make the cheese next to the nursery. I remember it dripping over basins covered with muslin. We always called her Na, but her real name was Elsie Gordon Cameron. She was married during the War to Leslie Jackson, a draughtsman at Rolls Royce in Derby. She died quite young, in her fifties, of cancer. During the war the gardens at the Hall were dug up for produce. The goats went, but we had ducks and hens in the orchard. We used to put down the eggs in isinglass in the cellar. I remember peering into the big crocks to see if the eggs were floating and therefore bad.

In the early part of the war my mother worked for the Women's Land Army in Matlock. Petrol rationing was not so strict then and she used to drive there each day. 1940 was a dreadful winter and I don't know how she managed it. Owen Twigge, who had lost a leg in the First World War, and Arthur Gibbs were the roadmen. They used to clear the snow. It always seemed to blow into the road on the bend by Gypsy Lane, as you come into the village. They just had simple wooden snowploughs and shovels: I don't know how they were pulled, there were so few tractors then. Perhaps horses pulled them. My youngest sister (*Mrs. Kilner*) remembers terrible leaks in the roof of the Hall that winter, with buckets on the top floor to catch the drips before the roof was replaced.

At the beginning of the war in 1939 my mother started a knitting party. Younger people came to it. I know it was in the dining

THE CROMPTON-INGLEFIELDS. The family came to live in Parwich Hall in 1931. Back: John Crompton-Inglefield, Gilbert Inglefield. Second from back: Rosemary, with baby Caroline on her knee, Patricia, Isma, Mrs. Gilbert Inglefield, and her baby; in front: Lady Crompton-Inglefield with child of Mr & Mrs Gilbert Inglefield.

room at Parwich Hall, and a lot of young people came to knit socks and balaclavas and things like that. My father was stationed in Lincolnshire with the Derbyshire Yeomanry, guarding Boston docks. Then it was thought the Germans might invade on the East Coast. My mother could get enough petrol to drive across to see him. Later, she did not know where he was and for two months there was no news.

It was feared there would be gas attacks. I remember a funny thing in the village that looked rather like a bird table on a pole situated on what were the allotments then, opposite the Hall. It was made of what looked like paper that would have turned green in the event of a gas attack. During air raids we sheltered in the drawing room. My mother brought us in together with the cats and canaries and sealed up the door, and there we slept until the 'all clear', which was sounded by the policeman blowing his whistle as he rode round the village on his bicycle!

In 1943 the Hall was shut up. I was aged 13 years. We children went to live with our Grandmother at Flower Lilies. Although we saw little of our parents we had a wonderfully happy time with our Grandmother. There were plans to use the Hall as an overflow for the convalescing soldiers at the Hospital, but I don't think it was ever used. Mr. Shields, the gardener, (no relation to the Shields that own the Hall now), just kept the gardens ticking over. The garden where the pond is now was used for vegetables for the hospital, and the front lawn kept for the soldiers to play football.

My mother joined the M.T.C. (Motor Transport Corps) and then the ATS. She went through the ranks and was posted as junior Commander with the 21st Army Group in London under Montgomery and narrowly missed the flying bomb which landed on the Guards Chapel. She had asked to serve overseas, but was refused because she had young children. Ironically she was then posted to Dover which was very heavily bombed. My father was in North Africa with the Yeomanry under General Alexander. He was wounded and was sent to the USA to lecture. Later after D-Day he served in Europe, crossing the Rhine with A P Herbert. During the 1944 invasion he was attached to General Sir Percy Hobart, Montgomery's brother in law, and worked on the 'funnies' tanks in Dorset in preparation for the Normandy landings. He had to practise getting out of a submerged tank. I remember once he came home on leave, but my sister and I were away at boarding school and had chicken pox, so we couldn't see him.

My father and mother were both demobbed in about July 1945. Just before the war my mother had bought a seaside house at West Wittering which had been requisitioned. We spent that first summer after the war there. I remember there was still barbed wire on the beach. I was at boarding school at the time, so I did not return to Parwich until Christmas. After the war, life gradually started to return to normal, though there was still rationing to contend with.

By the time the the war was over, the gardens at the Hall were overrun with ragwort, 'stinking Willie' as my father called it, so in 1946 he organised ragwort pulling parties for us. It was difficult with the petrol rationing to have any social life at Parwich and I was seventeen at the time (1947). In 1949 I went to London to work as a secretary in the Foreign Office. My younger sister (*Mrs. Lutyens*) joined the W.R.N.S.

Patricia Bagshawe

A PICNIC IN WARTIME

Charlotte Halliday enjoys a sandwich on a picnic with her mother, Mrs. D.L. Halliday, Diana Darling (a family friend) her brother Stephen, and Nanny, Melanie Jelinek.

VICTORY, PEACE AND REMEMBRANCE

[On] the eleventh day of the eleventh month of 1918, when the Armistice was signed which closed the First World War... [b]ells were rung, we saw the German prisoners of war leaving Alsop Moor for the last time, and in the evening the first Thanksgiving Service was held in Parwich Church. The church was crowded, and all were as one in grateful Sympathy when the Vicar exhorted us to "Rejoice with those that do rejoice, And weep with those that mourn," for the "bereaved" were with us, also the "anxious" who would not know for some days whether their loved ones would return to Parwich.

H. Birkentall

On 11 November, came Remembrance Day, a service that I loved almost more than any other; the hymns, *Eternal Father* and *Onward Christian Soldiers*; the Last Post; the poem *In Flanders' Field*; and finally, processing outside to the war memorial, often in the rain, always in the wind and cold, the vicar's robes billowing around him as he walked, and standing there beside my father, head bowed, looking at the wet, glistening gravel as the 2 minute silence was held. Best of all, though, was going with him and the men of the village, ex-servicemen all, up to the British Legion hall and hiding behind him while all the men drank beer and swapped stories. I am now an associate member of the Royal British Legion myself, partly because my son is a serving soldier (in Iraq, as I write) but largely because of those Remembrance Day services in Parwich when I was small.

Angela Dodds

Beatrice and Fred Graham
at the Victory Ball, 1918

"Empire's Honour", Ashbourne Town Hall, during World War 1; by Miss Lewis.

Snow blocking Kiln Lane 1947

Christmas

[An old woman] told us also how every Christmas a wagon with four horses appeared in the village, sent by my grandfather from Derby, laden with the useful and homely produce of a draper's shop, not for sale to the people, but for simple distribution, and there was always material for every need. "Most demoralising, most destructive of all spirit of independence," no doubt would be the comment of the modern political economist: but, as my husband afterwards remarked, the people in that remote northern village were hungry, and poor, and ignorant, and in those simpler days the one remedy appeared to be to comfort them and supply their needs. Somehow I do not think that the benefactors, now all gone aloft, will miss the final commendation, "Inasmuch as ye have done it unto the least of these My brethren, ye have done it unto Me."

Mrs. Curtis

Christmas Eve was posset-time. There was milk at all the farms free for all, and it was a common sight to see children going early in the morning with can and pail to collect the milk.

Most children preferred the bread and milk before the spiced-ale was put into it, but all enjoyed the hot mince-pies which followed. I was reminded while writing these notes that the word posset had not died out of the Parwich language. A friend of mine rang up to tell me that on returning from a cold drive they had posset for supper, and slept well and warm.

Helena Birkentall

At Christmas the Hall was festooned with lots of holly and there was a tree in the drawing room. This was decorated with baubles collected over the years. We had none of the themed Christmas trees you get now. There was a fairy on top with lights and beautiful tinsel. I think some of the tinsel I still use came from Parwich. The drawing room curtains were kept open so people could see the tree. The smell of the freshly cut Christmas tree has stayed with me for the rest of my life, it's so evocative, and I remember the excitement of waking to the stockings filled with an orange and chocolate money. At Easter time we had Easter egg hunts in the gardens. I remember the wonderful smell of dark chocolate.

One Christmas holiday we had a dance/party. The snow came down, and I thought no one would get to it. I remember sitting on the stairs. People came by train from Buxton to Alsop station. I don't remember who did the catering: catering was difficult and we had to get a licence to lay on a party with ham, turkey and mince pies. In 1947, during my last term at boarding school in the south, there was a terrible winter. I remember my mother saying each day she would walk with the dogs to see how the men were getting on with digging a way out of the village. A plane went down carrying coal.

Patricia Bagshawe

We had a great time at Christmas with the Christmas tree, and a real party on. During the war I wanted a tricycle and of course you couldn't get new ones but they managed to get me a second hand one and it had been all painted up, and I thought I'd got the world. The kids used to come back with me from school, especially after we could get the bus, and we used to ride this tricycle round the kitchen and in the sitting room, although the house was not very big. My mother loved it; she was like a mother hen, a bit like me in that respect. A friend of my mum's on the next farm at Gotham, gave me a very old doll when I was little. It had got ever such funny joints and the most beautiful face. It would be worth a penny or two now. We played and played with it.

We used to have the carol singers come all the way from Elton and my mum used to invite them in. I was in bed and I'd hear these noises, and I used to get right under the covers and think, gosh, what's going on? Maybe Santa's coming! Then you could hear them singing and it was absolutely lovely. Mum used to give them mince pies and sherry and cups of tea. In those days the church and the chapel used to go carol singing in Parwich too.

As I've said (p.27) my grandfather always used to kill a pig at Christmas, hang it up and salt the hams in the big thrawl with saltpetre which cured it better round the knuckle bone. I used to stir the blood.

Mary Rawlins

Pork Cake
Half pound salt pork chopped fine, then pour on one pint of boiling coffee and stir in two cups of brown sugar, one cup of Molasses, spices of all kinds to taste, citron, one pound of currants and two pounds of stoned and chopped raisins

Mary Emma Hopkinson

Sir John and Lady Crompton-Inglelfield had wonderful parties at Christmas at the Hall, and the Dodds children were always included. There was a huge tea in the upstairs dining room with maids and the butler, whose name was Winfield, to look after us. There were 'snowballs' of cotton wool wrapped round straw which were thrown around the room, until it was time to go downstairs to the drawing-room, where Father Christmas would arrive, ringing the front door bell and being announced by the butler. We were given big, glorious presents.

On Boxing Day evening, the Inglefields would come down to Hallcliffe so that the staff could have their Christmas staff party at the Hall. We danced and played marvellous games after dinner, starting with 'Strip the Willow' and an eightsome reel danced to the gramophone. There was always a game where a team had to guess a word which rhymed with another word, and my father and Sir John would be on the floor, rowing a boat, and somehow managing to go green, because one of the words of the charade was "sick".

Zelda Kent-Lemon

When the Inglefields were at the Hall we used to have a party every Christmas, with all the Staff. 'Course, we used to be knocking about with all the girls (I was in my teens) and that sort of thing, you know. And every Christmas Colonel Inglefield gave all the outside staff a goose. Then he'd give us a free night, and we'd have the run of the place till about two or three o'clock in the morning; Postman's Knock and everything!

Ken Wayne

When we were in the choir we used to go carol singing at the Hall at Christmas. We were asked inside and given coffee and mince pies and all sorts of things. In those days there were quite a few of us in the choir, two boys and four girls, and so many men and women as well. We used to go carol singing there and then up to Parwich Hospital.

I was clerk to the Governors when Sir John and Lady Inglefield were here. They always made you very, very welcome. Sir John did a lot for the village. The church never paid for any repairs, he paid for them, and when we were wanting a new village hall, Sir John put so much down and we did fund raising for the rest. That was in the 1950's, because I was at school and I was in the youth club then. Sir John used to hire a big marquee and have a summer garden party in it, and we used to have a stall every year.

Valerie Kirkham

I remember Advent and the excitement of the build-up to Christmas. The carol singers would come round, and as we grew older we became carol singers ourselves – with the church carol singers and also with the chapel group. They always went round the village on different nights because Mr Fearn, headmaster at the school, was both choirmaster for the church and preacher at the chapel. We loved it when we reached Hallcliffe, our home, because our mother would provide mince pies and hot Bovril which we thought was just perfect.

My memories of Christmas:
Everything dark outside, chill and, with luck, snowy; walking across the Green to the church on Christmas Eve to sing carols; looking up into the shadows in the roof and hugging ourselves, tingling with the thrill of being alive, being there; then home again, to bed; but first to hang up our stockings and to sleep. One Christmas Eve I woke when a shadow crept into my room and I heard the slightest crackle of paper as things disappeared into my stocking; I kept mouse still and quiet; I would not for anything in the world have let my father know I had seen him. Then the stocking itself: tangerine in the toe, a walnut or two, some tiny parcels and a chocolate Father Christmas sticking out of the top. Christmas Day, with church again and then a turkey lunch and Christmas pudding; then into the drawing room and an impatient wait until three o'clock when the wireless would be put on and we would all listen to the King's Speech, later the Queen's - standing for the National Anthem, stiff and straight backed just like soldiers, just like our father; and then we could have our presents! Our father would always give a little speech to say how sorry Father Christmas was that he couldn't be with us but that he, our father, was deputising for him and would like a helper, and in my memory I was always the helper.

In the evening we went up to the Hall for Christmas presents; and then we little ones would go home again to bed while the older members of the family changed and went back to the Hall for dinner. How exciting it was when, one by one, we were considered old enough to join them. On Boxing Day the Inglefields would come to us for supper, because that was the night when their servants had their own party – Boxing Night was always less formal, and we would play silly games like balloon tennis and generally be noisier and more relaxed.

New Year was not in the least bit exciting until we became "grown up" and were asked to the Hall by the Inglefields for their annual New Year's Eve party. There was lots of good food, champagne, and always charades, which I loved watching but hated having to perform, being by far the shyest and quietest of the four of us. I shall never forget seeing my father, the token Scotsman, having removed his trousers and wrapped a rug around his middle for a kilt, getting down on the floor and wriggling around under the carpet, while Colonel Inglefield, his false teeth removed, did his impression of a doddery old man suffering terribly from seasickness. Why is it that just about every word chosen managed to include that scene or one very similar? Perhaps it had something to do with the amount of champagne being drunk!

Angela Dodds

The best time of all was Christmas. The Crompton-Inglefields always invited us, the vicar & Mrs Hansford and the Beale family to tea, which we would have in the upstairs dining room and then congregate by the fire in the hall. A loud knocking on the front door would be heard. Winfield, the butler, would open it and announce, "Father Christmas, madam". We'd follow him into the drawing room where there was a huge tree lit by real candles and a heap of parcels underneath.

In the evening, when we were a bit older, we'd be invited to dinner at the Hall too. We'd have cold turkey and ham, followed by sherry trifle, and the table would be piled with cotton wool "snowballs" which we'd throw at each other till the cotton wool fell off and the straw inside could be unravelled to find the present inside. The mess we made was awful.

Then we'd go down to the drawing room where charades would be played. The dressing up box would be raided and more mess would be made. We always felt sorry for Winfield and Hetty, the housemaid, who would have to clear it all up. The generosity and laughter and kindness which surrounded us are memorable to this day.

Sara and Vere Dodds

King William:

In comes King William that valiant knight
Who shed his blood for England's right,
England's right and England's written
That's why I carry this awful weapon
Ho spice Ho spice don't be so hot
For in this house you don't know what we've got
Mince pies hot, mince pies cold
Baked in a porridge pot nine days old.

King William then stabs 'Enterer in' with sword and he falls to the ground.

From *Guizing: A local Christmas tradition unmasked!* By Rob Francis.

Postscript

The Present

Parwich, as I see it, is a mixture of modern and grey-haired history. These both live alongside each other in perfect harmony, but soon the modern will be forgotten or replaced, but the old will still stand tall. The bus stop I use so regularly once was used by many others, but as a pump house.

Parwich has some very old traditions. One of these I look forward to all year: Wakes Week. With its colourful bunting and jolly faces it is surprising how in one week the whole community is brought together to do what many have done for generations. My favourite is the parade, the colourful costumes and friendly competition. The theme this year was Glastonbury, and I came up with the idea of being a knight and horse. The day of the parade came and as I was waiting nervously at the shop, cheers and laughter filled the street. The brass band played and it was like being a knight who had just won a battle and was now collecting an award for courage and bravery: and like I imagined it, I collected 1st prize and I was overwhelmed with joy and excitement.

I also entered the Hill Race. I'm not very good but this year I'd been training, so when I was on the starting line I never imagined I would do as well as I did. I collected 1st Local Girl and 2nd Girl Overall. I was very pleased!

There was a power cut last year and it was so dark I couldn't see. We all moved around by candlelight. This reminded me of how people used to live; it was a bit spooky; but we couldn't cook so I wonder how they used to manage without electricity? Well, we solved it by going into Ashbourne to get some fish and chips and it seemed as if the rest of the village was there too!

Hayley Powell (Age 14)

The carnival parade, Parwich Wakes.

The most enjoyable time of the year in Parwich is Wakes Week. The fair comes and so does the burger bar. Then at night when it goes dark there is a band doing loads of the latest music. On the Sunday there is a treasure hunt which most children take part in and walk round the whole of Parwich trying to find clues, and on the Tuesday it is the Hill Race. The last night of all is Friday night and this is called the Odd Fellows Dance, and the old people go for drinks and food and there is a band called "Storm" produced by Parwich people and they are Brian Griffiths and Shaun Marshall.

Emma Greatbatch (Age 14)

I really like Wakes Week. We always have a good time, even if it rains. The fair comes and we play on the Village Green. We have chips and hot dogs and stay till it's gone dark. We chase each other round the play area. My brother once fell in the dam and got wet and Mum was cross but not for long.

Tom Stafford (Age 6)

The thing I like most about Wakes is the racing night. I don't mean the children's races but the ferret races and horse races. I always remember the first time I watched it and I won a lot of money because I kept choosing the winning horse. The ferrets sometimes turn around and go back up their tubes just when you think yours is going to come out and win.

Alexander Drummond (Age 10)

Ferret racing. Will mine win? Oh no, it's going up the wrong way!

The thing I like about Parwich is the church. In summer it is nice and cool but in winter I wish they would burn a few more candles to warm it up a bit. My mummy and granny take me to see the pretty flowers when somebody has got married. It smells nice but when the flowers are gone it smells fusty, like my granny's garage. I like to hear the bells ringing and chinging. I think it could be the hunchback of Notre Dame!

Georgia Griffiths (Age 6)

On Saturday the 20th September I went conkering. I phoned up my mates and arranged to meet down at the football pitch. I got out my bike and helmet and cycled down Creamery Lane to the football pitch. When we were there we found some big sticks and started knocking the horse chestnut trees so the conkers would fall down. After that we started to have battles with our conkers.

William Beesley (Age 8)

My granny lives in Parwich. I like going to granny's house. I like all her gnomes in her garden and I like her flowers. My Granny is a bit crazy. She loves her gnomes lots and lots.

Charlotte Bradbury (Age 6)

I like it when we dress up as our favourite book character at school. I was Tom Sawyer. We went to the library and we were allowed to get out some books. I got out eight. My picture was in the paper.

I like Wakes Week because I get to do the Hill Race and lots of other sports. There is a competition to see who makes the best costume. Last year I dressed up as Elvis Presley. I won second prize.

I like the Horticultural Show. This year I entered tomatoes, cucumber, marrow, runner beans, cactus and a geranium. My marrow won second prize. That is why I think Parwich is a nice place.

Sam Webster (Age 7)

One of my best memories of Parwich village is when we go round the village to play trick or treats on people. There are a lot of my school friends all around the village but no one is sure who is who because of the masks and hats we all put on. We sneak around and knock on people's doors. Some people have made special cakes just for us; others have brought all sorts of sweets and chocs for us but best of all we sometimes get coins. It's very exciting but also a little spooky. Last year we called at the village shop and they'd made bags of sweets up for us.

Harry Stafford (Age 8)

I remember going to Rathborne Hall when we were trick or treating. They threw cold spaghetti at us and had water pistols but we did get a lot of chocolate. In the summer we can cycle to the ford. I am good at catching fish. They are called Bullheads.

Rannoch Linnell (Age 7)

It was New Year's Eve, but not just any New Year's Eve, because in just a few hours time it would be the year 2,000 and it would be the turn of a New Millennium. As well as that, it was also my birthday! Everyone in the village had got a lantern and it had been agreed that at a quarter to midnight people should light their lantern and walk down to the Green. It was quite a cold night, and a slight frost, but that didn't dampen anyone's spirits as little glowing lights glided from all over Parwich towards the Green. As more and more people started to gather, a big circle was made, and the air was humming with jolly chatter (and a bit of alcohol).

Then we heard someone shout, "Ten, nine eight...." and as everyone else joined in, it rose in crescendo, and then there was a huge cheer as the year 2000 began. Then everyone joined hands and started to sway to Auld Lang Syne. Fireworks were exploding and people were laughing as the greatest birthday party came to an end.

Robert Drummond (Age 13)

The Future

It needs young people to get involved in village life. It is getting to the stage where the generation of my children (my eldest son is thirty) should be doing it, but they're not because they don't want to. We need to keep the school going because it is a good school, and I think it would be awful if you had to send your children or grandchildren out on a bus at five years old so early in the morning. If we don't watch what we are doing, in the years to come we are going to end up with a village of old people and tourists, because there is no Local Needs housing, or cheaper housing for youngsters to buy. We are going to have people moving away like my husband and I had to, and my son has had to do, which is sad because we need young ones to keep the village going.

Valerie Kirkham

I think Parwich is a very special place because there are lots of activities that everyone can join in, like Wakes, where we all can run a race or enter a fancy dress competition. But the most important thing that gives Parwich that special shine is that all the people are so friendly.

Allie Webster (Age 12)

Contributors to "Voices"

Charles Allen was brought up in Alsop en le Dale, and his detailed memories especially of the time when his father was stationmaster at Alsop en le Dale Station are relevant to a number of the women referred to in the book. See Parwich & District Local History Society Newsletter no. 10 September 2002 for a fuller transcript of the recollections used here.

Agnes Allsopp (maiden name not known). Agnes was the widow of William Allsopp who died in approximately 1551. All we know of her is contained in her will quoted. She managed a large part of her husband's estate up to her death in 1571. The Allsop family probably descended from the Saxon Lord of the Manor of Parwich and Alsop at the time of the Norman Conquest, and took their name from the village of Alsop en le Dale. The Allsops in Parwich were, from the late fifteenth century, successful yeoman farmers.

Jeanetta Katherine Allsopp (née Brownlee) was born in 1862 in Parwich, raised her seven children here and is buried in the churchyard. The Brownlees, originally from Ireland, came to Parwich in the first part of the nineteenth century.

Kathleen Allsopp (née Brownlee) spent her earliest years at Daisy Bank, up on what is now the High Peak Trail. Her family moved to Parwich when Kathleen was 7 years old and she continues to live in the village. Her husband, Eric Allsopp, was Jeanetta Katherine Allsop's grandson, and Kathleen is her great niece.

Patricia Bagshawe (née Crompton-Inglefield) lived at Parwich Hall from the time her father (Sir John Crompton-Inglefield) bought the estate in the 1930s. In the text people refer variously to the family as Inglefield and Crompton-Inglefield. A colonel in the Second World War, Sir John was knighted in the 1960s. The family sold the Hall in 1975 when Sir John and Lady Crompton-Inglefield settled at their London house. Mrs. Bagshawe, though living in Staffordshire, still retains some property in Parwich.

Helena Birkentall (née Hampson), born in 1875 at the School House, was the daughter of Fletcher Hampson, Headmaster of Parwich School from 1870 to 1911. She taught in Parwich School for a short time. Her brother, Fletcher Booth Hampson, was Headmaster here also. She wrote extensively of her memories of Parwich in the 1950s for the Parish Magazine.

Sandra Chadfield (née Wilton) is the daughter of Ambrose and Irene (née Lees) Wilton and, like them, lives in the village. Through the Lees side of the family she is related to many people either in, or connected with the village.

Frances Curtis (née Carr) was the daughter of the Rev. Carr, who was vicar of Parwich from 1822 to 1828. At this time Parwich Hall was used as the vicarage. Her mother was Ellen, the daughter of William Evans who had purchased the Parwich estate in 1814, though his main house was Darley Abbey, near Derby. Frances Curtis and her sister Susan Lewis inherited the estate from their uncle in 1892. She did not live here as an adult and the family sold off their various interests in Parwich between 1915 and 1925. Her book, "Memories of a Long Life" quoted in the text however contains many references to the village.

Mollie Dakin   (née Brownlee) is the sister of Kathleen Allsopp and lives at Carsington, near Matlock.

Angela Dodds, now living in Belgium, was the third daughter of Major and Mrs. Dodds. They came to live in the village at Hallcliffe in 1947 as tenants of Sir John Crompton-Inglefield. The family remained there until Major Dodds had died and the children left home. Mrs. Dodds moved to London, where some years later she married the widowed Sir John. She died in 2000 and is buried next to Major Dodds in Parwich churchyard.

Sarah Dodds, now living in Sussex, is the eldest daughter of Major & Mrs. Dodds (see under Angela Dodds above).

Vere Dodds, now living abroad, is the second daughter of Major & Mrs. Dodds (see under Angela Dodds above).

Eileen Ellis (née Steeples) spent her childhood in Parwich and started work at the Hospital here, but then her career took her away. Her father ran the local bus service and sold petrol from the garage in Creamery Lane. Eileen returned to live in the village relatively recently.

Clara (usually called Clare) Evans (née Sykes) was brought up with the travelling fair that came to Parwich Wakes every summer. Her mother, born an Oadley, was from a travelling family Her father started his career as a miner but it was not long before he and his new wife built up their own fair. Clara always said if she had to settle anywhere it would be in Parwich, and she married a Parwich man. She and her husband still live in the house they built themselves.

Roger Graham lives in Derbyshire but has never lived long-term in Parwich. He spent many holidays here as a child with his grandparents Fred & Elizabeth (Beatrice) Graham, who ran the Post Office here. Their courtship is recorded in an extensive correspondence, some of which is quoted here. His aunt, Mary Graham, or Miss Graham as everyone in the village knew her, took over the Post Office from her parents. She remained postmistress until 1984, finally agreeing to retire when she was 85.

Charlotte Halliday, a professional artist in her own right, now lives in London. She is the daughter of the famous artist, Edward Halliday. The family lived at the Fold during the Second World War as tenants of Sir John Crompton-Inglefield

Ella Hopkinson is originally from Suffolk and no relation of the Parwich family of the same name. She and her late husband, Harry Hopkinson, came to Parwich first in 1946 when he took a job at the Hall as under gardener. He did not get on with the head gardener and he left, only to be asked to return as head gardener. Harry continued to work at the Hall until his retirement. Ella still lives in the village.

Ethel May Hopkinson born in 1892, was the daughter of Mary Emma (below) and William Jackson Hopkinson. She married Gerald Lewis in 1928. Extracts from her book of sewing patterns are included in the text. Her daughter is Mary Whitechurch (see below).

Mary Emma Hopkinson (née Rippon) was born circa 1848. Her husband, William Jackson Hopkinson, was a cordwainer and bootmaker in Parwich. She kept her own book of recipes and remedies, which passed to her daughter Ethel, who in turn passed it on to her daughter, Mary Whitechurch.

Zelda Kent-Lemon (née Dodds) now living in Oxfordshire, is the youngest daughter of Major & Mrs. Dodds (see under Angela Dodds above).

Valerie Kirkham (née Flower) was born at Church Gates and was brought up at Dam Farm with her parents, Esther and Samuel Flower, and her grandparents, Samuel and Ada Willa Flower. Her maternal grandparents, Sydney and Ethel Lees, lived opposite Dam Farm at Church Gates. Val and her husband continue to live in the village.

Barbara Lowes (née Brownlee) was brought up at Slate House. She and her husband continue to live in the village.

Dorothy Marsh. A friend of Miss Graham's who lives in Ashbourne.

June Nadin. Brought up in Charlesworth, north Derbyshire, June married a Parwich man, Tom Nadin, whose father, George Nadin, was bailiff to Sir John Crompton-Inglefield. Tom and his family lived at School View. The couple moved away but returned to Parwich eleven years ago.

Mary Rawlins (née Keeling) was brought up at Upper Moor Farm. When she married her husband, Peter Rawlins, they settled in the centre of the village, where they still live. Peter's mother, Henrietta (née Twigge) was housekeeper for the Crompton-Inglefields at Parwich Hall, and his father, William, was the butler.

Eveline Shaw (née Chadwick) lived with her parents, Les and Gladys, and her sister and brother, Joan and Len, at the Croft, Parwich. Her father worked at Ballidon quarry.

Betty Stone (née Thurman) was born in Parwich at Littlewood Farm where her Aunty Annie Calladine lived. Betty visited relatives in Parwich throughout her childhood. Her mother was Ruth Thurman (née Lees) whose parents (Betty's grandparents, Samuel and Elizabeth Lees) lived on Gibbon's Bank. Mostly, Betty stayed at Shaw Croft with her Aunty Alice Ward, whose husband was a farm worker. Like Dolly Wayne and Sandra Chadfield, she was related to the local midwife, Mrs. Blackwell (née Lees) who lived at Church Cottage. The Lees family is large and complicated, and many people in the village are related through them. Betty moved away to Sheffield where Ray, her husband, was Head of Art at the University. They returned to Parwich after his retirement.

Joseph Thompson (1833 to 1909) though living in Manchester was descended from the Parwich Allsops through his mother. He wrote an account of his childhood memories of Parwich around 1900, which fortunately has survived.

Ann Vidler lives with her husband in Hertfordshire. She wrote down the memories of her husband's mother, Muriel Vidler (née Brownson), and of his grandmother, Esther Brownson (née Shaw). The Brownsons were a wealthy family living at various times in Alsop Hall and Parwich Hall. The family tradition is that they are descended from one of Mary Queen of Scots' retainers who settled here after the Queen's execution. Esther and her husband George kept a shop in what is now called Brentwood Cottage.

Catherine Elizabeth (Dolly) Wayne (née Lees) was born on Gibbon's Bank, Parwich, in 1913 in a house next door to her grandparents, Elizabeth and Samuel Lees. Her mother, Florence (née Holmes) was married to George Lees, and when Dolly was about 5 they moved to Ballidon, from where Dolly walked to Parwich school with her brother Tom. At age 13 her mother died and she transferred to Ballidon school for a year. After her mother's death she lived on the farm next door with George and Nellie Fox and later moved with them to Aldwark. She returned to Parwich to live at Fernlea a few years before the start of the Second World War. She was called up and was sent to Bliss's in Derby but returned to Parwich when she was transferred to Royce's. She married Arthur Wayne, a Parwich man, and has lived here ever since.

Walter (Ken) Wayne now lives in Great Longstone. When he was born his parents (Walter and Millicent) lived at Rock House and managed Gerald Lewis' creamery or cheese factory at Knob Hall. Later they took over the tenancy of the Sycamore Inn. When his father died his mother tried to run the pub herself, but in time handed it over to Ken who continued as landlord until 1968. His memories of his mother and other women in the village provide a valuable contribution to the book.

Mary Whitechurch (née Lewis) now living in Kent, was brought up in Guernsey. Her childhood was coloured by her parents' memories of Parwich. Her father, Gerald Lewis, came to Parwich in the 1890s when his mother Susan Lewis (née Carr) inherited the Estate (see Frances Curtis above). Susan Lewis lived for a while in Parwich Hall and is buried in the churchyard here. Gerald set up the Creamery in Knob Hall and the market garden in Monsdale Lane. He lived at Hallcliffe. In the 1920s he moved to Guernsey, and subsequently married Ethel Hopkinson, who came from a Parwich family. (see above)

Irene Wilton (née Lees) was born in Parwich, and lives here with her husband Ambrose.

The children contributing to the book.
The ages given are those which accompanied their contributions in the summer of 2003.

William Beesley (8 years); *Charlotte Bradbury* (6 years); *Alexander Drummond* (10 years); *Robert Drummond* (13 years); *Emma Greatbatch* (14 years); *Georgia Griffiths* (6 years); *Rannoch Linnell* (7 years); *Thayer Linnell* (5 years); *Hayley Powell* (14 years); *Harry Stafford* (8 years); *Tom Stafford* (6 years); *Allie Webster* (12 years); *Sam Webster* (7 years)

Other Sources

The publications of the Parwich and District Local History Society have proved an invaluable resource:
"Gardening in Parwich" by Peter Trewhitt and Barbara McCormick. (2002)
"A Parwich Walk" by Peter Trewhitt and Patti Beasley. (2002)
"A History of Parwich Church" by Brian Foden and Andrew Robinson. (2002)
Useful extracts have also been taken from the Newsletters of the Parwich & District Local History Society. These are published on the society's website, www.parwichhistory.com.

Acknowledgements to The Manchester Evening News for extracts from "Take a Tip", to the Ashbourne News Telegraph and the Derby Mercury; and to Mark Edmunds for a quotation from his book, "Ancestral Geographies of the Neolithic", Routledge, London & New York, 1999. Also to Joyce Douglas for quotations from "Old Derbyshire Recipes and Customs", Hendon Publishing Co. Ltd. 1976. Isobel Combes book for Landmark Publishing Ltd. "The Spirit of Parwich." (2003). The "Best Way Cookbook" (compiled from the "Best Way" pages of "Woman's World" "Cosy Cover". The Amalgamated Press, London 1907. [Ditto, No 3]. "Things Everyone Wants to Know". C. Arthur Pearson Ltd, Henrietta Street, WC.

Index for Voices